The Republic of Grace

The Republic of Grace

AUGUSTINIAN THOUGHTS
FOR DARK TIMES

Charles Mathewes

William B. Eerdmans Publishing Company

Grand Rapids, Michigan / Cambridge, U.K.

Published 2010 by
Wm. B. Eerdmans Publishing Co.
2140 Oak Industrial Drive N.E., Grand Rapids, Michigan 49505 /
P.O. Box 163, Cambridge CB3 9PU U.K.

Library of Congress Cataloging-in-Publication Data

Mathewes, Charles T., 1969-
The republic of grace: Augustinian thoughts for dark times / Charles Mathewes.
p.   cm.
Includes bibliographical references and index.
ISBN 978-0-8028-6508-3 (pbk.: alk. paper)
1. Christianity and politics.
2. Augustine, Saint, Bishop of Hippo.   I. Title.
BR115.P7M31677   2010
261.7 — dc22

2010009229

www.eerdmans.com

For Isabelle and Henry
whose world this will be

lift me up love
pick me up love
everyday

Contents

Teaching in a Time of War

ꞏ꒰ꞏ

As morning warmed toward noon on September 11, 2001, a teacher slowly wrenched part of his mind away from the catastrophe visible on his television and began to come to terms with his own, local problem. He was supposed to teach a class that afternoon, a class on modern theology. The reading for that day seemed now to have been selected by an evil genie: it was the theologian Karl Barth's essay "Theological Existence Today," proclaiming that we should "do theology as if nothing else mattered." It's a powerful essay; written in 1932-33, as the Nazis were coming to power in Germany, it argues that the world is full of terrible challenges and dangers, that it will ever unsettle our confidences and expectations, and yet that that peril should not deter us from doing theology — asking the perennial questions of the meaning of human life, the proper shape of divine love, and the purpose of history. Such questions as these, the essay proclaims, remain central human questions of every day, no matter what the experiences of the present moment seem to demand.

The teacher's thoughts twisted back and forth in his mind as he struggled with the question of what he should do. Could he teach this essay? Was it right even to hold class today? But could it be right to leave his students alone? If they did have class, should they spend the time talking about what had happened that morning, and what was happening now and what it all meant for the days and years ahead? (What *did* it mean?) Or should they try to go forward normally, trying to recover, if only for ninety minutes, the rationale for their presence together in study, in college itself? And if they went forward, how could he introduce the reading for the day? The Barth essay is challenging enough on normal days; it takes some imaginative stretching to get students to appreciate the vehemence and outrageousness of what he is saying. But today of all days the piece's vehemence and outrageousness would be no problem; today the problem would be getting the students to feel the seductive power of Barth's conviction in the face of the massive manifest evidence against it. How would they react to being confronted with such a strident, demanding claim? Come to think of it, how should *he* — the teacher — react? Can Barth's words be the words for a day like this? That question, once spoken, answered itself. He taught the Barth.

I am not that teacher; he's a friend of mine. But I wish I had been, for what he did seemed to me profoundly wise. It still does. This book is an attempt to extend his lesson further. It is the book of a teacher, not the book of a cultural analyst or a geopolitical (or ecclesiological) strategist. My aim is fundamentally pedagogical: to offer a primer in the Augustinian-Christian vernacular, a language of religious, moral, and political deliberation. This vernacular was once common currency among educated Christians in Western cultures — and indeed formed the lingua franca of those cultures themselves — but it has become almost completely lost. Those who learn it learn a way of thinking about the political machinations of states, the moral and religious struggles of individuals and communities, and how all the manifold features of human existence relate to one another and to the central driving force behind all history, God's living pursuit of an errant humanity, wounded in its attempt to escape the inescapable desire for God at humanity's core. Were this language recovered, Christians and non-Christians would find in it many crucial insights they would not otherwise possess.

My friend's class was not all Christian, of course; it was not a class in a seminary or divinity school. While he was teaching about a Christian theologian that day, on other days he would teach a secular philosopher or intellectuals of other traditions. This book pretends to no such wide-ranging scope. It discusses one strand of one religious tradition — Christianity — in the hope that extended attention to it will illuminate the challenges we face in a new and vivid way.

"In the *hope*" — there's the rub. For cultivating hope is the central political task of today — of every day, in fact. But hope is harder to cultivate than we think, and since 9/11 its absence seems to me increasingly palpable.

Part of the problem is simply the challenge that living in this new age puts to us. Many of us, myself included, have not managed fully to move past the events of 9/11. It has been more than eight years since that day, and yet many of us have yet to see 9/12. My memory of that morning is still fresh. I remember it all — the phone calls, the first images, the way the day turned from a bright and fair late summer day to rain by nightfall. Don't you?

And those not stuck on September 11 are still caught, it seems, on September 10. Books flood the market talking about life after 9/11, but most of them are simply variations on "this just demonstrates what I've been saying all along." This is not just manifestly false, it is actually destructive of the possibility of knowledge: such attitudes are not responses but mere reactions — consolation devices for those who can't bear the reality of our situation. For it is hard to bear. Hope helps us bear it, and so come better to understand what is going on in our world.

Understanding, the philosopher Ludwig Wittgenstein said, is knowing how to go on. Such a "knowing how to go on" is a kind of "understanding" that presumes no total comprehension of reality, or even of any single event, in all its fullness and detail; such comprehension is not ours in history. Henry Kissinger once asked Chinese leader Chou En-lai what he thought of the French Revolution, to which the premier replied, "it's too soon to tell." As with all events, the meaning of 9/11 will be revealed in its full effects; what those effects are, is still being determined by the actions of people all over the world, and will be for some time to come. An apocalyptically final understanding is beyond us at present. But we can at least attempt to acknowledge the event, and go on from it, into the future.

Hope has had a hard time since September 11. But things were not so good before then, either. In fact, true hope is more rare than we realize. After the end of the Cold War, a curious kind of vapid smugness took over public life, infecting everyone with its vacuous giddiness: a complacency with no fears about the future because it refused to admit that there would *be* a real future — that anything genuinely new would ever happen again. The general attitude seemed to be, "now we can all have more of the same forever and ever!" Such bovine placidity pleasantly complemented the hysterical optimism at the core of American civil religion. But it was not hope.

We can do better than this. We must: after all, ours is a political

3

world, and many of our most urgent problems are political — caused by decisions we have made and hence to some degree amenable to our correction. After all, we need not be victims of the rulers anymore. We are not subjects of kings, we are citizens of republics, sharing in our common sovereignty; genuine participation in the governance of our world is possible. Because of this, we have reason for hope. Indeed, I think the hope for today is more profound, and more profoundly insightful into the metaphysical truth of our condition, than are the anxieties that occupy so much of the surface of our lives. Despite our despair, there is much to be hopeful for today.

The fact that we do not see this hope is not due simply to the particular exigencies of our historical moment. The challenges are far deeper than that — deeper even than the "modern condition" itself. They are, in this dispensation, intrinsic to the human condition. Hope is challenged in our world, and through hope all the virtues, yet our received languages of moral concern cannot bring this issue properly into focus. This is a perennial problem for human life, though a too-shallow attention to the contingencies of the present can make us miss this. As C. S. Lewis put it, speaking in regard to another such crisis, World War II: "The war creates no absolutely new situation: it simply aggravates the permanent human situation so that we can no longer ignore it. Human life has always been lived on the edge of a precipice. Human culture has always had to exist under the shadow of something infinitely more important than itself. If men [and women] had postponed the search for knowledge and beauty until they were secure, the search would never have begun. We are mistaken when we compare war with 'normal life.' Life has never been normal." Part of our job, then, is coming to terms with the ways in which our ordinary condition of "never being normal" are incarnated in our particular time and place. But we must never forget that the challenges are far more perennial than they are merely of our moment.

So the challenges facing us are deep and abiding. What can an academic theologian do to help us meet them? He or she can teach; that's why I take inspiration from my colleague's actions on 9/11. Teaching, after all, is a form of hope — a hope that, against real difficulties, something of value and meaning can be communicated from one person to another. To teach is to say that the past has something to teach the future. It affirms that we can be better or worse prepared to inhabit the future that is coming, and that that preparation is in some complicated way due to how deeply we grapple with our past.

Well, that may begin to explain why an academic has something to say, but what about an academic theologian? The answer is simple. These challenges confront the whole shape of human life, and as such they must be met through the particular configurations that actual human lives take. A merely generic response to the challenges we face will not confront their true depth and breadth. The best way to address those challenges, I suggest, is in terms of the most fundamental cultural forms through which people attempt to live their lives. Christianity is one such form.

It may seem oddly limiting to write a book primarily addressed to Christians; that may seem a strangely narrow audience. But the appearance of narrowness deceives. It is ironic that explicit appeals to Christians are all-too-easily labeled "narrow" or "sectarian" when there are roughly 250 million Christians — of quite diverse flavors, of course — in the United States today, and more than 2 billion around the world. How "broad," in comparison, would be an argument addressed to readers of the *New York Review of Books*?

Many people are writing books today that tell us what our religious convictions should lead us to do, even, most presumptuously, what Jesus would do. This book takes a further step back and asks: How should these convictions lead us to see the world somewhat differently than those who do not share those convictions? What, that is, are the categories that a believer should use to see the world and its challenges, and how will such a believer use that vision to act?

Certainly we need advice on what to do. But advice does not help us think for ourselves, which is what we must do when faced with the New Thing God is always doing. Many books today on the right and the left tell us what to do — give us God's politics, or identify the godless enemy, or offer the political teachings of Jesus, or what have you. They often appeal to the "plain sense" of some Bible passages. But they ignore the fact that the Bible's advice is often quite contradictory; merely to grab the passages you like, in order to berate others who have grabbed onto other passages that they like, simply won't do. We should beware of that temptation, for even the devil can quote Scripture. For example, the U.S. Civil War was fought by two sides equally convinced of the theological rectitude of their cause. They talked past each other, in part because they both started from the same simplistic, proof-texting approach to religion. Abraham Lincoln, in his Second Inaugural Address, had it right when he noted that both sides "read the same Bible, and pray to the same God; and each invokes His aid against the other." We need more than a simple appeal to what the Bible says; we need to know how to read the Bible, and the signs of the times, and we can do the former only if we also do the latter. Lincoln provided it through his depiction of the Civil War in specifically theological terms, as God's judgment on the nation. (We will come back to this example later.) We need something similar.

Others have commented that Lincoln's Second Inaugural is more of a sermon than a political tract. And if we accept Marilynne Robinson's definition of a sermon — as a piece of prose expected to be delivered, and heard, "seriously and in good faith" — then in a way this book too is a sermon. Make no mistake — I do not want to preach at you. But I do want to make those of you who are believers alert to the challenges facing our common inhabitation of this world, and make you aware of what you can do about them, and make you alive to how undertaking those tasks will deepen and widen your faith. And for all, I want the book to reignite a fierce commitment to the common good of our society — to care for the least and most vulnerable, and to use your gifts and power and wealth as a force for good and justice in the world. I want it, in short, to help us to remember what it is to work together for a good larger than each of us (and each of our groups) — a genuinely common good. This is inevitably, inescapably a political task, involving compromise, negotiation, and bargaining. These need not inevitably sully the product of our labors, but they do inescapably accompany it. So part of what I'm offering here is a primer on politics for Christians — to help us find hope in public life.

Such hope is different from naive optimism. I do not want to be a cheerleader; I want to provide wise counsel: to generate a rich and more ambivalent sensitivity to both the possibilities and the perils that we face, alert to the tensions of codependence and contradiction between those possibilities and perils, and unseduced by all attempts to sell us any program that admits of that tension's simple resolution. In fact, so far from pursuing any premature reconciliation of the many conflicting challenges and opportunities of our world, we ought to accentuate our appreciation of them both — the prospects and the dangers — instead of blending them into a pabulum-like paste. (The wisdom of moderation here can sometimes mean little more than the fatigue of middle age.)

This approach is not only wiser than the alternative; it also better captures the eschatological tensions inherent in the Christian faith, because it accommodates the powerful energies of the "now" and "not yet" of the coming kingdom of God, the insistence to be in the world but not of it, the pronouncement of apocalyptic judgment and the proclamation of good news — all these dimensions, and many more, of the Christian faith work to magnify our sense of living between the times, at a moment when different forces are exquisitely poised in our soul before some final denouement.

This is not easy. As Reinhold Niebuhr put it, "it is no easy task to do justice to the distinctions of good and evil in history and to the possibilities and obligations of realizing the good in history; and also to subordinate all these relative judgments and achievements to the final truth about life and history which is proclaimed in the Gospel." More deeply than discrete positions, then, I want to introduce Christians to a way of living their faith more thoughtfully than they may currently be living it. I want to wake people up to the challenges they face to their faith, their prayer life, their ability to love, their ability to be grateful, their ability to be joyful, their ability to care. Christians need to believe again — to have real belief in God, but also belief in our capacity to challenge ourselves and change the way we have chosen to live. We need to turn from cynicism and scorn, from selfishness and avarice, from lassitude and despair, and to affirm that this is our world, and that its suffering and peril are not cause for retreat but urgent reason to recommit to serving God's purposes in it, that its vulnerability is not inducement to shield ourselves behind brittle walls but reason to care all the more. Behold, today we have set before us, as perhaps never before in human history, life and death, and as never before, we must choose to live.

We will not be, we cannot be, the agents of this world's salvation. But we can be servants of its conservation and betterment, caretakers of its sustenance, partakers of its blessings. And this is for Christians equally basically a political and a religious undertaking. In the Middle Ages, scholars wrote guidebooks for kings, known generically as "mirrors for Christian princes," wherein the contours of a virtuous ruler were displayed, the better for flawed human rulers to see and address their own shortcomings. Today we may use the virtues analogously, to detail a mirror of Christian citizenship — of faithful engagement in broadly political matters, matters pertaining to the common good, where there is no king, where "the sovereign" is *us* — you and I and our neighbors, those we like and those we cannot stand.

Because this is its aim, this is a book for all who wish to become theologians, and for those who wish to understand how theologians think. Who is a theologian? When he was asked this, the sainted fourth-century monk Evagrius Pontikos said, "a theologian is one who prays truly, and one who prays truly is a theologian." I would go further: Do you wish to pray truly, or to understand those who are gripped by this wish? If either of those is true, then this book is for you; welcome to the club.

Welcome, indeed, to the human race. For such questions are irrepressibly human, arising in the midst of everyday life. All theology begins with these questions, and in a way ends with them. After all, theology is simply reflection on how the people of God go about making sense of our lives as creatures of a God whose governance of the world has been made visible in the story of the people Israel, Jesus Christ, and Christ's people in the world.

Theology can sound intimidatingly obscure. But do not be intimidated. There are many who disparage "theology" as academic, and who disclaim their sophistication and say they'll write for "ordinary folks." Like graduates of Yale and Harvard who run for president, such people silently trade on their expertise even as they disclaim any "book-learnin'." This is deeply misleading. All of us think, all the time, about issues that get segregated into the prison of theology, and swaddled in the barbed wire of intellectual snobbery and anti-intellectual complacency (two sides of the same coin, actually). Thinkers over several millennia have prayed, and preached, and worked, and thought, and written on these matters, and all of that is the heritage of the least among us. That is not only a word of comfort, it is a word of obligation: it is part of your duty, as a creature with a mind, to think about these things.

That is not to say that this is easy. Learning to think about these things is hard work. To do it well we need some wise counselor as an exemplar. This book relies most on Saint Augustine of Hippo, the fourth- and fifth-century North African bishop; he will be our near-constant companion in the pages to come. Augustine is among the deepest of thinkers on these matters, both politically and theologically. In his writings you hear a real person grappling with real problems. No moderately careful reader of his work walks away from it with the feeling that he's trying to delude us about our problems, seeking to convince us that they can be "solved." Augustine is distant from us in many ways, but he was no snake-oil salesman.

Augustine's confrontation with human pretensions to empire and the meaning of history in his magisterial *City of God* is well known. But he is often misrepresented as a brooding, somber presence, gloomy about humanity's chances for improvement, anxious at the slightest effort toward reformation. But this approach does him injustice. It sands away his particularities and leaves him uttering platitudes, and the platitudes selected tend to be those that run against the tenor of the age. Because ours is a sentimental age, Augustine is often used to exfoliate the popular optimism, in order to leave us with a "realistic" — which often means pessimistic, even cynical — vision.

Well, now. Platitudes can be news to some people, of course: those who still believe that everyone can be reached by calm discussion; that human society is fundamentally not a fragile thing; that people are, deep down inside, good; and that things are going pretty much as they should go. But Augustine is not the most appropriate tutor for correcting such people; who or what would be, I will not speculate here. Furthermore, by tasking him with such kindergarten duties as these, we miss his distinctiveness. Augustine's insights, and his "contributions," such as they are, emerge only when he is read as he wanted to be read, as a fundamentally Christian thinker speaking most primarily, most of the time, to Christians, and Augustinian interventions into the public sphere itself will largely be indirect, refracted through their advice to the body of Christ.

And anyway, despite his reputation today, Augustine himself was no pessimist. He proclaimed a God who offers us a deeper joy than we can imagine, and he understood our lives as preparations for that joy that has been prepared for us — a time in which we can begin to be healed in order to be one day able to bear that joy. He is not a complacent theocrat who warrants crusades, holy inquisitions, and the divine right of kings. Nor did he demonize political life, despairing of finding in it anything but the grimmest restraint of humanity's worst vices. Nor is he, or the tradition he represents, fundamentally escapist or otherworldly, luring people away from a tough-minded confrontation with the truth of the human condition with lullabies about heaven. If he espouses something that some see as "otherworldliness," it is meant not to disparage or flee from the world, but to patiently endure its vicissitudes and rightly enjoy its transitory joys, in order to prepare ourselves for its transfiguration into the true creation it was meant to be all along. More than anything else, he wanted his audiences to see reality, in all its almost overwhelming messiness and contradictoriness. That means that he was, above all, profoundly ambivalent about the world we inhabit. Humans live in an irreducibly ambivalent and ambiguous condition, requiring a structurally and existentially ambivalent attitude toward human political authority.

Today we find such ambivalence hard to countenance in others, much less affirm for ourselves. We live in a time that is deeply intolerant, perhaps even fearful, of ambiguity and ambivalence, and we are often hostile to those among us who offer anything less than an unqualified endorsement of our created condition. But in fact, that condition is as deeply ambivalent as it was in Augustine's age; what has changed is merely that our world is far better equipped with devices and desires that enable our escapism than Augustine's ever was. How many people among us have killed our own meat? How many have seen loved ones die? How many have even had a tooth pulled without novocaine, for pity's sake? The degree to which we have shielded ourselves from the more unpleasant fundamental facts of reality, from suffering and death, is astonishing; just as astonishing is our avoidance of the fact of that avoidance. More than ever before, it is possible to go through life relatively successfully (until the end, at least) ignoring the basic condition of our existence. Our hostility toward Augustine, our suspicion of his ambivalence, is not a sign of our more mature moral and spiritual condition; it is rather an effect of our ability to avoid reality more successfully than he could.

Inattention to reality may seem like an odd failing in a person, and a relatively rare one. But what I mean is not what we often call "absentmindedness," the condition whose victims frequently walk straight into walls, or go to work with their laces untied and their zippers undone. It is far more insinuating than that, and more pernicious as well; remarkably gifted people can suffer from it. The celebrity interviewer Larry King once spoke with the brilliant physicist Edward Teller, the father of the H-bomb project in the United States, on his radio show. During the conversation a remarkable fact emerged: for all his work on nuclear weaponry, Teller had never once seen a nuclear weapon tested. King was, to say the least, intrigued. Why hadn't Teller thought it worthwhile to see one of the bombs he designed explode? Teller was blasé about it; it was a simple matter of already knowing all he needed to know about nuclear weapons. Seeing a test would change nothing, he said, for he had done the math: "Once the math works, the bomb will work."

This, I submit, is the danger we face: a willed blindness to the basic character of our situation. It is a fundamental human flaw throughout history, but it is an especially prevalent problem today. To correct for it, you must learn, patiently and meticulously, to notice the world for what it is, recognizing not just the things you expect to see there, but also those things that do not fit into your expectations. And that means you will never be able fully to affirm one thing — the contrary examples will serve as a counterpoint, to perforate any too-seamless confidence. That in turn entails that honest apprehension of our condition will never be wholeheartedly on one side or the other of anything.

That is the nature of Augustine's ambivalence, and it should be ours as well. Both politically and even more broadly existentially, we face the difficult task of trying to inhabit an inevitably sinful life, both retaining a sense of its sinfulness and yet not trying to deny that it is, after all, our life, blessed with its own real goods. We should do so recognizing that our inhabitation of it involves a certain kind of suffering on our part.

To understand our life in its full ambivalence — recognizing our real joys while also acknowledging the distance we have yet to travel to the kingdom, and thereby bringing us face-to-face with the discomfiting condition of having to endure as much as enjoy our lives — Augustine uses the language of the theological virtues of faith, hope, and love. If life in this world can be led as a form of training in virtue for the life to come, then perhaps the civic virtues are themselves, in a way, the theological virtues in a strange land. And so they are. Engagement in civic life — just like every other part of our ordinary, mundane lives — is fruitful for cultivating our character; engagement in the earthly city helps fit us for the heavenly city to come. This is the aspect of Augustine's thought that we can develop further here.

Convincing you of all this is the aim of this book. After an initial stage-setting chapter 1, Part I (chapters 2 through 4) explains how we might live our lives through the theological virtues, and it explores how living our lives through that effort can alter our vision of what is going on in the world. While the virtues have a natural structure, we always meet them somewhat deranged — both deranged in themselves, as we only partially inhabit them, and deranged in their order, as our world always presses more obviously and immediately upon one than another. In the contemporary setting of the "war on terror," the proper order to address them is hope, faith, and love, as existence presses most immediately on our hope, with terror; then on our faith, with temptations toward various idolatries; and then last (but probably most profoundly) on love, with the temptations toward a consumerist pursuit of finally shallow and diversionary pleasures. Understood in these terms, we exist in the midst of three interacting dynamics — sometimes canceling each other out, sometimes reinforcing one another — that collectively challenge our ability to be the sorts of Christians shaped by the virtues that we are called to be. I abbreviate them as "9/11," "11/9" (November 9, 1989 — the day the Berlin Wall fell), and "millennial capitalism," and I speak about these sequentially in these chapters. This is an important lesson: good Christian sight is a matter of discernment, and what we see, and don't see, is just as much a matter of concern as what we do and don't do. This is why this part is called "Seeing as Christians."

Part II (chapters 5 through 7) turns the gaze around and asks: If people do come to see the world in this way, what do they look like to others? To answer this we must step back from the immediate challenges of the moment and ask about the fundamental challenges that our inhabitation of those virtues must confront throughout history, and how Christians' inhabitation of those virtues may make them appear both strange and appealing to others. So these final chapters are a bit more programmatic, and reflect more broadly on the vocabulary and general orientation implicit in this book's proposal. In these chapters I aim to offer the rudiments of a richly *theological* language, in an Augustinian dialect, for understanding our world today, in order to help Christians deepen their believing into a way of life, and especially a way of being citizens, as a discipline of soul-formation for themselves and as a witness to others; this is why this part is called "Looking Like Christians."

With all that said, let's get to it.

CHAPTER 1

Prophecy after the End of History

ずんん

H ere is the science-fiction writer William Gibson, in an interview in
the *Washington Post* in the fall of 2007:

> If I had gone to Ace Books in 1981 and pitched a novel set in a world
> with a sexually contagious disease that destroys the human immune
> system and that is raging across most of the world — particularly
> badly in Africa — they might have said, "Not bad. A little toasty.
> That's kind of interesting." But I'd say — "*But wait!* Also, the internal
> combustion engine and everything else we've been doing that forces
> carbon into the atmosphere has thrown the climate out of whack
> with possibly terminal and catastrophic results." And they'd say,
> "You've already got this thing you call AIDS. Let's not — " And I'd
> say, "*But wait!* Islamic terrorists from the Middle East have hijacked
> airplanes and flown them into the World Trade Center." Not only
> would they not go for it, they probably would have called security.

All this is to say, anyone who claims to know the future is probably in
need of medication. Still, there are some large-scale patterns of change
— changes, speaking metaphorically, not in the weather of our days,
but in the climate of our age — to which we should be alert, for they
shape this book's project, namely, the task of inhabiting hope, and more
broadly the theological virtues, in profound ways. Those changes, and
how this book will confront them, is the topic of this chapter.

Such a survey is a good place for a book like this to start. For the worldly problems we face are profound: the powerful growth of global capitalism, which enriches many but also seems to leave others immiserated, or worse; environmental degradation; demographic challenges, as part of the world grows old while another part has a dangerous "youth surplus"; and on top of all that, the wracking spasms of what we may call the "Age of Sacred Terror." And to be frank, few would claim we are successfully addressing them. The developed countries of the West spend most of their time bickering among themselves, and cynically use that bickering to distract their citizenry from the real problems of the present and foreseeable future, and all those citizens, like the narcotized masses of Aldous Huxley's *Brave New World*, sleepwalk through life on an endless diet of inanities and triviality.

I. Enduring Hope

You agree with this? That just confirms that our political imagination — for secular and religious people alike — is deeply cynical, even despairing. To an astonishing degree today people are resigned, but they obscure the truth of their resignation from themselves by the self-congratulation of thinking themselves more realistic. In fact, the surrender of the torment of hope's necessary indeterminacy is profoundly unrealistic about the world, and as such is disastrous for both the world and ourselves. We live in a time when many kinds of pressure are put upon hope, and it faces many challenges to its flourishing.

But it is not just that conditions are hostile to hope; it is also that we do not know what true hope is. Our pallid cynicism represents hope to us as that cynicism's mirror image, wild utopianism. But that reduces hope to what cynicism can imagine — which is very little, and mostly false. But hope is not simple utopianism. That is a mistake often made by cynics. Cynics grasp part of the present as determinate evidence for the future, and presumptuously project a clear picture of what they expect into the future, and they imagine that the hopeful do the same. But such approaches miss the mystery, even the terror, at the heart of hope, how it ruptures all our presumptions. Hope is not a solipsistic chipperiness that leaves you insensitive to innumerable drubbings from reality; rather, hope is a means of *accessing* reality, of getting at it, seeing the hopefulness at its center without occluding or deflecting or other-

14

wise avoiding the depth of pain, injustice, and wrongness in the world. Hope sees all that is there, the bad as well as the good, but realizes that a hasty acquiescence to what is immediately apparent is not realism, but one more form of the false consolation of complacency. Hope is surprising — indeed, it is the capacity to be joyfully surprised. In this way hope is readily called transcendent, and even, in a way, "otherworldly." But as we will see, this "otherworldly" hope is at the center of even *this* world.

How could this be? Hope is our capacity for recognizing the difference between *what is* and *what should be* — and it is the source of our energizing desire to resist accepting that gap as we find it. By telling this difference, hope makes more palpably vivid both the way things should be and the way the world currently is, and by making both more vivid, leaves those who have hope bereft of the usual evasions and rationalizations. Hope definitely implies that the way things are is not yet the way they will ultimately be. But it is not just a not yet; it empowers us in the here and now as well. When we feel hope, we feel that things have a chance — a chance, not a guarantee; that is enough to keep us up at night, tantalized by it, tortured by it, caught finally with the challenge of living in this world while knowing that things are not the way they are meant to be.

In a deep way, then, hope is not a muscle we can individually develop, nor is it a consolation or painkiller; it is a kind of patient waiting, a patience that affirms that what we see is not yet fully determined, that the world is much more than what we can presently know of it, and that even those things that we do presently "know" may well turn out to be very different from what they seem now to be. We cannot *will* hope into existence; it is a gift, a grace. Hence our experience of hope is not one we enact or create in ourselves, but one we confess and suffer.

Nonetheless, hope's patience is not resignation: its patience emerges from the confidence that, as Václav Havel put it, "repeating this defiant truth made sense in itself, regardless of whether it was ever appreciated, or victorious, or repressed for the hundredth time." Nor is hope a merely subjective feeling, a self-aggrandizing act of reckless courage willed in the face of an indifferent universe; hope is elicited by the world, brought forth in us by what we see the world to be. (In fact, part of hope is this prelude to the explicit possession of hope — that is, to see the world in such a way as to elicit hopefulness in us is already a hopeful vision.) To say "I have hope" is to say something not only about yourself, but also about the world you understand yourself to inhabit: that this world is not a quarry of despair, but a realm in which the surprising can happen. Furthermore, there is a sense of community and solidarity in hope: to be hopeful is to realize that we are not alone, we are not abandoned. Hope itself may *be* that solidarity, for at times it can seem an alien force in us, acknowledged or confessed, not something we have willed but a visitation or annunciation from a yet-unrevealed kingdom. Yet even as it seems strange to us, it is not utterly alien; it is something we can identify with and inhabit. It has an intelligible core, so to speak: it tells us about *our* destiny, not just the destiny of our descendants who will come later. Elicited by the world, an experience of solidarity and loyalty, and promising something real to us — these are truths crucial to hope.

Hope is in this way a transcendental, and even what theologians call an *eschatological*, reality: an energy that looks beyond the conflicts of history to a suprahistorical resolution of those conflicts. Hope is transcendent because it looks for genuine novelty, not more of the same — a novelty that comes like a thief in the night, able to alter radically our lives in ways we are incapable of doing ourselves. But hope is also eschatological because while it exists in the present as an affirmative power, it also insists "not yet"; it looks forward to a radical refiguration of our lives and the world as a whole, a refiguration that will purify our ideals and resolve our conflicts, redeeming our partial goods and semi-achievements, giving us what we long for at every moment in history but cannot receive *from* or *in* history. Hope is the hope that, though we are creatures who move through history — stretched out across time, part of us "lost" as memories of the past and another part not yet arrived as the coming future — we will finally be given our whole existence fully, all at once, in a radically transfigured dispensation, which Saint Paul calls the "new creation."

Yet we are not called just to wait around until this hope hits us. We are not simply supine before the winds of the moment; for such hope is always *real*, and our failure lies in our lassitude at cultivating our capacity not directly to be hopeful, but to see the hope that is offered to us. There is much work we *can* do to cultivate hope, for we must learn to be receptive to it — in a way, to suffer it, for in truth hope is disconsoling; where despair and presumption both try to *resolve*, to settle, hope is unsettling. Indeed, hope is part of a way of being in the world, a virtue whereby we come to shape ourselves as perpetually unsettled, or of recognizing our unsettledness — a way of enduring our begrudging recognition that the future is going to be genuinely surprising — surprising in a way whose "surprisingness" will never end.

But here is one peril we face: our prospects for inhabiting this hope are challenged by the fact that we are living in a way that increasingly makes hope unintelligible to us. And our very languages of moral and spiritual understanding cannot easily bring this challenge into focus. For us, history is increasingly just one damn thing after another, nothing more than a perennial series of temporary delays between the sparking of an appetite and its desultory, momentary satiation. Our understanding of history increasingly lacks any sense of an ultimate horizon against which we can measure our lives' significance or discern an event's true meaning. We think our past is fully past, the future will simply bring more of the same, and any longing for a recovery of full historical existence can be expressed only as a kind of abashed nostalgia. For us, eschatology has been replaced by next-day air.

And yet we would delude ourselves if we thought our problem were simply a matter of our era in history — as if in the past things would have been all better. For the failure here is more a failure of nerve than of intellect. The truth is that humans are much less comfortable with hope than we like to think we are. "It's not the despair I mind, it's the hope I can't stand," cries John Cleese in the movie *Clockwise*. And he is not alone; hope isn't easy, after all. It must be learned: we need, civically and religiously, to learn how to endure hope.

How, then, can we become hopeful people, and hopeful citizens? That is the fundamental question this book wants to help us answer. Many thinkers suggest that "the struggle of the age" is the battle between faith and godlessness, or between blinkered dogmatism and enlightened skepticism (and we can tell which side you're on by which description you choose). And yet it is the struggle to possess and acknowledge this hope, against the despair and cynicism so common today, that is the deepest political and religious struggle of our age. This book is written by one who wishes to be on the side of hope. To help us face our challenges, we should understand those challenges as best we can. That is our next task.

II. Interesting Times

When Harold Macmillan was prime minister of the United Kingdom, a young journalist asked him what made politics so difficult, and he replied, "events, dear boy: events." It should be clear that the "events" have not stopped since Macmillan's day. If anything, they seem to be coming faster and faster. But a too-narrow focus on the demands of the immediate moment will distract us from attention to larger, slower-moving changes in our world. We all can see the events that shape our day-to-day lives: wars, marriages, children, jobs, political scandals, that sort of thing — the sort of thing that would appear in a newspaper. But there are larger, more fundamental changes, changes that take place not over days but over years, decades, generations — the change of expectations of the role of women in society, for example, or the expectations of what the government will do for its citizens, or what citizens owe the government, or what humans owe the world. We can distinguish these as analogous to the difference between the weather and the climate. The weather is fickle and fluctuates, on one level, unpredictably, though at a deeper level it obeys the logic of the seasons. But more deeply still, there may be climatic changes occurring, so gradual as to be imperceptible over one human lifetime, yet changes that affect human life far more dramatically than whether it rains or snows or is sunny tomorrow. The weather depends on the climate, but you can never discern the climate simply by looking out the window. Events aren't the only things that happen.

Seen in this light, the events of the past few years are all mostly weather. There are deeper "climate changes" taking place, which we would do well to note. In this section I want to talk about those climate changes. It is at that level that the inhabitation of hope for Christians, and everyone else, is becoming more difficult.

A. *The Moral Revolution*

Since 9/11, probably the most shocking single event for humans was the Indian Ocean tsunami of December 26, 2004, which killed at least a quarter-million people and left millions destitute. Some commentators compared the responses to the tsunami to the responses to the Lisbon earthquake of 1755, and noted that in 2004, unlike 1755, relatively little commentary addressed the implications of the tsunami for our thinking about the existence of a good God. But such discussions, or the absence thereof, were not the most interesting thing about the worldwide response to the tsunami. The most interesting thing was the worldwide response itself. Unlike Lisbon, the tsunami did not primarily provoke speculative philosophical discussions, and those only in Europe; it provoked food drives and massive financial donations from around the world. The question most asked was not "what kind of God could allow this suffering?" but "what human errors permitted this suffering?" and "how can we help in the present to alleviate it, and how can we act in the future to ensure that it does not happen again?" The difference in response was not because people in the eighteenth century were more callous or parochial than we are today; the root of the difference lay in the relative power of humans before the onslaught of nature. In the eighteenth century, natural disasters would largely provoke wonder and awe, because that was the only possible response for humans to have to them. But today, we can act in response to them, and if we cannot prevent them, we will at least try to repair them.

This desire to repair all injuries, and our burgeoning belief that we have an obligation to do so, witnesses to what thinkers such as Charles Taylor and Michael Ignatieff have called the "moral revolution" of modernity. This "moral revolution" is actually two equally radical and interrelated transformations: one in our understanding of our character as moral beings, the other in our expectations for what a successful human life should look like.

First, Charles Taylor has noted the construction in modernity of an "extraordinary moral culture," one with ever-higher demands for concern for all other humans. Today, as never before in history, we genuinely feel the demands of other people on us, no matter how far away they may be from us, simply because they are human. Taylor is not the first to note this. (That title goes to Sigmund Freud and Friedrich Nietzsche, who discerned these changes in the nineteenth century.) Nor does this mean that humans are becoming any better at meeting the requirements of the obligations we feel — that we are becoming more morally good, that is to say. But what has happened is that now we feel a wider range of moral obligations in ways we never did before. It is not that we are more moral; it is that more of our situation feels moralized to us. Very few eighteenth-century Englishmen would have concerned themselves with the death rates of Africans; today it is a real concern to many.

The second transformation is visible in the assumption, common in our world, that suffering is an *accidental* fact about human life, not inevitable, but able to be eliminated or fixed. There has been a change in our attitude to suffering and pain — from an attitude fundamentally of acceptance of those realities as natural and inescapable facts about the human condition, to an attitude fundamentally of outrage and revolt against those facts. Today, resignation in the face of suffering is not wisdom, but insulting, morally troubling — perhaps spiritually troubling — to us.

These twin transformations have combined most dramatically in the rise of "humanitarianism," the idea, universally affirmed if imperfectly practiced, that all humans across the world stand in states of sensitive obligation to one another, and that those obligations may require us to act at times to care for or help those who live half a world away and whom we will never meet. From the Red Cross to Live Aid to the Indian Ocean tsunami and Darfur, this sort of concern has become increasingly a part of our lives. This moral revolution, that is, mobilizes our concern for strangers far away, and makes us work actively — however minimally, however lamely, however clumsily and haltingly, yet in a fundamentally new way — to ensure their well-being, driven both by a sense of obligation to them and by the conviction that their suffering is not inevitable, that the poor need not always be with us, that the world's wounds can be healed.

This revolution is genuinely something new under the sun. It presses upon us new questions: political ones, about how properly to organize international society; moral ones, not so much about "am I my brother's keeper?" as about the extent of and limits to our fraternity; and metaphysical or theological ones, such as "why should we care about those far away at all?" These questions all ask after what can sustain our moral energies in the face of so vast an extension. In all these ways, this moral revolution is a powerful force for good, and one we should celebrate and promote as much as we reasonably can.

But this moral revolution carries new problems along with it. Its insistence on the global contingency of suffering, vulnerability, and evil is at once its strength and its tragic flaw. It encourages in us awesome moral energies, but ties those energies to the conviction that our exertions will one day be rewarded with the elimination of our true enemies — evil, suffering, and death. Of course, our moral energies are often most provoked by confrontations with evil and suffering. But is it wise to tie the justification of those energies to our chances of overcoming such realities? Evil and suffering seem ineliminable characteristics of the human condition as we inhabit it. If we root our moral energies in the conviction that they can be eliminated, the inevitable discovery that they cannot results in endless vexation and, perhaps, a deepening resentment of and cynicism about those very moral energies.

Something like this can be seen in the wrenching soul-searching that has preoccupied much of the humanitarian aid movement over the past few years. An earlier age's utopian hopes have been lost, and replaced by a far grimmer (and indeed, I would argue, despairing) insistence that we simply care for *these* people, *here* and not ask any larger and fruitless questions about "why" or "wherefore," questions whose answers, it is implied, can only lead to demoralization and apathy. If, as Santayana put it, fanaticism is doubling your efforts when you have forgotten your aim, such changes suggest that our moral revolution threatens to become fanatical.

How can we avoid such an outcome? It is always possible simply to try harder: to insist that the solution to modernity is more modernity, that the problem is our residual if partial captivity to archaic premodern notions of self and community and world, and our solution is to more fully accomplish our liberation, make all of us properly free agents and individuals. All such solutions are forms of what philosophers call "immanentism," the conviction that the patterns of nature and history are all that we need to flourish, or all that we have, anyway, and that we must find our goods in the immanent goods of this world, and not look to a promised happiness somewhere "altogether elsewhere" than this.

But can we be wholly immanent? Augustine thought not; he rejected all claims that all our problems will be settled by getting more of what we already have. For him, humans need a god: we are doxological beings, and cannot live without transcendence; whenever we attempt it, we invariably either try strenuously to abase ourselves or end up worshiping some fabricated idol as a gilded consolation prize — an idol such as a suffering-free, wholly just universe, for example.

I think Augustine was right about this. While modernity's moral revolution is a very good thing, it cannot sustain itself outside of a framework of transcendent hope. And it cannot create that framework by itself; that hope must come from outside it; it must be, that is, a hope grounded on and funded by more than what we can empirically discern in the world as we have it. Of course, when so theological a notion as hope is expressed in our world, some wish to dismiss it as mere otherworldliness, an archaism of interest only to nostalgic antiquaries. That is, I think, a mistake; I think such a transcendent hope is finally the only solid ground on which to base a moral life such as we are called to live in our world.

Of course, many reject my view, and nonetheless seem in no worse a moral position than me; sometimes they are quite obviously substantially superior to me, morally. Despite our current disagreements about the necessity of such a transcendent source for hope, we can and should still work together on tasks of common concern and projects of common calling. Therefore, while I have suspicions about the ultimate adequacy of a wholly this-worldly approach to human life, I do not want to sound as if someone could not reasonably disagree with me. Many, quite reasonably, do. The moral revolution is thus something that all of us can share in, and indeed encourage, even if we ought (I think) to be wary of its tendency toward self-consuming excesses.

B. Totalitarianism, Nihilism, or Idolatry?

In saying this I may sound as if this book is fundamentally an apologetic tract, meant to convince readers that they need to get religion — the argumentative version of a "come to Jesus" meeting. But that is not what this book is about. "You can no more argue, through torture, a man into belief," said Cardinal Newman. Readers will have their own considered views on these matters, and I do not want to waste their reading of my book on a task better left to the grace of God. Those who are fundamentally unsympathetic to the book's starting point may still find value in its analysis, but convincing them is not my main concern. I want instead to analyze our cultural setting to understand how the Christian life may be rightly lived in that setting. I do not seek to condemn our modern world, but to see how best to inhabit it. And the moral revolution points up to some still deeper dynamics in the modern condition that it will be good for us to have in view.

Recall the claim made earlier: modernity is a crisis. By talking about modernity as a crisis I mean to note the way that modernity forces upon people a certain intensity of decision, an expansion of the scope of their self-conscious agency. (*Krisis* in the original Greek means a "decisive moment," a moment where one must make a decision.) On the most banal level, this simply means that we who live today face many, many more choices than our ancestors did. Where we live, what we do, who and how we love, whether and how we worship — those decisions are pretty much left "up to us" in our world, and those are just the big ones. On a deeper level this expansion of choice, of human agency, suggests a more ambitious goal: the goal of a human life defined through and through by its own choices, the ideal of the wholly "self-made" individual. This goal is unrealizable, of course, though our efforts to achieve it have led to some very good developments in the modern world, and some very bad ones.

So "more modernity" is not a solution; it is our condition. Modernity just *is* this condition, which the British sociologist Anthony Giddens has called "radical reflexivity," that condition in which we are forced to recognize that "who we are" seems increasingly a contingent matter, a matter of accidents of birth and biography, of choices that almost never seem inevitable.

What is this condition doing to us, as individuals and as communities? To answer that, it helps to understand how thinkers have understood our predicament. Today we face two such visions; I call the first the "totalitarian" vision, and the second the "end of history" vision. Though both have useful insights, neither is fully adequate. Understanding the strengths and weaknesses of both will help us articulate a fuller view than either alone will allow.

For the totalitarian vision, the main worry is the tyranny of power. Such thinkers, drinking deep at the well of twentieth-century history, find the struggle of contemporary history to be between humanity's desire for genuine liberty and our fears of one another, culminating in, as Tzvetan Todorov put it, "the simplified division of the world into good people and bad people." The central fear of this sociopolitical imagination was powerfully captured in George Orwell's terrifying vision, in his prophetic 1984, of "a boot stamping on a human face — forever." Here the worry of absolute power culminates in a vision of absolute violence — of the idea that behind everything there is violence. The nightmare is a condition of perpetual war — war of governments against each other, and using those wars to mount terror campaigns against their citizens: a world of ever-increasing violence and soul-crushing terror.

But is humanity becoming more violent? What evidence we have suggests the opposite. Both domestically and internationally, first in Europe and North America and then spreading outward in the twentieth century, the past few centuries have seen a remarkable decline in humans' tendencies to violence. Personal assault, vendettas, rape and sexual violence, feuding — less individual and "private" violence seems to happen today than at any previous time in recorded history. This is true at the international level as well as at the intranational one: the main worries on the geopolitical scene have moved in the past century from "evil empires" to "rogue states" and "evil actors." Though it may sound mad to say after the century we have just witnessed, in fact humanity in 2009 is far less prone to violence than humanity in 1909, or 1809, or before then. In terms of relative destructiveness, no large war has yet surpassed the Thirty Years' War of 1618-1648, which annihilated fully a third of the population of Germany. Even in the relative near-term this is so: the Cold War gave the appearance of peace because there was no great-power war, but in fact, global conflict rose steadily in the third world throughout, and especially from the 1960s forward. It was only after the end of the Cold War and the demise of the Soviet bogeyman that these wars began to be noticed in the West. Far from suggesting that humans are getting more barbarously violent, the evidence is substantial that we are becoming more and more peaceable.

So the expectations of those captured by the totalitarian imagination ill-fit the evidence we possess. But if they are wrong, what will shape the twenty-first century? A different set of worries — worries caused not by an excess of strength and political energy but by the absence of such energy — offers an answer to this question.

This worry goes like this: our world has changed with the demise of Communism and the triumph of liberal democratic capitalism, no matter what the various local and parochial insurgencies against it proclaim. (Contemporary self-styled "leftists" like Hugo Chavez can sustain themselves only by being parasitic on the global capitalist economy; Chavez buys his domestic popularity with the petrodollars he gets abroad.) Today, in this second view, we increasingly lack a rich language of moral and spiritual concern, the sort of language that enables us to

live fully meaningful lives. The debased version of consumerist life offered to us feels inadequate to a growing number of people, but when
anyone tries to complain about our condition, and gives voice to those
complaints in their full existential and intellectual depth, a response is
provoked in the rest of us that is finally a cynical dismissal of the viabil-
ity and staying power of any real alternative.

Why is this? The answer, on this view, is simple: liberal capitalism
continually subverts the various efforts people make to cultivate and
sustain the conditions for meaningful and morally energized lives, the
very sorts of lives that liberal capitalism needs humans to lead — dedicated, morally serious, focused on substantial long-term goals — in order for it to survive. Every institution, every social structure meant to
resist the commodification of reality that liberal capitalism embodies,
eventually succumbs to becoming just one more lifestyle option within
the machine. Liberal capitalism, in short, eats its own hope.

Some thinkers talk about this problem using the language of nihilism. They fear that the people cultivated by such a society will simply
believe in nothing, will lose the capacity to be existentially committed.
Such thinkers see evidence to support this claim; for example, Bernard
Henri-Levy has argued that most contemporary wars, especially those
in Africa today, differ from most earlier wars in being about nothing —
in being less a crusade or some politically coherent action and more
simply a matter of sheer opportunism by some groups against others,
the soldiers involved more akin to gangsters than any Greatest Generation, and everyone trapped in the kind of life that Mad Max would understand. And there is always the thought that, at its heart, this world is
at the stage that Samuel Beckett depicted in the final moment of his terrifying *Act without Words*, where the sole actor, having been defeated in
his efforts to use all available props to kill himself, is given, just before
the lights go out, this final direction: "he looks at his hands."

There's something right about this diagnosis. Especially, but not only,
in advanced industrial societies, we do see the rise of a corrosive
ironism that undercuts the ability to take conviction — religious, political, even moral — seriously. But nihilism is not the best language to describe this; I would rather put it in terms of idolatry. By "idolatry" I
mean the absolutizing of a partial or relative value, the raising of a
lesser good to our ultimate aim, the fabrication of a false god. Talking
about our challenges as idolatry lets us acknowledge that no one is

without commitments, that, even if people do not admit it, they are pursuing what they see as genuine goods — most obviously, the material goods needed for a flourishing life. But the pursuit of such goods becomes idolatrous when we try to use such material goods to suffocate our immaterial longings. Understanding it in this way, we must seek to create and sustain structures of meaning that can survive the corrosive effects that go along with the many benefits of liberal capitalism: we must continually reconfront the challenge of cultivating convictions in a context where convictions are difficult to sustain; we must struggle to be the kind of people we should be — people who strive to be good and who inhabit, albeit ambivalently, this liberal-capitalist order.

There are always dangers in any appeal to "the big picture." Such appeals always give license to look away from concrete realities of our world into more or less woolly abstractions; we use such abstractions more typically to delude ourselves than to force us to face realities we'd otherwise not see. But still, some such set of abstractions is inevitable. This book is nothing if not a big-picture book. It offers an interpretation of our condition, and recommends one way in which we may fruitfully inhabit it. It argues that 9/11, the "war on terror," and the Iraq war are all, in an important sense, noise — events whose drama may distract us from the deep background changes that have been occurring, largely unnoticed, for a number of years, and that in fact give those events their proper meaning. And it recommends that these changes make it urgent for us consciously to adopt a mode of existence that better enables us to cultivate the theological virtues. 9/11, that is, is epoch-marking, not epoch-making; as a symbol, it does not signify an entry into a new age, but rather a sharp reminder to reflect on our larger modern condition.

The Christian faith has something to say about this. But how it says it, and what language it uses to say it in, is more idiosyncratic than many recognize.

III. The Republic of Grace

Hope is a preeminently *political* virtue, best cultivated not in individuals but in communities. It is by thinking about hope that we are most likely to admit the fundamental inadequacy of sheer individualism and recognize the need for communities to form our individual characters. The myth of the lone hero is, by and large, just that: a myth. This is not to deny the value of genuine individuals at all; to the contrary, genuine individuals are pretty much possible only in the context of such rich community upbringings.

Because it is found more primarily in communities than in individuals, the challenges to hope described above are best addressed by communities. But what does that mean? We typically picture a book's audience as composed of solitary individual readers, consuming the book in silence and interiority, for reasons of individual enrichment and edification. There are lots of books that basically serve as manuals or handbooks for an individual's living, a guide for being an individual in our culture today. Being an individual is a real achievement today. In the land of the blind, the one-eyed man is king, and books addressed to individuals do offer helpful ways of not succumbing entirely to the commodifying whirlwind in which we live.

But this book is not like that. It is not a theological self-help manual, a guide to individual improvement, a book of advice addressed primarily to individuals. Certainly all individuals — non-Christians and Christians alike — can read the book on their own, and I hope they will learn a great deal from it. But as an explicitly Christian effort, this book is directly addressed to communities interested in shaping themselves and one another in certain ways — ways that may seem at first fundamentally political but in fact are far broader and deeper than that.

A. An Epistle to the Churches

The communities I am primarily speaking to here are the Christian churches — more concretely, the community of all those Christians attempting to live into their faith through and in community with one another. What do I mean by the churches? I mean, simply, those communities where the grace of Christ is most intentionally and intensively *apprehended*, its reception *cultivated*, and through that cultivation most palpably and vividly *endured*. This all happens in several ways.

First, in church we undergo the practice of *apprehending* grace: both recognizing it in our lives and, once we have recognized it, with its assistance enthusiastically confirming its presence therein. By this apprehension we learn to tell two stories: one, the story of our lives as lives in which we can discern God's gracious providential governance; and two, the story of God's saving action for the world, in Christ, in ways that find a place in that larger story for the story of our lives. This latter story makes us ever more aware, both of the presence of that grace in our lives and (as a consequence of that recognition) of our always-increasing need for its presence ever more fully.

Second, this grace, once apprehended, is further *cultivated* by the communal response, in the Spirit, to those stories and the actions they narrate — a response directed to God in prayer, praise, and thanksgiving and in acts of charity and peacemaking in the world, through the world to God. This happens in church services, of course — as we'll see, church is a place where our perception of the world is (hopefully) altered in order to help us see grace more clearly. But equally importantly, this cultivation happens outside the explicit context of church services as well — though never without the aid of others undergoing the same journey. Grace "inspires" us to change our everyday lives in very practical ways, and in and through those changes, aided by our fellows, we become in a way "habituated" to grace's acting in and upon us, and thus more sensitive to its presence, and more responsive to its promptings, in our lives.

Third and finally, once we have apprehended this grace and begun to cultivate it, we come to understand ourselves as *enduring* its reshaping of our souls and its infiltration of our consciousness. This is an experience in which we are not the primary actors. In a way it is like medicine; medicine affects our body in certain ways, causing it to change, and while it is our body that is doing most of the changing, it could not do it without the medicine. So too grace is a kind of medicine healing our souls, and a central part of our activity in receiving grace is a patience, a suffering, an endurance of the workings of grace on our very agency, our capacity to act.

In short, this grace is apprehended, cultivated, and endured by finding ourselves in the story of the triune God's dynamic, sustaining, and redeeming love of creation, and then finding out how that story carries on, with us in it. Again, while this practice is most commonly given its first form, perhaps, in worship services in church, hopefully over time it comes to encompass all parts of our lives, so that the spaces we call "churches" are not truly where the church resides: rather, the "church" is found in the midst of ordinary, everyday living.

As places where such activity occurs, the churches are subunits of the "republic of grace." What do I mean by that? Well, I mean something close to the literal meaning of "republic." Our word "republic" comes from the Latin phrase *res publica,* the "public thing," and originally referred to the object of collective and explicit reflection and deliberation in early Rome. There, the "public thing" was the flourishing of the whole community of Rome — from the moral health of its citizens and families to the political health of the community, relative to its own internal standards and to its strength in comparison with its neighbors. To think about "the public thing" was to ask questions concerning those topics; it was to think not just about the good of oneself or one's family, but about the good of the polis, the community as a whole.

The churches are a "republic of grace" in this original sense. They are a "public thing" because they are a public institution — objects of common collective attention and concern for their members, and publicly assessable for all who care to look at them. And to faithful eyes, the churches exist because of, and as a manifestation of, grace — the grace of God revealed in Christ, who founded the churches, is found *in* them, and continues to guide them.

Addressing this book to members of churches, not to citizens of political communities, is a bit odd. As an explicitly Christian attempt to teach, the nature of this teaching is peculiar. It is peculiar in two different ways, not only in its *content* but also in the *form* the advice takes.

First, it will shape its answers while alert to and informed by the theological tradition that sponsors it. *Lex orandi, lex credendi:* "The law of prayer is the law of belief." This is one of the oldest of Christian theological rules. It means that proper theological formulations, formulations of what it is right to believe, always attend to how people want to pray, to how the community means to talk to God. The voice of the people as they pray to God in thanks and praise offers a fundamental standard of theological propriety: for behind the people, guiding them, is the Holy Spirit. Theology is a way of making sense of our active gratitude, expressed in "prayer," where prayer is broadly construed as our works as well as our words. It is an attempt to understand the Holy Spirit — to catch its rhythm, so to speak. Theology is a way of dancing, where another takes the lead.

As a work of theology, this book wants to help Christian churches pray better, and so the book must hold itself accountable in a certain way to the Christian community's considered theological views.

Focusing on this one audience does not mean I want to be exclusionist or triumphalist, providing ammunition for one side in the culture wars. God knows there's enough of that going around today. Instead, I mean to argue, to Christians and non-Christians alike, that Christians can have a distinct way of thinking about these questions, one based on their ongoing need to cultivate their faith. When they reflect on the challenges of contemporary life, Christians share a set of civic worries with non-Christians, but they have peculiarly theological worries also, and they must attend to them as well.

Even here, however, non-Christians are not banned from participating in the conversation. After all, many secular critics of Christianity are spot-on and should be heeded. On the other hand, even many nonbelievers today agree that the received secular solutions to the challenges enumerated above seem tired; so many non-Christians may find that a richly theological interpretation is peculiar enough to offer new insights into these civic debates. After all, there is nothing new under the sun, and the Christian traditions have dealt with similar concerns before; hence they offer resources to help, and all of us — believers and nonbelievers alike — would be fools not to attend to them.

There is a second way that this book may be distinctive. If we want to ask the question "what is going on in the world today?" in distinctively Christian fashion, we find we must undergo a crucial dislocation from our usual point of view. Most of us reflexively ask that question from the relatively parochial "we" of national identity and national purposes; a few of us, resisting that nationalist captivity, ask it instead out of a sense of "we" as citizens of the world — say, of universal values, or the U.N., or some other political imagination of that sort. But Christianity's perspective is neither finally nationalist nor cosmopolitan. It speaks neither to citizens of this or that nation, nor to citizens of the world, but to those who would be citizens of the kingdom of heaven. Proper Christian formation challenges the way we take the division of the world into nation-states as "natural"; it helps us articulate our intuition, never fully absent, that we share with others around the world a common humanity, and that that humanity asks of us not only respect for them, but also honor for the way they manifest the glory of God in their own wondrous and fearfully made individual lives.

Calling the churches a "republic of grace" draws together superficially "political" and superficially "religious" concerns in ways that reveal all of them to be both religious and political — indeed, in ways that call into question whether so tidy a divide is as easy to make as we so often assume. After all, politics is not simply a set of merely mundane negotiations about how to split up our worldly cares and concerns; it is also asking existential and metaphysical questions about who we are and what kind of world we inhabit. On this account, politics is *itself* a graceful reality, in some ways and at some times a "symbol" of heaven: a distant anticipation of what the kingdom of God will be like. Conversely, to ask questions about the churches is to ask questions about how well this political community is developing its members' capacities to sing the new song to God that they are asked to sing, and through that "singing" to show forth to the whole world in their lives as well as through their lips what God is calling them to be and to do.

The churches are supposed to do this because humanity's purpose is to praise God. This trains us for our flourishing: on this account we are called to become fit to bear the joy — what C. S. Lewis called "the weight of glory" — that is our eschatological destiny, to delight in creation as a gift and to give due gratitude for that gift to the Giver, and to come to receive rightly the proleptic gifts of that eschatological joy in the here and now. As the fifth-century Greek theologian Gregory of Nyssa put it: "the human voice was fashioned for one reason alone — to be the threshold through which the sentiments of the heart, inspired by the Holy Spirit, might be translated clearly into the Word itself." As our voices were made to sing, so we were created to praise. The human is an ecstatic creature, born to praise and delight, to be "self-transcending," to sing a new song.

Theology takes as its topic this theme: the prospects for humans to be taken up, in and through praise, into a vivifying communion with God even now — the ultimate goal of all theology is to help Christian communities pursue the deepening (in its members' souls, through various broadly "ascetical" practices) and widening (in others, and society as a whole) of the body of Christ on earth, the church. To be a Christian is to be called to a certain kind of service, severe yet joyful, and theology consists essentially of recommendations to the faithful about how they can increase their ability to participate in the life of praise that is the flourishing of the body of Christ.

This is why theology sees the task of addressing our political anxieties as part of the larger question of the proper formations of our dispositions, our character — in short, our souls. But concerns about the shaping of souls are hardly the exclusive province of Christians. Thomas Jefferson once said that in a democracy people generally get the government they deserve. But the reverse is equally true: over time, the government gets the people it deserves, for a government has enormous power to shape, and misshape, its citizens, for good or ill. Anyone — in fact, everyone — will share those concerns.

B. Faith, Hope, and Charity

This book uses the theological virtues of faith, hope, and charity to explore these themes. The virtues provide a rich vocabulary in which to undertake a realistic and fine-grained analysis of the human's moral and spiritual condition. And in turn when we faithfully engage in public life, those virtues are themselves enriched, challenged, and reformed by that very engagement. Christians have much that is good to contribute to public life, but public life can also be a means of deepening their own appropriation of faith, hope, and charity. Through interpreting current events in light of how our world enables and challenges our cultivation of these structuring virtues, we will acquire a better understanding and appreciation of those virtues themselves, and the way of life they seek to express.

Understanding our lives in terms of virtues is not without its dangers, though. For this book, two sorts of concerns are particularly pressing. First, why *these* virtues? Why not what are called the moral virtues, classically enumerated as justice, prudence, temperance, and courage? To talk in theological terms seems at once to distance our discussion from expressly moral concerns; why do that? In fact, however, to talk about the theological virtues as shaping moral life is an old move, and we are only following Augustine in doing it here. He said that all the moral virtues are reducible to the theological virtues, and indeed that the three theological virtues are in turn themselves reducible to one: love. We will see this manifest in the pages to come in concrete terms, but to speak generally, we may say that to talk about the shaping of life first and foremost in a theological language is not to reject moral concerns, but rather to put those concerns in their proper context, as part of the larger life of a humanity seeking God.

Second, and more fundamentally: Why a language of virtue at all? In classical antiquity the virtues were achievements — heroic victories gained in struggle against the recalcitrance of our flesh. They were originally terms borrowed from warfare and sports (and possibly magic), and suggested struggle and a fairly crude form of manliness. Furthermore, from Christianity's perspective, the virtues trigger deep imaginative structures that encourage us to depict human agency as fundamentally an *achievement* of agents themselves. In thinking about our lives through the prism of the virtues, we promote a salutary level of self-reflectiveness, but that very self-reflectiveness can encourage a pathologically narcissistic self-regard in a way that obscures how much others (our neighbors and God) help us and also closes us off to seeing those others as other selves.

The value, and the danger, of such virtue language for Christian life was recognized as early as Paul's epistles (see Eph. 6:11ff.: "put on the whole armor of God," etc.). But it was Augustine who decisively changed this language's focus from activity to passivity, emphasizing not achievements but sufferings — not ways of accomplishing something but ways of being vulnerable, of being susceptible to God's efficacious working in one's soul.

The virtues are not only a generally useful lens for such thinking; each of them highlights one distinctive contribution that Christian citizens can make to public life. Considered individually and collectively, then, these virtues are very richly oriented toward proper Christian aims. Understanding our lives through their organizing framework gives us the fundamentals of a distinctively theological way of talking about our lives, and therefore of understanding them. This is especially important now because, by and large, the churches lack such theological interpretations and the theological languages that could ground them. Too often we unreflectively accept the workaday languages of our fallen world as primary, as "natural," and try to cram what we can of what our faith says within their confines; what doesn't fit gets lopped off or left to wither from lack of articulation. (For example, what we can call the Westphalian mind-set urges us to see the world's division into nation-states as fundamental, unchallengeable, and "natural" — but this mind-set itself goes back no further than the Treaty of Westphalia, in 1648, and can be intelligibly challenged, as we will do later in this book.) Very little effort is given to the project of transforming the way we see the world — to giving Christians a rich and useful language through which certain aspects of the world become more prominently visible and others become less prominently visible. Yet such a transformation is central to what Christian faith is all about.

I do not say this out of a longing for Christian "purity," out of the temptation many feel today toward some sort of Christian identity-politics. (Such fantasies are themselves little more than unknowing collaborations with other parts of the language of "the world" such as identity politics.) I say this because believers' reliance on "worldly" languages is pragmatically unwise, for typically the available secular languages are meant, more or less intentionally, to deny certain fundamental theological claims — merely by the fact that they are meant to work well whether or not we affirm those claims. A language that functions successfully "even if there were no God" is a language that Christians may well find useful, but they should use it with real care and never allow it to become their fundamental language. A better understanding and more systematic articulation of what the Christian churches are trying to do — to, with, and through their members — will help Christians be both better Christians and, assuming they think their Christian faith is an organic part of all aspects of their lives, better citizens of their communities, their nations, and the world as a whole.

Hence the peculiarity of this book, addressed as it is to a peculiar audience. Typically a book today about moral life after 9/11 would ask about the strength of civil society, the wisdom of our governments' foreign policies, our use of energy, or the prospects for dialogue between "the West" and "Islam." And all those issues come up here. But as a thoroughly "churchly" book, this book is asking the question "what is going on?" from the perspective of those who are trying more fully to inhabit that church, and who are trying also to build up that church as a reality in the world today. This doesn't mean that we utterly dismiss more apparently "worldly" concerns; it does mean that we can ask questions about the fundamental categories that we typically assume to be "natural," given and incontestable realities of our lives.

For example, we can challenge the world's apparently "natural" division into nation-states by asking different questions, about missions, international aid, and humanitarianism, ones about migration and immigration, childhood poverty, and matters of building up a community respectful of all its members, from the youngest to the oldest; most generally, we find ourselves asking for ways to help cultivate a culture of cultivating praise. How, precisely, are these questions solved, and what sorts of answers can we expect of them?

IV. Prophecy and Empire

Where is the wisdom we have lost in knowledge?
Where is the knowledge we have lost in information?

T. S. Eliot, "The Rock"

Every morning brings us news of the globe, and yet we are poor in noteworthy stories.

Walter Benjamin, "The Storyteller"

Terror, empire, luxury amidst mass poverty and squalor, falling towers — we've been here before. But while we draw on past thinkers to help our present challenges, we must be alert to the danger that the momentum of our received ways of thinking about things may subtly misdirect our appreciation of current events.

Many fall prey to this trap. For some, the road to 9/11 was an unbroken string of squeamish liberal evasions that permitted evil men to gather and lash out. Or it was a series of provocative imperialist arrogances that finally got the blowback it deserved. Neither of these is true; they suggest a too-tight chain of causes connecting one moment to another. But what, then, can we say about the connections between 9/10 and 9/11? What is the good of looking to the past if our challenges are wholly "unprecedented"?

A. Prophecy

Recall my colleague late in the morning of September 11. His particular dilemma is this book's dilemma as well. Both attempt to speak a very old word to a new world. The tools the book uses — the thinkers, the concepts, the arguments — are very old indeed; what can they bring to our deliberations? How is this myth anything more than nostalgia? Whenever I teach something that I call, without embarrassment, one of "the great books," I always recall a savage line in Samuel Beckett's play *Endgame*: "Ah, the old questions. The old questions, the old answers! There's nothing like them!" Are we not just offering "the old answers" to "the old questions"?

Things are not as bleak as all that. Much of the time, everyone will agree, the old answers will do. We are creatures of routine, of habit; much of our lives is spent busying ourselves in order to avoid acknowledging how rarely things really change. There are very few moments of inescapably genuine novelty, of true revelation in our lives — when a parent or sibling dies, when we discover we are really in love, when a child is born. Genuinely to experience the newness of the new is always to court being traumatized by it — where "trauma" means being unable to connect up before and after, and so being stuck in between, unable to retreat to the past or live genuinely in the new situation.

Sometimes people say "everything has changed." But people have been saying that for a very long time. There is an old *New Yorker* cartoon, in which Adam and Eve are in the process of being expelled from Eden, and Adam, turning to Eve, says: "my dear, we are living in a time of transition." So claims about the unprecedented nature of our situation have, themselves, many historical precedents.

The real problem is not with the activity of finding connections and analogies. For after all, events *are* connected, and these connections can be crucial, even to events we thought were already "past." When my father died, what I had seen to be local squabbles between two adults now took on the appearance of a remarkably childish strategy of avoidance on my part. When my daughter was born, I reflected on my past and discovered that what before I had understood to be evidence of my hard-driving work ethic now looked like an unbroken record of mammoth selfishness. The new challenges the old; it can cause what happened in the past to be redescribed, at times radically.

The problem is that the connections we make may obscure the particular distinctiveness of each situation, considered in itself. After all, each event is so particularly, peculiarly itself, that any story we tell about connections of events at least threatens to do violence to the quirky quiddity, the "whatness," of the events so hastily smashed together in an analogy.

The problem lies in how we try to make connections. For we think there is an easy translation from one setting to the other, and so we think only the details change. We call these details *information,* or data. Of course, we need information, and a lot of it. Being a thoughtful Christian today, and being a citizen, entails a rough understanding of the way our world is put together; and hardly any of us are even partway to such an understanding. (This is indisputable: in general, the state of our knowledge of the world is deplorable. I hope this book can point readers toward sources that can help them achieve such an understanding.) But information is useful only in situations where continuity overwhelms discontinuity. Beyond that you are in the realm of analogy, where statisticians fear to tread. And we are all too much statisticians these days — all too much enraptured by the flood of data available to us. But data will not save us, and in a book like this, a litany of facts can easily become an avoidance mechanism.

Here we see something of the true nature of prophecy. Prophecy is not meteorology, the simple prediction of future events. It is more existentially interested in the present, the *now:* What is the living God doing today? How should we sing to the Lord a new song? In this way, prophecy is the mode of being wherein we learn to be joyfully surprised. And this learning is mostly lost to us now. Our prophetic muscles are atrophied, badly in need of great reinvigoration.

More than more information, we need something else, a kind of insight that is not immediately detachable from one situation and applicable to a new one, an insight that is only ever incompletely inexpressible but that, in the hands of the wise, can shed light on many different situations. *In the hands of the wise,* note — it is not enough that anyone can do this, they must be already able to hear it. And what do the wise hear? They hear — and they communicate to others — not information, but what Walter Benjamin called "counsel." They teach, however indirectly and by subtle insinuations, a way of listening to the world, a way of listening that lets us hear the faint echoes of the past in the fresh clamor of the present. In learning how to listen, we learn to hear those faint echoes, echoes to be sure, but by their faintness signaling the distance of the analogies they propose. More prosaically, they help us recognize patterns, but without letting our apprehension of those patterns blot out our apprehension of the novelty of our present situation.

For the particular "old" word here offered claims to be the ever-new

Word, announcing the glad tidings of a new creation coming into view. Again, my colleague's response on the afternoon of 9/11 is right: here the act of teaching is an act of hope — proclaiming that we are still in a position where we can hear Karl Barth's words, where they still have a meaning for us. They have a meaning for us because they are *prophetic*. And prophecy is not a light matter. My colleague's dilemma renders palpable the prophetic, the hopeful stance, the stance of counsel.

Yet wise counsel would caution us to tread gently here. For if the besetting sin of the modern information-maximizing mind-set is to imagine that there is a fundamental continuity across all historical movements, the besetting sin of the prophetic is to imagine that the past simply repeats itself in the present. A hasty equation of past and present is always a temptation. That temptation stems from one of the most powerful and potentially perilous convictions of Christianity: namely, that we live in the *epilogue*, the "afterword," after the truly important events of history — the fall, incarnation, crucifixion, and resurrection — have already occurred. Now, it seems, we are merely waiting about for the final denouement. The end of history has already been "scripted," quite literally, for Christians; we know already what is going to happen — namely, the second coming. Prophecy, in this setting, can seem like sheer repetition, a broken record.

There is something very dangerous in this. It can encourage us to conceive of the time to come until the end as empty, meaningless time, bearing nothing good or significant. It can lure us away from seeing the realities before our eyes and toward pondering abstractions and promises whose fulfillment seems perpetually deferred. It can flatter us into a false confidence that we know what is happening, and what will happen. It can tell us we don't need to look at the world, to seek to understand it, genuinely to live in it, because we already know the real story, and nothing else, as the Barth essay put it, can matter. In short, this conviction can become escapist and apocalyptic.

It *can* be. But it need not be so (mis)used. Surrendering to this temptation — what I call the *apocalyptic* temptation — is always a possibility. But it is not an inevitability. For proper Christian faith does not deny that we will continue to be surprised, nor that such surprises are good or significant. After all, the Christian God is a living God, and in Christ God is doing a new thing, a newness as old as creation, a newness whose perception we've lost after the fall. This new thing's novelty is so radical as to not be fully visible to us now; it will become visible only at the eschaton. Faith in this God demands a kind of training, a cultivation of our capacity to discern God's working in all aspects of our lives. It requires us to see the world as sacramental — a matter of signs that God uses to communicate with us, to commune with us. Such a faith requires, and elicits, a profound suspension of our apocalyptic temptation to draw conclusions, to say we "know already" all that is to come. It is, in a word, not an apocalyptic but an eschatological faith.

The distinction I make here, between an "eschatological" imagination and an "apocalyptic" one, will reappear from time to time throughout this book. In much literature on religion these terms are sometimes used interchangeably, but for complex reasons I do not do that here; so it will be useful for you to know what I mean by these terms. The "apocalyptic" imagination is the temptation we feel to assume we know already what is going on and what will be going on. It expresses the presumption that we already know, by and large, the details of how things will turn out at the end of history; history is scripted in advance for this mind-set, and it pretty much knows the script. In contrast, the eschatological faith — urged on us by thinkers like Augustine — confidently confesses that it knows that "all will be well," but it also humbly confesses that it does not foreknow *how* all will be well. It requires us to look and see what is going on in the world, to attend to it eagerly, hungrily, for the signs of the times, and not to presume we know already. Rather than lure us away from careful attention to the world, it demands that we scrutinize the world all the more assiduously.

This puts Christians in an odd position vis-à-vis historical existence. For Christians typically understand themselves to be living in a time of fundamental emergency, of *krisis*, but history itself is this *krisis*, this "time of transition," so there is an air of "nothing new under the sun" about the proper Christian attitude. Recall the line of C. S. Lewis discussed in the introduction: "The war creates no absolutely new situation: it simply aggravates the permanent human situation so that we can no longer ignore it." And yet there is real novelty on this view in the ever-new character of God's word. Because of this, we should not treat the world as "more of the same," but recognize a profound tension between the old and the new. The transition from the old to the new, or rather, living in the time of that transition, is what Christianity is all about. That is to say, in thinking historically, Christianity's potential strength and its possible weakness are one and the same. This book seeks to provide counsel for our continued existence within that tension.

Here Augustine can teach us. For he has counsel to deliver. Indeed, he is misread unless he is read as primarily offering counsel. He definitely has convictions and views that he wants to convey, but for him those convictions, absent the larger transformation of our character that he demands, would be superficial. In his age, as now, the central problem of human life was the human heart at war with itself. This was the old story about human existence, and Augustine's counsel as regards it has never been bettered.

B. Empire

But it is not enough to say that Christians are always looking at the world to be surprised. There is a difference between being flummoxed and being surprised, and prophets always have something to say about the new thing. Christians bring to their encounters with "the new" a set of categories that shape the contours of their surprise — what it is they will be surprised *at*, and how they will respond to that surprise. Central here, historically, is the concept of *empire*.

"Empire" is an old concept, one of the oldest in Christian thought, visible at least as early as the book of Revelation — or perhaps Isaiah, or even the story of the Tower of Babel in Genesis. It has decisively shaped contemporary suspicion of and worry about domination. And yet it is not finally a political concept, but a theological one.

In its deepest roots in the tradition, "empire" is what happens to human rule when it unmoors itself from proper service to God; empire is what humans do — to themselves, to others, and to the whole of creation — when they decide they will not only be *like* God (which is bad enough) but will instead try to *be* God, to supplant God's sovereignty with their own. Oliver O'Donovan puts it nicely when he says that, from the earliest political texts of ancient Israel forward, "world-empire was a bestial deformation." Christianity's vision of the world is not properly understood unless one recognizes the role in it of the divine's eschatological confrontation with what it identifies as "the powers" of this world — the rebellious energies potent in (and in a way subjugating) fallen humanity, energies that attempt to make the world self-governing, separate from God; Christianity has always interpreted these powers through the language of empire. Properly to inhabit the world — properly to survive in our world in an age of sacred terror — properly to be prophetically engaged in the *saeculum* — we must come to terms with humans' misuse of power and authority, and this means coming to terms with what gets classified under empire. For Christians, then, to think about life in this world after the fall is to think, directly or not, about empire, and to think about empire is to think about worldliness.

To think about politics via the category of empire is a valuable and powerful thing, but it has its dangers, and we should be alert to them. Historically the idea of empire has typically been a crude tool used to bludgeon one's way through political life rather than a lantern to light the way on that dim and tricky path. It is usually taken to suggest that all human political involvement is inevitably the work of the Antichrist (if you think Americans hate politics *today*, they have nothing on Christians of the first or second century), and much Christian political thinking that tries to avoid this trap often does so only by simply baptizing political authority with divine sovereignty. Even today some Christians are tempted to eschew politics altogether, while others demand a this-worldly kingdom based on the possibilities of justice. Even today, that is, we have a hard time thinking about *politics* itself — as the need to get along with others in an (apparently) interminably mixed (and mixed-up) world. To think about politics via these categories, then, risks the dangers endemic to all thinking about politics, for such thinking is much harder than we first imagine.

This book is an effort to think about life today — political life most immediately, but life in general as well — under these new-yet-old conditions. As such it is not first and foremost an argument but an introduction to a language: a language that brings to articulate self-consciousness, and thus to reflective vision, what it means to live in our inescapably political world. It does this to provoke articulate thought of the appropriate scope and depth to address the full nature of the challenges we all face.

Let me be clear. I am not primarily trying to convince you to share my judgments, but to enter into a more serious way of thinking about these matters. It is quite possible to understand and affirm the vocabulary through which the book analyzes what is going on, and yet to dissent from its judgments about what will happen and how we ought to live in this world. And readers can certainly understand this vocabulary but decide to dissent from it, even if they find quite plausible the practical diagnosis and prescription that that vocabulary enables. I am happy for this book to have as many friends as it can find, in whatever ways it can find them. But even if it finds no friends, I hope it at least provokes others to do better than they have yet done in thinking about what is going on and how we should respond.

For this much, I think, is incontestable: today we need, not a theory that explains what has gone wrong with the world and who is to blame for it, but an account of who we are, what our condition is, and how we should live in it, so that we can live as best we can in the world — the world that we find ourselves in, not the world that we tell ourselves *should* be.

We'll see what that amounts to in the pages to come.

PART I

SEEING AS CHRISTIANS

CHAPTER 2

9/11: Terror, War, and Hope

⌁

W hat are the odds of you, or someone close to you, being killed in a terrorist attack? Vanishingly small. What about dying in a car accident? Significantly larger. Roughly 43,000 people were killed in the United States in 2001 by automobile crashes. That's more than one 9/11 every month. In fact, after 9/11 Americans' fear of flying caused more people to drive long distances, which increased the number of auto fatalities significantly; according to one estimate, approximately 350 extra lives were lost in the three months following the attacks from the increase in people driving over flying. The casualties of 9/11 weren't just those who died in the Pentagon, World Trade Center, and the airplanes.

None of this is to say that the danger of terrorist attacks is illusory. But part of their danger is the way they misshape our expectations of the future, amplifying certain imagined dangers while diminishing others. Indeed, the actual deaths in terrorist attacks are, properly speaking, incidental; the aim is rather to affect the shape of some audience's expectations about the future. Terror, that is to say, is a profoundly *un*literal act.

The twentieth century saw many changes in the nature of political life, but among the most powerful was the discovery, or creation, of the mass politics of fear and hysteria. Certainly before 1900 there were ways in which political leaders and actors whipped up mobs and used the psychology of terror for their own purposes — the early Jim Crow era in the American South is one example, as is the anti-Jewish pogroms of medieval Europe — but the twentieth century perfected those skills. We live in what some social theorists have called a "risk society," wherein recognition of the power of decisions we make has created a situation where we have become aware of *risk* in a new way; our sensitivity to risk renders us also susceptible to manipulation by terror. Citizens increasingly appeal to their governments not simply to address their material needs, but to manage their immaterial fears. One of the greatest political discoveries of the century was, as Hannah Arendt said, the discovery that terror could be controlled and used like a weapon. Terrorists use it; states use it; politicians use it; even advertisers use it.

None of this is meant to insinuate any kind of moral equivalence between what political campaigners in the United States do, or what anti-American European politicians do, and what al-Qaeda or the IRA or the Red Brigades or Kim Jong-Il (or even Vladimir Putin) does. All I am saying is that the general political life of today often cultivates in us just the sorts of dispositions and habits of fear, anxiety, and threat perception that are most inimical to proper hope.

This chapter addresses this problem directly by engaging with the effects of 9/11 and the "War on Terror" since then. Insofar as this is a war on terror, it is not a traditional, literal war at all. There are no front lines, no home front, no enemy territorial base. But despite its melodramatic connotations, the metaphor of "war" is appropriate, for it captures the character of the conflict as a violent struggle between two sides on matters of genuinely existential concern. (The dead since 9/11 number at least [at least!] 100,000 — so it's been fairly existential for *some* people.) Nonetheless, we must beware overliteralizing this war — confusing the spirit and the letter, as it were — for the nature of the contest is crucially spiritual, psychological, and symbolic in ways it is essential to grasp. This chapter argues that it is a struggle between despair and hope.

In using the language of "hope," we must keep alert to the ways it confuses the crisp lines we often want to draw between "secular" or "worldly" matters and "spiritual" or "religious" ones. For hope has a way of overrunning all the boundaries we like to set for it. It is clearly a worldly category, as it energizes and orients worldly action. Yet it is also a category that reaches beyond any worldly confirmation or motivation, speaking out of, and toward, some supraworldly ideal of justice. Hope is, in its origins and in its ultimate end, I argue, a theological reality, and yet (and just because of that) it profoundly illuminates the this-worldly dynamics of our "secular" political life.

Or so this chapter will argue. Part I summarizes Augustine's own "war on terror" — namely, his campaign against the Donatist Christians in North Africa — as a prelude for thinking about our own situation. Part II attempts to explain the real nature of the conflict we are engaged in, and to suggest how that conflict will continue through the coming decades. Part III proposes a political psychology of terrorism, arguing that the challenge is best understood as a temptation toward resentment and despair, and hence toward a certain hopelessness. Finally, part IV draws counsel from Augustine's approach to the Donatists to understand the nature of our situation as Christians in this world, and how we should endure the conflicts between terror and hope that riddle our lives today, and will for many years to come.

I. An Augustinian War on Terror

Augustine was involved with a "war on terror" of his own: a theological, cultural, and ultimately political struggle with a group called the Donatists. He tried to confront that conflict in a properly Christian way. Both in how he taught his congregants and in how he urged the authorities to behave he has much to teach us.

The Donatists were those Christians in North Africa who, in the fourth and fifth centuries, held to the more traditional and local ways of the faith, against what they saw as the corrupt and outsider imperial Latin churches, which they saw as interloping carpetbaggers. Donatism began as a complaint, a century before Augustine's time, by some of the faithful against certain high church officials who had betrayed the church by handing over church Bibles and perhaps other information to pagan Roman authorities out of fear of persecution and who, after the persecutions ended, wanted to return to the church and to their ecclesial offices. Once the persecution was over, these authorities were permitted by the larger church to return to the fold. But many among the local churches of North Africa — which had a reputation for parochial nativism, for toughness, and for enduring bloody persecutions with great resilience — wanted nothing to do with priests seen as cowardly, duplicitous, and in the service of Romans (no matter that they were catholic Romans; "a Roman's a Roman," one can almost hear Donatists say). So they refused to accept them, and set up parallel ecclesial bodies, which took most of the people (in many cities, *all* the people and the buildings) with them. The issue at its most basic was a matter of moral and religious propriety and rectitude: Donatists demanded, as they saw it, a certain integrity among their priests, and they saw the Latin catholic priests as irremediably corrupted by their descent from traitorous bishops. And they simply wanted nothing to do with them.

Augustine thus entered a North African church that was split between two warring factions, with his faction visibly the smaller and weaker. Augustine's first response to this challenge was debate. As he said in a letter to Vincentius (bishop of a faction of Donatists called Rogatists), "[m]y opinion at first was that no one should be coerced into the unity of Christ: that we must act only by words, fight only by arguments, and overcome by reason alone, lest we should have those whom we knew to be true heretics becoming false catholics." Furthermore, this debate was expected to be mutual, with force being used by neither side: early on, in a letter to a then-Donatist bishop Maximinus, he said, "let there be no terror produced by gangs of *circumcelliones*," that is, groups of hard-line Donatist vagabonds who roamed the countryside like outlaw gangs, using violence and assassination against the Catholic clergy and their allies in North Africa.

Augustine never jettisoned debate as a default option. Until the end of his life he always tried argumentative means of persuasion toward the Donatists, and urged others in his congregation and through letters to do the same.

This was rhetorically powerful. He sought accommodation, always insisting that it was the other side that was not accommodating. Furthermore, he worked to undercut the Donatists' cultural ethnonationalism by insisting that the catholic church could be authentically "native." But over time, his wish to manage matters by nonviolent debate foundered on the rocks of (what he described as) Donatist intransigence. As he wrote to the Donatist bishop Januarius, various Donatist radicals attacked priests, ransacked churches and monasteries, and ambushed catholic religious processions, "disturbing our peace and devastating us by their most appalling crimes and mad acts of violence." This *"compelled* us" (note the use of "compulsion" here) to ask imperial authorities to combat the worst of the Donatists with the threat and at times the use of force to throw them out of their churches, to force them to enter in communion with catholics upon pain of death, to employ physical violence to foster inner belief.

In no way did Augustine think that urging such compulsion was a theologically or morally inconsequential matter. He recognized that there was a theological problem with the idea of coercion, which is why he tried to offer reasons for it. More surprisingly still, he urged the turn to coercion for profoundly "civic" reasons. He framed his argument to the imperial authorities not first of all as a theological matter of saving souls, but as a civic matter of protecting people, presenting the extremist Donatist radicals, the *circumcelliones,* as threats above all to the *civic* order. So he wrote to Emeritus, a Donatist bishop: "when our people seek help from the powers which are ordained, they do so not to persecute you, but to protect themselves from the lawless acts of violence perpetrated by your people."

Yet his civic-mindedness was not the whole story. Augustine was convinced that fear could shape souls in good ways, that it could be a vehicle for positive formation, which is what he understood by discipline. As he wrote to another Donatist bishop, named Vincentius, "[m]y opinion at first was that no one should be coerced into the unity of Christ. . . . But this opinion of mine was overcome not by the words of those who opposed it, but by the examples to which they could point by way of demonstration. For, in the first place, my own city stood in opposition to my view. Once wholly on the side of Donatus, it was converted to catholic unity by fear of the imperial laws." Fear, he thought, is a useful force for shaping souls, and no realistic political psychology can do without it.

But Augustine thinks of "fear" and "compulsion" far more broadly than we typically do. The word he uses in his letters, especially in numbers 93 and 185 (to Boniface, count of Africa), is *cogo* (to collect), not *compello* (to compel). *Cogo* is not a matter of simple compulsion; furthermore, Augustine seems to think of it as etymologically related to thinking (*cogitando*), as the prerequisite for it — because we must have collected things for us to think over. Outward *cogo* can lead to inward *cogito*. On his understanding, compulsion is the use of external power in the hope of enabling (not straightforwardly causing) an inner change. Think about teaching and learning: teachers "compel" their students and put them in a situation to learn. Doctors compel their patients' bodies with medicine and hope the bodies use the medicine rightly to heal themselves; God, the supreme doctor, uses suffering's "harsh medicine" along with pleasant lessons to educate and reclaim sinners. The same is true for civic authorities; rebuke and reform, *correptio* and *correctio*, are intimately related. For Augustine, coercion was not punitive but therapeutic, a matter of using what Frederick Russell calls "constricting circumstances" to coerce. God can use fear as well as hope; indeed, the two may be far more intimately related than we imagine. Rulers should lovingly chastise their subjects; magistrates can make some behaviors unpalatable, by taxation or punishment, in the hope of effecting changes in behavior. Heretics' "blasphemous folly, like some tumor, is healed by deterrence, rather than punishment by surgical removal." The external threat of punishment may induce people to avoid overt behavior, and over time the hope is that the law enters into their souls to shape it — and so they eventually become not only grudgingly nonrapists, for example, but people for whom doing sexual violence to another person's body is, strictly speaking, unthinkable.

Augustine regularly intervened for leniency and insisted that disciplinary correction must be moderate. As he put it in a letter to one Donatus, proconsul of Africa (not a Donatist, despite his name): "We desire that the terror of judges and laws shall be an opportunity not to slay them but to correct them, lest they fall under the penalty of eternal judgment." But nonetheless, state coercion was for him *an opportunity* — not a necessary evil but possibly, in this setting, useful and commendable. This had seriously damaging consequences. His account, with nuances forgotten and ambivalences effaced, underwrote in part a millennium and more of political thought about the use of political force to coerce.

Yet we cannot let our disappointment with Augustine be the only thing we take from this episode. His ultimate civic rationale for forcing the Donatists' conversion was not directly to gain them for the church, but rather to subvert their greatest pretension to religious purity, thereby indirectly rendering them more susceptible to accepting the merciful grace of God. He was no Grand Inquisitor. His fundamental purpose in this matter was not the use of the sword to gain bodies for his one true church; it was more fundamentally defensive, an attempt to let witness peaceably play its worldly role in a situation where some were willing to use violence to resist that action.

There is another insight here, easily overlooked. Augustine's response to the Donatists has often been summarized as an exemplary case of "Constantinianism," collaboration with the kingdoms of this world. But in fact, his most important words were not to the authorities of the *imperium Romanum*, but to his parishioners in the "catholic" churches of his diocese, and believers in North Africa in general. This is visible especially in his preaching to his congregants. Sermon after sermon grapples with the problems of manifesting rightly ordered love, and in a setting in which rivals such as the Donatist churches violently contested the "catholic" churches. Here we find Augustine's most direct response to the challenge of the Donatists. In these sermons he asks: How should his parishioners face the dualism of the Donatists, and the violence of their most fanatical adherents? It would be all too easy, Augustine suspects, to react to them by returning the compliment, mirroring the Donatists' own behavior and demonizing them just as they demonized the catholics. He recognizes the power of such polarization, but he knows it is based on a reactionary fear that refuses to recognize the many connections they have with each other — the many complicated strands of attachment and affiliation that run across boundaries of faction and party. Furthermore, it would simply reproduce the Donatists' mis-vision of the world. Their problem, after all, is that they assume a dualism between world and God and seek to abandon the world; to this temptation Augustine reminds his parishioners to ask, "Were there no saints in the world at large? Was it right for you to condemn them unheard?" Rather than leaving the world and the neighbor, we should more fully engage them and recognize their radical ambivalence for faith. For Augustine, congregants do this by manifesting with their lips and in their lives a willingness to see others as their neighbors, deserving their love and esteem.

And we do that, Augustine insists, through hope, hope for the possibility of love between the two sides, between "us" and "them" — a sense that we are, at least potentially, more united than divided, that we are better together than apart, that no one is ultimately a stranger or enemy. There is no security in attempting to inhabit such hope, Augustine warns. But none should be anticipated, or even hoped for, in this life. As Augustine says, "Expect not security in journeying; if ever we wish for it here, it will be the birdlime of the body, not the safety of the man." Our hopes must seek only a transcendental satisfaction. This condition of suspension, of waiting, is hard to take, but it is our condition, and any attempt to end it by telling a story that excludes our ultimate end — or, as in the Donatists' case, suggests that we know with too much certitude which side our neighbors will be on when at last that end arrives — is dangerously premature. Instead, we should seek to be "trained by longing" for the eschaton. But this training takes place here, and we cannot escape it, or the conditions of this journey, before our completion.

Augustine's strategy is simple. In situations where "religion" and "politics" are already mixed together, we should not necessarily seek to disentangle them *directly* — for all such efforts may backfire. Instead, we might accept what may look like the instrumentalization of the church for civic ends, in order to achieve certain finite civic goals by resisting the bad theological pretensions of the spiritually self-righteous. The civic peace this strategy secures lets us pursue our fundamental spiritual project of confronting the challenge of living hopefully in such a situation.

The danger of the civic instrumentalization of religion is that it can defeat one threat to the hope of faith by collaborating with another. So even as we respond to those who would terrorize us, we must stay alert to how the defense may turn out to be just as hazardous as the danger. But it is a risk, Augustine says, we are well advised to run.

II. A Semiotic War

In these ways Augustine has much to say on how we should endure a "war on terror," and how we should respond to it. Can we apply those lessons? Like Augustine, this chapter means to advise churches not polities, citizens not presidents; our aim is not to guide U.S. policy, but to understand what is going on, in order to help believers do the best job they can in believing under these conditions.

The first thing to recognize is the inescapability of the "long war" itself, and come to terms with the need to endure it. But that will entail the popular acceptance of a certain low-intensity conflict and the long-term discovery that the "war on terror" is really a war over hope. I explain this more fully now.

What does it mean to "win" a war on terror? I do not mean this as a rhetorical question. What will "winning" look like? Many who resist describing the struggle as a war do so because they do not think the language of "victory" can have any meaning in this sort of conflict. The limitations of the metaphor of a "war on terror" are profound. The enemy is not a symmetric rival; despite its rhetoric, al-Qaeda does not threaten to annihilate or conquer the United States. It has no traditional force structure that can be defeated on a battlefield, but is more like an elite cadre of venture capitalists of terror, funding innumerable start-up terror cells, generally for single operations. Furthermore, the goal of this war is not territorial conquest or liberation; al-Qaeda's violence is ultimately more "expressive" than strategically instrumental. Its attacks are not meant directly to effect strategic changes, but to do so only as *interpreted* by audiences. As Christopher Henzel puts it, "al Qaeda's immediate goal is not to destroy Israel or even drive the United States out of the Middle East; rather, it is to 'orient the nation.'" None of this denies the literality of the violence: real people die. But the actual deaths are instrumental, a way of communicating to various audiences. Because of this, the nature of "combat" with this opponent differs dramatically from that of traditional wars. Fighting al-Qaeda is in fact more like fighting an ad agency than like fighting Nazi Germany.

Given that fact, can we really call this a war? Certainly. But the Western nations may just be bit players in this war, even though it may seem that they are the great actors in it. We need to imagine what victory in this war looks like, and to do that we must understand the nature of the war being fought today. It is not a war as we have traditionally understood it, but a semiotic war — a war by signs, over signs, and in a sense about signs. But signs of what? Referring to what? To answer this question, we must distinguish the spirit from the letter and understand just which war is actually being fought.

For Augustine, signs are related to hope, for signs are promises of the real things to which they refer, and so the fact that it is a "war of signs" means it is a war about our hopes. What seems to United States audiences to be a war of terror is more properly a war over hope — a war to see who will most shape the hopes and fears of the populations caught up in it. It is not a "clash of civilizations," even though al-Qaeda would like it to be interpreted as such; it is a civil war in the Islamic world, a war caused by despair — not only in the *dar-al-Islam* but also in the Muslim ghettos of western Europe — a despair about the prospects for a real future for a very proud civilization.

Ironically, in fact, the roots of this war do not lie fundamentally in failure but, in a way, in partial success — in the partial success of modernity, and the frustrations attendant upon that very partiality. Muslims are asking real and fundamental questions about how to practice their faith in a world of global capital flows, information networks, and liberal democratic nations. The collapse of the secular pan-Arabist ideologies of Nasser and his generation; the collapse of the traditional Islamic authorities' (the *ulama*'s) monopoly on religious orthodoxy with the rise of literacy; the bureaucratically sclerotic, corrupt, and stagnated state-led economies; the enormous "youth bulge" entering the labor force; and the popular recognition, fed by the explosion of media of all kinds, from satellite dish TV to cassette tapes, that much of the rest of the world has it much better than the status quo in the Middle East: all this suggests growing resentment and anger as the gap between expectations and reality widens for these nations' citizens. (This was all well noted in the 2002 Arab Human Development Report, in which a group of Arab scholars blamed the region's failure to progress on "deficits" of freedom, knowledge, and women's empowerment.) In this civil war the main combatants embody various responses to despair. On the two ends of this cross fire, tyrants still govern according to kleptocratic "principles," such as they are, and radical Islamists engage in a sanguinary nostalgia for a long-ago "pure" caliphate, by which they mean an institutional denial of modernity. Caught in the cross fire are the vast majority of Muslims, who are from time to time tempted by the parodic patriotism of their leaders and the nihilistic nostalgia of the insurgents, but who believe there is still something more.

Given all this, the world is caught in the middle of a very long struggle — probably stretching over decades — between those who seek to relate positively (however critically) to Western modernity and those Islamic actors who seek simply to demonize and oppose it. This is the truth behind Pentagon officials speaking about "The Long War." This war will not most fundamentally be fought on the battlefield. It is not centrally a military action, but instead a struggle over the future, or better, a struggle to move from one way of life to another, a struggle that has caught many people in its midst. The Bush administration failed to recognize how the West's enemies flourish precisely in this ambivalence. Poll after poll suggests that Islamic views of Western societies, and especially the United States, are profoundly ambivalent. Alongside images of American prosperity and happiness are other characteristics — appalling moral lassitude; weakness of character; lack of respect; lack of integrity; grotesque, institutionalized, self-interested consumerism — that characterize America for many Muslims. But are the benefits of the "American way of life" inextricably intertwined with the morally compromising ones? Al-Qaeda thrives in the murky space where the answer to this question lurks.

There is no quick solution regarding these matters; they have generational timescales. The best weapon, the only real weapon, against despair is hope, and certainly a multigenerational promise to help Middle Eastern countries transition to something approximating representative democracy *could* inspire such hope. But it will take a long while. The social and political alienation and economic stagnation show no signs of alleviation in any of the countries in the Middle East, and the demographic pressures that seem so massive now will only become more profound for the next several decades. Citizens of the world must become accustomed to living with the threat of terrorist violence, and they must find a way to live as best they can with this fact. It will become less a discrete event or era and more the climate of existence itself.

This will be a challenge, because the U.S. populace is notoriously optimistic about war: they believe that wars can be won neatly, decisively, and quickly. These expectations must be adjusted to the reality that this war will not end in any neat and quick manner. In fact, in a way, the war on terror cannot be won; it can only be managed until it goes away, as the United Kingdom's experience with the IRA demonstrates. The United States will have to learn to live with the fear of sudden horrific violence, the danger of which will not recede for a decade or more. And yet the U.S. populace must not allow itself to be resigned to this terror, for both mundane and theological reasons. The war must be, as it were, "seminaturalized" — made so much a part of everyday experience as to become "the new normal," yet not so normalized as to become a part of reality that does not seem odd or unusual.

The Cold War offers a partial model of this. It was not the individual character of U.S. administrations from 1948 to 1989 that secured the West's victory; rather, the institutions put in place by American statesmen and their allies in the 1940s "bound" future U.S. policy in quite significant ways — ways that kept America engaged in world affairs after World War II in a manner unprecedented in its history. But the analogy fails at a crucial point: for the USSR was granted legitimacy as a nation-state — too much legitimacy, many would say, but whatever one thinks of that, the legitimacy entailed that the United States understood itself as having to learn to live with the Soviet bloc. Few thought the West could ever "win" the Cold War in the way it did; most imagined it would just be a permanent condition of our world. One complication in the current struggle is that the West cannot grant al-Qaeda the legitimacy of a state, the kind of legitimacy that would more easily allow the United States to lock in a structural opposition to it. Institutionally speaking, al-Qaeda does not seem worthy of that respect: they are too contingent, they look like they don't deserve to exist, and so we have a hard time accepting that they do and that, legitimate or not, we have to recognize their existence as a semipermanent fact. So this situation is psychologically even more precarious than the Cold War — for it involves accepting a long-term struggle but with an opponent that lacks the paraphernalia of Westphalian legitimacy that would make inhabiting such a struggle slightly more endurable.

The Bush administration did a poor job both of institutionalizing this struggle and of explaining it to Americans. It did very little to infiltrate this conflict into the background facts of our condition — to "naturalize" it, as it were, in serious ways. (Again, tax policy here is important, but so are matters of immigration and military policy.) It wanted the population to stay outraged, but all that does is cultivate fear and paranoia. In fact, they have probably made future administrations' work here more difficult. The Bush administration repeatedly showed short-term political savvy in avoiding making hard choices and evading the serious costs of its decisions. This is a serious strategic failure. Particularly in this sort of war, leaders must speak about strategic goals, and what achieving those goals will cost. That is to say, the U.S. populace needs a certain secular political analogy to hope: an articulate vision of what will be done and why, a vision of what our world should look like if these efforts meet with success, and why they are worthwhile in the absence of any absolute guarantee of success. It is the leadership's obligation to offer the framework within which such hope can be cultivated. These are the tasks the Truman administration undertook from 1947 to 1952 (and what the Eisenhower administration did after them). One can only hope that the Obama administration will offer a richer response to al-Qaeda than the Bush team has done.

So this is where we are: in the first years of a period of tumult that will last for several decades, getting worse before it gets better. Not a happy thought, but a realistic one.

Given this, it behooves us to know who our opponents are in this conflict. We turn to that next.

III. Us and Them

Religious traditions are often accused of thinking in profoundly dualistic ways, of fantasizing and demonizing their opponents rather than coming to grips with the reality of their enmity and the concrete nature of their complaints. Appeals to Augustine to help confront our challenges may seem deeply wrongheaded. But Augustine's thought is especially sensitive to our all-too-human tendency to demonize our enemies, to replace our actual opponents with imagined bogeymen, and he uses various stratagems to identify and subvert those tendencies in our thought. Here we will see how.

To understand our opponent in this conflict is a delicate endeavor. Such understanding cannot make opponents too familiar to us, because that would threaten to render them indistinguishable from us. Yet it cannot render them too alien, for fear of making them too unlike us. It must do something in that hazy in-between.

Consider a simple question. What does it mean to seek to "understand" evil? Initially I suspect the decent mind recoils from such an undertaking. If "understanding evil" means to render it intelligible in the sense of excusable or even rational, then such "understanding" is, I would argue, intellectually delusionary, psychologically futile, and morally hazardous. But this question can be taken in another, deeper, sense: here understanding is simply the project of depicting evil as something within the realm of human behavior, as something that *we* could conceivably do.

It is probably impossible not to feel the tug of the first form of understanding. Yet we should resist it as strongly as we can. That we could be like these "others" in different circumstances does not mean that we are in fact relevantly similar to them, and hence lacking any standing to judge them. Judging requires both sufficient proximity to secure a good sense of the matter at hand and sufficient distance to ensure that one is not improperly confusing one's own interests and concerns with the situation.

This question is important because we need to know "the enemy" precisely in their *enmity* to us — their rationale for why they do what they do. To do this we must resist the all-too-human reflex to alienate them *as* "the enemy," to see them as fundamentally different from us, fundamentally nonhuman. (This is not to deny others' sole responsibility for their particular acts of malice; it simply identifies the disquieting fact that this behavior is, in some way, done by creatures inescapably, disquietingly *like us*.) Yet we must also resist the counterreflex to depict (and tacitly excuse) them as "just misunderstood." Instead we have to see them as continuous enough with us to be recognizably human, but take no comfort in the fact of their bare "humanity" as somehow securing them from the possibility of being, paradoxically, monstrous.

Here Augustine's approach to thinking about evil can help us. For him, the attempt to explain evil will inevitably fail, because the motives for malice can only mimic rationality; they cannot actually be properly rational. Evil is finally unintelligible, precisely because for something to be intelligible it must be something intelligibly done by creatures affirming the created order. But evil, qua evil, is not affirmative at all: it strikes at the foundations of creation itself, at the ordering principle of the cosmos, which is purely good, and so it is a sort of mysterious, irrational counteraction. To seek to understand evil is to undertake an investigation into sheer appearances, and especially the appearance of intelligibility of malice itself. When we say we "understand," for Augustine, what we mean is that we can know what it's like from the inside, as it were: because we've been there, we have been wicked, to some degree. This internal recollection of malice is revealed by Augustine not to be fundamentally any sort of demonic magnificence, but rather a kind of grandiloquent pettiness and jealousy, which should inspire in us not any sort of fear and awe at evil, but a kind of bemused pathos about those caught in its lure. And one main purpose of this "revisioning" of evil is to disenthrall us from evil's self-presentation as powerful and dramatic, in order to replace it with a picture of evil as pathetic and absurd.

We can begin to see this if we turn from imagining what terrorists are like to looking at what we know about how they actually are. What does a terrorist look like? Would you recognize him if he was sitting beside you on the bus? Probably not. Studies suggest that suicide bombers are, on average, better educated and better off than their countrymen.

Many of them are trained in that most modern of fields, engineering, and almost all are highly educated middle-class professionals. Based on a study of the educational backgrounds of seventy-five terrorists behind some of the most significant recent terrorist attacks against Westerners, Peter Bergen and Swati Pandey found that Islamic terrorists "appear, on average, to be as well educated as many Americans." In contrast, they argue, "[o]f the 75 terrorists we investigated, only nine had attended madrassas, and all of those played a role in one attack — the Bali bombing. Even in this instance, however, five college-educated 'masterminds' — including two university lecturers — helped to shape the Bali plot." Think about the most famous ones: Osama bin Laden is a multimillionaire who was a feckless rich kid in his youth; Ayman al-Zawahiri, bin Laden's number two, was a pediatric surgeon. Many of the great heroes of the twentieth-century jihadi movement were inescapably modern: Sayyid Qutb, for example, was a journalist, not a classically trained Islamic scholar. Even the "musclemen" have credentials: Ziad Jarrah, one of the founders of the 9/11 Hamburg cell, was a dental student who then became interested in aircraft engineering. Mohammed Atta was an architect. Omar Sheikh, the kidnapper of Daniel Pearl, graduated from the London School of Economics. The new breed of global jihadis are neither the urban poor of the third world nor antimodern Paleolithic traditionalists. As the French scholar Gilles Kepel puts it, they are "the privileged children of an unlikely marriage between Wahhabism and Silicon Valley, heirs not only to jihad and the umma but also to the electronic revolution and American-style globalization." Many are in their thirties and forties and fifties; about three-quarters of them are married; and most have children. These are not wild-eyed crazies, foaming at the mouth; like middle-aged people everywhere, these people are invested in the world. They know what it is to read a course syllabus, to fill out applications, to surf the Web. They grouse about expense forms. They have careers, ambitions for promotion, hopes for retirement. They would appreciate the comic strip *Dilbert*.

And al-Qaeda runs pretty much like any other major organization: Mohammed Atef, a major al-Qaeda leader (until he was killed in Afghanistan in November 2001), wrote several memos complaining about the expenses that "brothers" incurred to buy, among other things, air-conditioning units; during a meeting before 9/11, bin Laden himself predicted "huge waves" (of actions and recruits) following some "big actions," and said: "Everyone is required to participate to their fullest by advising and cooperating within the charts of organization. Charts have been prepared to suit future events and the resulting disciplines." (*Charts?* It sounds like he's preaching from the "total quality management" handbook, talking about ramping up the out-product from the synergistic co-action of all the stakeholders, which will require a deeper buy-in from all the team members, people!) And bin Laden ended this particular meeting by reminding everyone that "[c]orrespondences must be in writing; [including] incoming and outgoing mail; [and keep] discipline in appointments." Life inside al-Qaeda probably feels more like *The Office* than the Death Star.

There's a serious point here. "These people" — the shadowy figures we are urged to fear, by themselves and by our side — are in important ways like you and me; there is a recognizably human, even modern, intelligence behind what they do. To understand what this means, I want to construct an Augustinian political psychology of terror. By a "political psychology" I mean a general picture of what motivates political actors to act in a certain way. This set of motivations needs not be wholly conscious, but it is still crucially their own — that is, we cannot claim it as an honest picture of people without showing how it gives a useful account of them, and not just of their outward actions — how it can explain something of their inner life as well as their outer one. This political psychology understands terrorism as human behavior — continuous, however distantly, with "ordinary" human life — where "ordinary human life" is a far broader concept than many scholars would like it to be, and that it can include some of the most bizarre and disturbing behaviors one can imagine. We should both appreciate the mundane reasons for terrorism and acknowledge and (so far as is possible) understand the rather grand ideological or religious worldviews that terrorists themselves often invoke and purport to inhabit. When we do this, we can appreciate both the limits of understanding and the limits of nihilistic rationality; this helps us resist the temptation to overrationalize and thus misunderstand what is going on.

But we are getting ahead of ourselves; to see why this is so important, we should see why the available alternative accounts are mistaken. One common opinion is that terrorism is motivated in the end by behavior, by U.S. foreign policy. As Francis Fukuyama puts it, "for the broad mass of public opinion in Muslim countries, we are disliked or hated not for what we are, but rather for what we do." Terrorism is simply a rational "backlash" against flawed and/or wicked Western (overwhelmingly American) policies, in particular European colonialism, the existence and behavior of Israel, and U.S. support for autocratic regimes. The proposed solution to Islamist terrorism is simple: change the policies, and the terrorism will dissipate.

There is much truth to this view. Much popular frustration is directly provoked by American policies, and even more is indirectly stoked by America's (and its allies') support for oppressive and autocratic regimes across the Middle East, and most vividly by American support of Israel. But while this may be a crucial source for anti-Americanism in the Middle East (and beyond), it is not an adequate picture of what motivates terrorists in particular. "The West" is not attacked by the whole population of the Arab Muslim world, let alone by all of the *dar-al-Islam;* "the West" is attacked by a select few. Fukuyama's account implies too easily that their motivations are continuous with those of the majority. (And polls repeatedly suggest that while Muslims in the Middle East dislike the United States, they do not translate that hostility into active or even latent support for terrorism against it.) Furthermore, if the "root cause" of terrorism lies in the conflicts in Palestine, Afghanistan, and Iraq, al-Qaeda should be manned by Palestinians, Afghanis, and Iraqis. But it is not; it is manned and guided by "born again" fundamentalists from Saudi Arabia or Egypt, or from the Muslim diaspora in Europe. Nor is there much continuity between the terrorist movements and the more "legitimate" political activities of protests, collecting charity money, or working within systems to change them from the inside. To suggest that terrorism is simply a rational political strategy defames the innumerable political activists in the region by associating them with people who just want to kill. A humid atmosphere of general animus does not condense into the poison drip of terrorism; we must look elsewhere than the former for an explanation of the latter.

Another account of the terrorists' motivation is captured in Michael Ignatieff's dramatic phrase "apocalyptic nihilism." On this account, the terrorists are fundamentally interested in destruction, in mass casualties, and do not care about their own lives. Their aims cannot be rendered ultimately intelligible to us at all, and any such project risks becoming an apologia for them. This view is terrifyingly pessimistic; on it, we cannot deal with the threat primarily by treating "root causes," for its root causes are not accessible to rational engagement. Nor can we deter the terrorists, for they are manifestly not interested in their own self-preservation. We must kill them before they kill us. In such an account, the Bush administration's change from a fundamentally conservative defensive strategy to a more risky offensive one is the only realistic option available. The only good terrorist is a dead terrorist.

This argument captures several crucial facts that the previous one does not: first, the intransigent character of this form of terrorism, once mobilized, and second, these terrorists' commitment to destruction as central to their project. Unlike perhaps other forms of terrorism — such as the PLO — the Islamist terrorists represented by al-Qaeda are in part provoked and radicalized by Western policies, but once radicalized they are no longer amenable to dialogue: they have started down a road that ends only in death, theirs and others'. This is true of bin Laden, at least from what we can tell from his various statements. As Bruce Lawrence notes, in bin Laden's messages,

> no alternative conception of the ideal society is ever offered. The absence of any social program separates Al Qaeda not just from the Red Army Faction or the Red Brigades, with which it has sometimes mistakenly been compared, but — more significantly — from the earlier wave of radical Islamism in the mid-20th century. Both Sayyid Qutb in Egypt and Abu'l Ala Mawdudi in Pakistan tried to transform their societies into a just Islamic order. . . . In place of social objectives, bin Laden accentuates the need for personal sacrifice. He is far more concerned with the glories of martyrdom than with the spoils of victory. Rewards belong essentially to the hereafter. . . . Despite references to the glories of the Ottoman Empire, bin Laden does not clamor to restore a caliphate today. He seems at some level to recognize the futility of a quest for restitution. He sets no positive political horizon for his struggle. Instead, he vows that jihad will continue until "we meet God and get his blessing!"

Clearly, with such an opponent, there is little to do but fight.

But there is something disquieting about the language of "nihilism" used in such accounts. Calling someone a nihilist may be comforting to us, but it is not finally analytically adequate, either descriptively or predictively. We should take claims of nihilism seriously, but not literally:

such claims psychologically do not adequately capture the full nature of human motivation, which is never wholly and purely destructive but always has some sort of positive vision, however inchoate or inarticulate it may be. This philosophical axiom is supported by empirical evidence about al-Qaeda, which suggests that there is something more than just nihilistic rage against modernity here. After all, terrorists are not recruited from the immiserated, the uneducated, or the sexually repressed; they are not modernity's outcasts, "medieval fanatics." As I said earlier, like its predecessors, radical Islamist terrorism is a largely bourgeois enterprise.

So while there is something true about both the "backlash" and the "nihilist" accounts, a more comprehensive account is available through a richer psychology, such as Augustine offers. His psychology recognizes the complexity of emotions such as pride, humiliation, and resentment. These emotions' complexity consists in the fact that they are, for sympathetic witnesses, inhabitable and understandable without being fully rational: we can sympathize with those caught in these emotions, without endorsing them as true assessments of "the way the world is," and what to do within it.

Consider the experience of humiliation, which is essentially the experience of one's own lowliness and subordination to another. The sense of being humiliated is a powerful presence in the Islamic world, particularly in its Arab heartland, shared by many in the population (though by no means all, and by no means in the same way). Islamic philosophy of history was progressive, the story of the expansion of the *dar-al-Islam* across the face of the earth. And for many centuries, almost a millennium, history went that way. But then things went wrong, and now a remarkable civilization, the greatest in the world at its apogee, seems oppressed on all sides: beset by enemies, manipulated and exploited by superpowers, part of its heartland colonized by European Jews, with its people poor, divided, uneducated, and its elites rotten at their core. For some Muslims, Islam seems to have lost its honor, to be in a state of perpetual immiseration and humiliation.

For those who feel this shame in this way, this humiliation can only be put right by the return of Islam to domination. For the logic of humiliation is a zero-sum game; the humiliated want to humiliate in turn, because that is the only way they believe they can expiate their shame. They are condemned by their humiliation to a worldview based on resentment, a resentment that implies, against its overt disavowals, jealousy of others' superiority. But this jealous resentment lacks a positive, self-affirming side; those who are resentful in this way are not resentful because they feel equally worthy of recognition, as if they have equal right to the goods (or the kinds of goods) that the other has. Their resentment is a doubly negative emotion; it negates the other and the self. Resentment has an object to which it relates, and so is not simply captured in the narcissism of nihilism, the way that nihilism seems to think only of its own negating of the whole world (including, at its extreme, itself). But in a way like nihilism, resentment's object is depicted wholly in negative terms — as an object to be destroyed. Resentment, then, is deeply connected to hate, to the desire to annihilate some "other." Yet resentment is hostile to the self as well. It culminates in escapist despair, for the resentful do not want to be another version of the person they hate, much less their humiliated selves; rather they want to be altogether different, to be somebody else, somebody who not only does not feel this resentment but who has never felt it. Resentment breeds self-loathing — or rather, the hostility toward others that is the visible aspect of resentment is complemented by a self-loathing that is equiprimordial with it. Resentment, in short, is a fundamentally negative judgment on the world as a whole.

One can appreciate the roots of this anger, and its attractions. We are all seduced by them from time to time. Resentment and hatred are easier and less demanding emotions to live by than love, and they may well be much more effective, at least in the short term, in mobilizing a movement. And when the object of your hatred is a group, a race, a class, or a nation, that hatred can easily underwrite a general picture of the world, and a general attitude toward it.

But recall what we said earlier: understanding this resentment, even recognizing our own occasional captivity to it, does not mean endorsing it. To humanize something — to make it something a human could intelligibly feel, which is to say something imaginable from one's own perspective — only makes dimly visible a rationale for malice; it does not make that malice normative, make it what we *should* feel. The problem with this resentment, simply put, is that it reveals a profound despair, or hopelessness.

What triggers this despair? It is not enough to point to perceived injustices in the West's Middle East politics; a tipping point is reached by some few, not by all. While recent events have given them a focus, their willingness to turn to violence is rooted in a different alienation: a feeling of being in the midst of, tantalized by, and yet excluded from Western society for a long time. This is a feeling especially common among Muslim immigrants to Europe, from whom the terrorists operating in the West are mostly drawn. As such they bear relevant similarities to other marginalized youth groups (typically composed of children of immigrants) who, when "locked out" of a society's mainstream, create their own societies in the form of gangs. In this way, political facts motivate and give shape to their despair, even if they do not fundamentally cause it.

Ironically, despite the anti-American rhetoric of these movements, the role that Europe plays in these problems is more profound. European nations have an anguished relationship with their Muslim immigrant populations, who are most often perceived as the monolithically impoverished and inassimilable "other" by "native" Europeans. Furthermore, European societies, especially western European societies, are deeply secular societies; they tolerate individuals' religious freedom but put enormous pressure on the faithful to keep their religious beliefs private. Islam is traditionally a richly public religion, and so Muslim collective identities and their public representations become a source of anxiety not only because of their religious otherness as a non-Christian and non-European religion, but more importantly because their religiousness itself threatens European secularity. None of this should give credence to fears about "Eurabia." Immigrants to Europe generally do very well; they're happy to have jobs and the promise of secure lives. It is a problem of the select few, and those few are actually not themselves immigrants but more commonly the children of immigrants, born in Europe without connection to their parents' homelands, yet also refused full membership in the lands of their birth. Often unemployed, marginalized in their societies, dismissed with racist insults, a substantial population of disaffected and angry young men has arisen, most of whom simply opt out of public life but a small proportion of whom become radicalized.

Their radicalism is an essentially modern phenomenon, driven by the "de-territorialization" of Islam by modernization and globalization (occurring primarily in western Europe), which strips Muslim identity of all the social supports it receives in a traditional Muslim society. Islam is a minimal creed, because it was embedded in very different cultural settings, and traditional Muslim societies were quite diverse — more diverse, culturally speaking, than Christian cultures. (The differences between life in medieval Spain and Hungary were nothing compared to the differences between life in Morocco and Java.) So the abstract core or essential "content" of Islam is, in a way, quite small, when compared with Christian or Jewish culture. It is in a way too easy to transplant into different cultural settings, and when the culture of one of those settings has no natural space for Islamic faith, the faith sits uneasily alongside the culture, disconnected from it. And that, according to some thinkers, is what has happened to European Muslim immigrants; especially in the second and third generation, their faith becomes "deterritorialized": without roots in the lands from whence their ancestors came, they find themselves unable to identify with the ethnic nationalisms of the lands in which they were born. In this setting these disaffected youths suffer from anomie and ennui — a distinctively modern kind of boredom and emptiness — and seek a cure for it in an imagined "tradition." The radicalized proportion is not minuscule — the French scholar Olivier Roy puts the numbers at around 10 percent of the Muslim populations of Europe — but it is not by any means a majority.

Yet while they have been radicalized in Europe, they have fixated their hostility on what they see as the heartland of the West, namely, the United States. This is ironic; after all, in the American Muslim communities, the effective support for these terrorist actions has been zero — American Muslims are among the most successfully "integrated" citizens imaginable. Furthermore, throughout the 1980s and 1990s Muslim militants waged "jihad" not primarily against Israel, and certainly not against the United States, but against invading Europeans — in Bosnia, Chechnya, and above all, Afghanistan — and in situations where the United States typically took the side of the native-born Muslims. The rationale for focusing blame on the United States emanates, in part, from the size of the United States' footprint in the world. (Where French or Russian or Chinese hypocrisy has consequences, those consequences are relatively limited; but U.S. hypocrisy has ramifications for every person on the globe.) But equally important, it may be due, paradoxically, to the very allure of the United States in these radicals' eyes. After all, it is the homeland of all they purport to despise, and yet it may well have some attractions for them; so it must be fought ever-more vigorously externally, in order to help extirpate its influence internally, in their souls. As Zachary Shore has put it, European Muslims (and many other Europeans and non-American Muslims) are ambivalent about America and about the degree to which they themselves are "Americanized." As such they are not simply anti-American, they are "ambi-American" — people for whom the violence of their vehement hatred toward all things American is directly related to the depth of their attraction toward those same things. And ironically, their vehemence is the greater, the greater they feel tempted by the United States.

The ambi-Americanism is actually part of a larger ambivalence, an ambivalence to modern life itself. For while such extremists are hostile to "Western modernity," the nature of their dissent is itself distinctively modern. They are not just frustrated and angry young men; they are frustrated and angry in a distinctively modern way. As Olivier Roy argues, their vision of a global *umma* is both a mirror of and a form of revenge against the globalization that has made them what they are.

Bin Laden offers these young true believers a "pure" version of Islam, by which he means one that is disembodied — stripped of its local saints, customs, and traditions, all traditional to Islamic faith. He offers them an identity, a way to know who they are: righteous members of a global Muslim *umma* to which they can belong despite their diasporic scattering and material entanglement in the *dar-al-Harb*. And the identity he offers them is quite modern, answering to the unwittingly modern needs of these young men; their faith, he says, is demonstrated not by conformity to a host of external social customs and observances, but rather by a radical act of inner belief. Outward material manifestations are important, but only as signifying that inner "spiritual" belief. For these believers, the pious intensity of individual faith is all-important, which is why bin Laden can demand a jihadism of all believers. All of this — the import of the "pure" original (but profoundly innovative) Islamic vision, the concomitant argument that the tradition as developed has demonically misled believers, the insistence on the individual's direct relation with Allah — suggests the distinctive modernity of bin Laden's message. Indeed, in a way it echoes Christian Protestantism. Many voices have called for a "Reformation" of Islam, a Muslim Martin Luther. Few realize that that Luther may already be out there, but not on our side.

Islamic terror movements are not composed of nihilistic fascists, as many (including some terrorists) suggest: they do have a positive vision. Yet that vision, while it may be in some sense positive, is ultimately fantastic — they are not ultimately motivated simply by disapproval of discrete and alterable U.S. policies; al-Qaeda expresses a hatred for "the West" that is inspired by what the West represents as well as by what it does. Certainly many forces conspire to make a terrorist and fuel a terrorist movement; it is probably best to understand al-Qaeda as centrally (but not exclusively) motivated by a complex cocktail of psychological resentments that cannot be brought fully into view by those suffering from them, and yet do in fact motivate their actions.

How should Christians live in this context? How, in particular, should Christians cultivate their hope in this setting? Most concretely, what advice might we hear from Augustinians to help us inhabit this situation? Surprisingly, there is quite a lot. The next section unpacks what that is.

IV. The Hope of Terror versus the Terror of Hope

Recall Augustine's conflict with the Donatists, recounted at the beginning of this chapter. For Augustine, the crucial struggle in that conflict was not with the Donatists, but rather with the very temptation that made the Donatists what they were — the temptation, that he and his congregants felt, toward demonizing the Donatists, as the Donatists had demonized them. This temptation toward dualism threatened to close off his congregants from the Donatists as fellow humans, in a common mortal life. So along with his agitation of the authorities against radical Donatist terrorists, Augustine also urged his own congregations to understand that the main work they should undertake was *witness* — for their churches' own sake, for the sake of the larger society, even for the sake of the Donatists themselves.

What practical lessons may we take from Augustine's project? Well, for Christian believers simply as believers, as people concerned with building up their faith, the lessons are several. First of all, it is deeply counterproductive to understand the conflict as one with two actual "sides," on one or the other of which every member of the world is enrolled. The war is radically asymmetrical; even though it targets "the West" as a whole, it is not representative of "the East," whatever that might mean. Because of this, the only intelligible counteraction is one that resists the dualistic logic of the terrorists themselves. This will mean that communities in the targeted lands must direct serious attention at deepening and enriching their own communities, rather than at attacking "them." That, after all, is what the asymmetry testifies to: "we" have something to defend and "they" do not.

Obviously Christian churches have a great deal to contribute in this undertaking, not least by serving as exemplars to the societies in which they exist. Practically the tactics are manifold, but here are several. First, Christians may well help in this "war" by engaging in a dialogue with their Muslim neighbors, seeking to articulate a certain kind of cultural critique as well. One of the things Augustine's project urges Christians to do is to get a grip on the genuine concerns from which terrorism draws whatever legitimacy it has. After all, we need not cede all worries about our world to extremists — we can voice them within traditional Christian and Islamic languages of moral concern, without turning to terror bombings. We should do this not to "understand" in the sense of "empathize" with terrorists, but rather to begin to construct and popularize another way of being related to those concerns, a way that will offer people more constructive relationships with their misgivings about modernity.

Furthermore, we can grasp one crucial thread in Augustine's work, his insistence on giving the "enemy" hope. After all, he saw that terror and hope were mixed on both sides, and he tried to speak to that. It was not simply a matter of "understanding" all others; he recognized that some people had been radicalized to such a degree that reasoning with them would be, at least as a first step, counterproductive; they had to be met by force. Yet while God uses fear as well as hope, the ultimate inducement was hope. Augustine recognized that terror and hope were mixed on *both* sides, and he tried to appeal to both sides' hope, rather than their fear, as a way of helping alleviate the problem.

In this project Christians will find good and powerful allies in this cause in the very many serious Muslims who are struggling with these same issues. Let me be clear: this is no simple alliance, quickly accomplished or even easily begun. Nor is the aim of this alliance a this-worldly convergence on all beliefs, let alone conversion of one side to the faith of the other. There are deep differences between Christianity and Islam, to be sure. But the resources for conversation and deep and powerful critique between the traditions are immense, and deeply rewarding. There are serious voices on both sides able to engage each other not simply as "modern people" but as believers. That engagement must begin now, and must go forward for centuries to come. It may have geopolitical consequences in coming generations, and those would be nice; but more immediately it may have spiritual and intellectual consequences for the participants and their audiences as well, and those could be seen on a much shorter time frame — a time frame of decades, not centuries. This is how the faithful of both traditions, acting over the long term outside of the political structures of our world, can accomplish something that no worldly government can.

For an analogy, consider the dialogue between Judaism and Christianity that emerged after the Holocaust, or Shoah, in the twentieth century. Thinkers and faithful in these traditions finally decided that there was no way for them not to be engaged in a rich and powerful conversation. This conversation has been slow in making progress — it has always had discordant voices, on both sides and within each side — and it seems even now only at the beginning of the process. But that is no reason to stop here. There is much more to do. The advances in understanding and dialogue between elements of the two traditions have put the traditions in a better position to understand each other than has been available for almost two thousand years.

How exactly does this hope appear in politics? Clearly it is not, on its surface at least, a distinctively Christian hope. While the churches must dedicate themselves to the propagation — in themselves and to others — of the gospel that has been given to them, the larger communities in which they exist will not simply urge on the world a Christian hope. Yet political hope is somehow analogous with that hope, for forms of hope, however inchoate they may be, saturate human life. Indeed, terror and hope are far more complexly related than we initially realize.

To see this you must recognize that hope is fundamental, in a way, to terrorism. What is terrorism about? Again, as I said above, it is rage, oriented not so much at people but at a way of seeing the world. Terrorism is about denying the legitimacy of some way of seeing the world, about changing our perception of the world itself. This is the logic behind the anarchist Peter Kropotkin's aphorism, that "terror is propaganda by the deed." Al-Qaeda understands this. First, their violence is aimed at challenging the "taken-for-granted" feel of our vision of the world — making us realize it is contingent, that things are not necessarily the way we take them to be, that our world could be radically other than it is. Terrorists say, "You think we attack innocents? But it is precisely their designation as 'innocent' that we contest — it is precisely the moral schema in which they are called 'innocent' while we are called 'terrorists' that we contest." In their terror strikes, al-Qaeda is attacking the *necessity* of the world being what it seems to us to be. That is the central aim of their violence: they are contesting the "naturalness" of our world. (Only secondarily do they offer a rival "literality," an alternative vision of what the world should be.) Other movements do this too, many nonviolently. (That's what all politics and advertising do.) Terrorism is different, insofar as it does so out of a fundamental violence, a negativity. So terror's *hope* is not fully coherent — it is intelligibly negative, in what it says *no* to, but not intelligibly positive, with no way to connect its random (for they must be random in some sense, for they target an entire population) acts to any intelligible positive aim. Even if the hope of terror is in this way hopelessness, nonetheless to see terrorist acts as human acts, you must see them as motivated by a kind of hope.

Conversely, all hope, even Christian hope, has a kind of terror attached to it as well. By "terror" I mean that, even though we do not know what hope promises us — even though in hope we stand in a way beyond knowledge, resisting its claims to complacency — we know that hope will change us, in ways that we do not fully understand, and indeed in ways that we do not, at present, fully wish to understand, much less undergo. After all, hope recognizes the need to transform our sense of what is "literal" about the world, to remake what we take to be "natural." It does not promise more of the same, nor does it urge us just to go about our business and get on with our lives. So we cannot allow ourselves to become too thoroughly unafraid or purely mundane. Yes, it criticizes our apocalyptic tendencies, but it does so not because we are being apocalyptic, but because we are being, as it were, not apocalyptic enough, unable to recognize the radicalism of the changes we will have to undergo. Terrorism and hope agree that our world is much more fragile than our torpid, habit-chained way of life lets us acknowledge. Terrorism exploits that fragility for worldly gains. Hope wants us to cultivate our recognition of this fragility in order to realize that this world can be seductively immanent — can lure us into forgetting ourselves and falling into *divertissement*, a word we might translate (loosely) from

Pascal's French as "the channel surfing of the soul." The world as we live in it is *factical*: fabricated, not necessary or natural or inevitable — not, that is, the ultimate framework whereby we live, move, and have our being. And the point of hope is to remind us of that fact, in order to help us begin to live in it as anticipating another, greater world yet to come.

So hope is fundamentally an attempt to communicate the *volatility* of the world, the idea that the way things are can change, change radically, sometimes for the worse, but also, sometimes, for the better. This hope is not optimism, for it does not visualize a route from the way things are now to the way they will be. It is rather a profound apprehension that "the way things are now" is *not* the final word. It is, in its most general form (and this is nothing if not general), just this apprehension: an apprehension not immediately about God, nor about our purpose in life, but about the fact that the world we live in is not the last word. As such, it is a perception that many non-Christians can share; and as such, it is both joyful and terrifying. And while we pit hope against terror, it is equally important to hearken to the terror that is proper to hope itself.

This hope is profoundly secular, but also suprasecular in a way, insofar as it suggests that our received perception of "the way the world is" is itself more an imagined necessity than a real one. This hope is available to anyone, no matter how secularly minded and this-worldly he or she may be; it speaks in a way that is not alien to a purely mundane existence. Yet while being firmly *in* the world, it is a window to a deeper vision of the way the world might be, and as such it can destabilize certain close-minded secularist confidences in profound ways.

This is how and why Augustinians insist that in their own terms Christians must come to understand and express a vision of the "war on terror" that understands it in terms of the deep political psychology sketched here. The point is to avoid a metaphysically dualistic vision of the universe as split between us and "the enemy" — for such a dualism would be itself a form of despair — even as we recognize the reality of the presence of actual enemies in the world today, and instead see this war as far more fundamentally a struggle between terror and hope in the hearts of many people, East and West, North and South, today. This is the fundamental struggle, a struggle over hope — as so many great geopolitical struggles are — and just as the Cold War was won in the battlefield of people's hearts, so there will this war be won as well.

Conclusion

It is interesting to think about how many apparently nonreligious terms in fact have a religious heritage. A word we have had recourse to throughout this chapter — "enemy" — is a good example of this. For it is the core meaning of the ancient Semitic root term *shaitan*, the antecedent of the word "Satan" for Judaism, Christianity, and Islam. "Satan," that is, means simply "enemy." Enemy is a political category, to be sure, but it has old theological roots.

We do ourselves a disservice if we ignore the ways our current political conundrums and conflicts rely on a deep history of theological formulations — not just enemy, but "election," "executive," the "will" of people, "nation." All these terms and many more have deep theological backgrounds and present resonances. Those who would tell you that that background is wholly irrelevant to our present perplexities merely manifest their own ignorance of that background. Then again, those who would tell you that that background is wholly determinative of our present condition — whether they be in al-Qaeda, or representatives of other self-proclaimed radical orthodoxies, or their fellow travelers — merely reveal their own misapprehension of the challenges we face. Political problems have a relative kind of autonomy and integrity that cannot be immediately translated into straightforward theological problems. The challenges are simply too complicated for any such move.

Our job is broader than that of simply forgetting about theology or of tracking back our present-day crises to debates in medieval church councils. Our job is to see how the crises of our world challenge the simple idea that we can only work in a self-professedly "political" register, or self-professedly "theological" one. We must speak and think in ways that sound like one register at one moment, from one perspective, and then like the other at the next. Ours is a genuinely *theo-political* world, and we significantly hobble our chances responsibly to confront it if we attempt to reduce our problem to one or the other.

CHAPTER 3

11/9: Empire, Hegemony, and Faith

In lists of important American political thinkers, the name Stephen Decatur, Jr., never appears. But he is responsible for one of the most famous of all statements in American politics, and hence bears some responsibility for the reflections it has provoked across two centuries. A famously fierce U.S. naval officer during the War of 1812 (and before that), between 1816 and 1820 Decatur served as a navy commissioner in Washington, D.C., and was active in the Washington social scene. At one of his dinners Decatur offered an after-dinner toast that would become famous: "Our Country! In her intercourse with foreign nations may she always be in the right; but right or wrong, our country!"

At the moment, in all likelihood, the toast probably seemed charming and moving, an expression of fervent love of the sort that many of us have proclaimed after a bit too much drink; patriotic beer-goggling, if you will. But upon reflection, the articulateness of Decatur's toast does seem to raise some questions worth pondering. Is it right to support one's country even when "she" is in the wrong? But does this mean that we cannot support *our country* itself, but only a right cause, whether it is our country's or some other's? What, after all, does "loyalty to one's country" mean? I imagine the guests left nourished, amused, and ruminative.

This chapter unpacks the issues raised by this toast, reflecting on the kind of commitment we ought to have to our country, whatever country that is. To think about such commitment inevitably entails confronting the language of faith. The deep meaning of "faith" is quite revealing here.

"Belief" is too thin, too shallow a term, for what faith — *fides*, fidelity, commitment — is. Faith is where our home is; it is our primal identity, what we "rest" in. To have faith means to be *determined*, in two senses. First, it means to be determined as regards one's convictions — to be confident and persevering in them. Second, it means to be defined in terms of a determinate identity — in the sense of moving from an indeterminate and amorphous sense of self to a more definite, determinate sense. In these ways our "faith" defines us, gives us a determinate identity, which is manifest in the confidence with which we hold and express our convictions. If we understand faith in this way, it explains why preachers have been preaching so vehemently against idolatry for millennia. Idolatry is dangerous not only because it directs our loyalty to a wrong object, but also because it significantly de-forms us, our very being.

The nature of our commitments to our polity, and particularly the relation of those commitments to other, presumably higher, religious or moral commitments, is often raised today, but the terms in which it is typically put obscure the real question being asked. Typically the question is asked indirectly: Is America an empire? This question is not just a request for a factual answer; it also expresses a nest of anxieties. One is a general one about the ongoing health of the nation-state system, facing the crisis of globalization; people look around for someone to blame, and responsibility seems best ascribed to the United States. Another anxiety emerges from the collision of the core values of the United States as a republic, and from the theological heritage of "empire" discussed earlier. If America has become an empire, is it not a monstrous perversion of what it started out to be? And are not its citizens themselves complicit — both victims and perpetrators in a grotesque crime? This question, that is to say, has multiple purposes and meanings, but behind all the formulations is the question of faith — the degree and kind of commitment we should have to the U.S. political order qua political order. On one level, then, the debate about American empire is actually a debate about the nature of the American polity and the quality of commitment one should have to it — the extent to which one can have, as it were, *faith* in it. Lurking here is a deep worry that the kind of faith America today demands of its citizens is demonically opposed to Christian faith.

Let me put this issue another way. Not all the challenges to proper flourishing in our world are due to 9/11. Those events took place in the context of a remarkable (and until then, underappreciated) revolution in geopolitics, a condition in which the power of the United States overwhelmed that of other nations, and was being used in ways perceived as quite revolutionary. The United States was already the linchpin of the world system on the morning of September 11. But no one knew how vast its power truly was. And then, when its power had been revealed, almost at once, the United States changed from being perceived as the fundamental stabilizing force in the world to a fundamentally destabilizing force — from a conservative power to a revolutionary one. To many, it is as if an elephant, upon being stung by a bee, decided that it had to ensure that there were no more beehives in the forest, and if that meant knocking down most of the trees, so much the worse for the trees. The world must be radically transformed, as the National Security Strategy of 2002 argued and as former President Bush said in a speech to the U.N. in September of 2004: "Our security is not merely founded in spheres of influence or some balance of power; the security of our world is found in advancing the rights of mankind." Those expecting a radical departure from this approach in the Obama administration are going to be disappointed. America is unbound, and has been since 11/9 — November 9, 1989, the date of the fall of the Berlin Wall. On that day, what Walter Russell Mead called the "wars of the British Succession" that ran from 1914 to 1989 were settled decisively in favor of the United States.

So it has come about, in these early years of the twenty-first century, that to be an American is to be a citizen of a state so powerful, so dominant over other states that the only comparisons sound almost mythological — to Rome at the height of its empire, to Han-era China. But those comparisons are flawed only because the United States is far more powerful relative to other nations, and far more likely to stay that way for the foreseeable future, than were either of those states. Today the United States is, quite literally, in a situation of unprecedented supersovereignty, hegemony, and clear domination over all other powers. And that is, for America and the world, surprisingly bad news.

But American empire is not the *usual* bad news it is taken by many to be. There is a large literature about the United States as a bad empire now, waging perpetual war. I agree that there are good reasons to worry. But much of this literature is marked by an essentially Manichean demonization of the United States — a demonization that is simply an inverted mirror-image of the triumphalism that idolaters of America affirm. American hyper-hegemony is not so terrible if you consider the alternatives. As Augustine might say, hegemony and *imperium* are not in themselves bad things. *Imperium,* after all, originally just meant "rule," and while it has gathered ominous theological connotations, rule itself seems simply necessary. The issue is properly the use to which hegemony is put. Order is preferable to anarchy, and order generally entails some hegemon, for there is no stable third alternative in this world. Order and hegemony become bad, for Augustinians, when they are misused for ends other than justice and the tranquillity of worldly order.

In any event, a geopolitical analysis here is not of central importance. The real worry is deeper. The real worry is that, speaking in religious terms, the symbolic dominance of the United States over every other rival perpetually tempts its citizens toward an idolatrous faith in the nation's power, and tempts others toward an idolatrous demonization of the same. This chapter explores these worries, and especially the inevitable tendencies toward national hubris and demonization in situations of hegemony. If 9/11 is best intelligible as a struggle between fear and hope, 11/9 designates the struggle in the souls of communities and individuals about the right attitude to take toward the fact that our world needs ordering principles that are not merely manifestations of the divine will — rarely, political entities — and that in our world today, *a* if not *the* central such entity is the United States. After unpacking the resources Augustine gives us for assessing the propriety of patriotism (in part I), this chapter discusses the particular shape and likely perils of American dominance (in part II), talks about the dangers of a jingoistic patriotism (in part III), and then sketches the contours of a more flourishing and faithful form of political commitment (in part IV).

I. Splendid Vices

Augustine had thought deeply about the dangers of a deforming and false piety toward one's political community long before modern political thinkers discovered the same worries. What distinguishes him from others, however, is his insistence that this is an inescapably *theological* problem.

Before Augustine's time, Christian thought about the relation between this-worldly kingdoms and the kingdom of God was beset by
deep and apparently irreconcilable tensions. As I said in the introduction, the earliest Christians thought of worldly politics largely in demonic terms. Christians had originally been opposed to Rome. But the
vehemence of this opposition combined with a shallowness of thought
and produced a particularly brittle vision of religion's relationship to
worldly power. After Constantine made Christianity the empire's official
religion, this vision became obsolete, with no really viable alternative
available. Many Christians thought the conversion of the empire effectively baptized it. The most powerful example of this view was the
fourth-century theologian Eusebius. In a number of texts, most notably
his *Ecclesiastical History,* he narrated the world as increasingly coming under God's sovereign command. In the final dispensation, Eusebius suggested, the political and theological realms will fuse, and the emperor
will be the nexus of both on earth — the this-worldly source of civic
peace and theological grace at one and the same time. History was near-
ing its end; we can begin to discern the ultimate pattern toward which
all things have been moving all along. This complacency was never universal, but it did mesh well with the perennial human temptations in
what was in hindsight foreseeable ways.

The sack of Rome in 410 shattered this optimism. As sacks go, it was
a relatively gentle one; the Visigoths were given free rein in the city for
three days, provided that the city itself was not destroyed. But its effect
on people's psyches — not least those of Christians — was profound.
Such is visible in one eminent contemporary of Augustine, Saint
Jerome. Before the sack of Rome, Jerome had already begun to cringe
for a disaster. "Describing the power of the city in a glowing passage,
the poet Lucan says: 'If Rome be weak, where shall we look for
strength?' We may vary his words and say: 'If Rome be lost, where shall
we look for help?'" For him, the sack itself seemed to strike at one of the
pillars of the cosmos. Soon after he heard of the sack, Jerome wrote to a
correspondent:

My voice catches in my throat; as I dictate, sobs choke my speaking.
The city that took the whole world was itself taken. Yet before the
sack, there was famine so that few citizens were left to be made cap-
tives. In their frenzy the starving turned to hideous food, tearing

one another limb from limb that they might have flesh to eat; even the mother did not spare the babe at her breast. In the night was Moab taken, in the night did her wall fall down. "O God! The heathen have come into your inheritance; your holy temple have they defiled; they have made Jerusalem an orchard. The dead bodies of your servants have they given to be meat unto the fowls of the heaven, the flesh of your saints unto the beasts of the earth. Their blood have they shed like water round about Jerusalem; and there was none to bury them."

He was later to describe hearing of the fall of Rome and experiencing it as if "the bright light of all the world was put out" and "the whole world perished in one city." "The world sinks into ruin, yes, but shameful to say our sins still live and flourish. The renowned city, the capital of the Roman Empire, is swallowed up in one tremendous fire; and there is no part of the earth where Romans are not in exile. Churches once held sacred are now but heaps of dust and ashes, and yet we have our minds set on the desire of gain. We live as though we are going to die tomorrow; yet we build as though we are going to live always in this world." A lot of this is simply the melodramatic rhetoric of the age. But beneath that was a real panic. For Jerome and many of his contemporaries, the sack of Rome was as much a theological event as a political one. It did great symbolic violence to every inhabitant of the *imperium Romanum* who understood that *imperium* not simply as a state among other states (after all, there were few enough such states at the time), but rather as civilization itself, beyond whose borders lay only anarchy. Their easy affiliation of the empire with the divine will left them bereft of any way to understand the act except in apocalyptic terms. Rome had fallen; surely this was the end of things.

Augustine's response was markedly different, and revealed an altogether more profound assessment of the conundrum. The earliest text we have of his that mentions the sack of Rome offers a brief précis of the view that he would elaborate enormously in *City of God*. The moral of the sermon, as of his later magisterial work, is simple: the status of the city of God on earth is inescapably and systematically ambiguous, and will remain so throughout human history. The sack, then, cannot bear the clear apocalyptic meaning that many Christians like Jerome assumed it must; rather, the sack, like all of history, is *obscurely* involved in God's governance of the world. The meaning of the events will only be apprehensible for humans from the end of time, and not a moment before.

This does not mean that worldly events bear no theological significance; that would be in its own way as much a false consolation as the apocalypticist's claim to apprehend God's precise meaning with full and certain clarity. History does express God's purposes, and is sacramental. The point is simply that it is God's history, not our own proper possession.

So Augustine embeds the sack of Rome in a larger theological scriptural history of God's dealings with human cities, for one of the texts on which the sermon was preached was Genesis 19, about God's dealings with Sodom. What this scriptural history teaches us, for Augustine, is that in all things God "imposes discipline before he executes judgment" so that, even if "the threshing-floor bears a single threshing-sledge to remove the stubble and purge the grain," the behavior of God cannot be seen to be other than loving: "The city was corrected by the improving hand of God rather than destroyed." Judgment was unquestionably being brought, though the mercy and love that must be in it are hard to discern, but nonetheless the faithful know to search out God's ways in the murkiness of the lived experience of pain and suffering.

The point for Augustine is not to promote a Pollyannaish vision that "I'm OK and you're OK." The point is that we live in a time in which God's governance can be confidently affirmed, but the particular determinate direction and sense of the meaning of that governance — what God "means" by discrete historical events — cannot be smugly proclaimed. We must live in the tense situation of attempting to discern God's purposes without resolving that tension by claiming to know "really" or "finally" or "conclusively" what those purposes ultimately are. This is not due simply to the bare assertion of a hidden providence for Augustine, for if God's "lash falls upon the just and unjust alike," we must still ask, "if Daniel confesses his own sins, who is there who is just?" That is to say, no one is righteous, no, not one, and so we must learn to take what we must suffer as the punishment due to us for our betterment. "The burden borne by the pious should not, then, disturb us; its role is to train them." Suffering is a tool that reforms us in order to avoid the absolute and endless suffering of hell. On this account, the key is the *use* to which suffering is put, for we have a narrative within which to make some sense of suffering. Our temporal victories are temporary, impermanent; the danger is not just that we attach too much import to them, but also that we attach the wrong sort of import to them, imagining that they give some direct access to the deep meaning of God's plan for history rather than — as is truly the case — indirect training in becoming fit for the heavenly kingdom.

In all this Augustine may seem to be heartless. But in fact what he was doing was simply laying out the consistent logic of the conviction that God is the Lord of history, but a Lord whose ways are not our own. Augustine was not worried that he would make people imagine God was abusive — God had promised life eternal for the blessed — he worried rather that people would assume that God's ways were too easily discernible in the immediate events of the day.

He had reason to be concerned. For it was just this idolatrous over-confidence that had manifest itself in the fundamental mistake at the heart of Roman patriotism — a patriotism that was all the more overtly religio-political by being called, in Rome, *pietas,* a kind of "piety" toward the city and the gods and one's family (three things not easily separated for the Romans). Roman *pietas* — a tight-lipped, narrow-minded, sharp-edged conviction about what was right (Rome) and what was wrong (everything else) — was famous throughout antiquity as, ironically, the cause of the rise and grandeur of Rome. Augustine had to confront it.

He did so through the brilliant idea of "splendid vices" (a phrase he himself seems never to have used), an idea that tells us much about his vision of improper, and proper, political attachment. The idea of splendid vices was his answer to one of the deepest questions Christians asked — how did the pagan Romans succeed so long? Augustine's answer was ingenious: they did not have love of God, but they had a force of distantly analogous power — love of the city, manifest as a love that sought the city's ever-greater glorification. While "love of praise is a fault," as Augustine says, when one centers one's life around love of the right kind of praise, given by a respected group of judges with very severe standards for what is praiseworthy, such a pursuit of praise will make us "less vile," as it requires a rigorous self-discipline for that pursuit. And so it was with the Romans: by centering their psyches ruthlessly around the pursuit of glory — ultimately the glory of the city but most locally their own glory, as servants of the city — the Romans managed to check their other appetites. Because of this, Augustine argues, the Romans in the best of times had what he called "civic virtues," a certain probity and rectitude in their behavior.

And yet they never had *real* virtues, for real virtues are rooted in the love of God. Their commitment to justice, or prudence, or honesty, or decency, was always contingent upon the greater good of Rome; were that threatened, anything goes. Rome was, in a way, their "god," the deity around which they organized their lives — what, in a word, they sacrificed to. This is why Augustine saw the Romans' problem as properly a theological problem — because he saw such adoration of the nation for what it was, which was idolatry. The Romans had worshiped a worldly end, and when that worldly end had ended, they had no rightful complaints about injustice. They had simply been mistaken in the object of their loyalty. But such was always the way of absolute patriotism.

This was clearly a quite sharp critique of a certain kind of patriotism. But it is not a recipe for indifferent otherworldliness. Augustine thought that Christians should not rest complacent in diagnosing and dismissing Roman virtue; rather, the remarkable achievements of the pagan Romans should spark them to still-greater deeds. Yet even this rivalry was not between two rival egotisms. Christians, Augustine insists, do not "rest" in the narcissism of glorying in their own achievements, nor do they attribute them to the greatness of some worldly city; instead they "refer" the glory they gain to God's greater glory — that is, they identify their acts as part of God's greater story, not a story they are telling on their own. As such, Augustine thinks, Christians are actually better patriots than the pagan Romans were, for they never misvalue the good of their city: they only ever properly value it.

All of this is visible in an exchange of letters Augustine had with an important Roman Christian noble in North Africa, Marcellinus. Marcellinus had written him, reporting the charges of some pagan Roman nobles about Christianity's deleterious effects on believers' commitment to serving the common good of the polity. These nobles argued that Christ's teaching must be incompatible with the morals of citizenship, of those who interest themselves in public affairs. And Marcellinus found it hard to disagree with them as vehemently as he thought he should; after all, he says, Christ taught us "not to return evil for evil, to turn the other cheek, give our cloak when one asks for a tunic, go twice the distance with one who asks us. These commands are contrary to the morals of citizenship." How, he asked Augustine, might one respond to this?

Augustine had heard this as well. "When [these men] read the divinely authorized command not to return evil for evil . . . they charge our faith with hostility to the commonwealth." He suggested to Marcellinus that the crucial point to press in response is that "a city [is] but a group of men united by a specific bond of peace," and that this peace was secured best by those with the proper character. Because of this, while much of the Christian morality was not immediately applicable to public affairs, "more relevant to the training of the heart within than to our external reality," its attention to character is especially important:

> It is in this cesspool of evil characters, where the ancient ethos has been abandoned, that the presence and assistance of heavenly authority is most needed. This exhorts us to voluntary poverty, to restraint, to benevolence, justice and peace, and to true piety, and to other splendid and powerful virtues. It doesn't do this only for the sake of living this life honorably, or only to provide a peaceful community for the earthly city. It does so also to win everlasting security for the heavenly and divine commonwealth of a people that will live for ever. Faith, hope, and charity make us adopted citizens of this city, so that as long as we are on our pilgrimage, if we are unable to reform them, we should tolerate those who want the commonwealth to remain with its vices unpunished.

Ultimately, then, the theological virtues do not disable civic virtue; they properly *enable* it. For Christians engaged in public matters, the virtues are both salvific and civically beneficial. A true patriotism anchors itself in true eternals — justice, goodness, temperance, mercy — and in the eternal God. Beyond the wholly this-worldly aims and ends of the pagans, the Christians see what they gesture at and seek to promote — namely, the one true God and that God's glory. Only by being so properly otherworldly can one be truly worldly.

With this picture in place, we are now ready to think about the challenges to such a theologically framed patriotism in the world of today.

II. *Novus Ordo Seclorum*

That such a religious patriotism faces challenges in our world is easy to see. Nation-states today are uneasy with the idea of attachments and commitments to realities beyond their imagination. Especially for citizens of the United States, the temptation toward a kind of idolatrous patriotism is no less real than it was for Romans at the apogee of their empire's power. To understand the particular contours of this challenge, however, we must understand the curious condition of America's hegemony in the world today — a hegemony that is simultaneously less voluntary and more vehement than previous ones have been.

The story of American hegemony is not a story of the United States *deciding* to become the hegemon. Most empires arise inadvertently, accidentally. Intentional imperialistic designs normally fail; they scare too many people too quickly and too thoroughly. The United States is no exception. American hegemony is not an act of naked, or even covert, imperialistic designs; it is crucially dependent on what other nations did not do. The United States is so powerful, in part, because it is unrivaled — without a viable counterweight for at least a generation. In another way, however, its rise to prominence has been driven, and shaped, by motives close to the very essence of America. Understanding both dynamics is a prerequisite to understanding our geopolitical condition today. The United States is a revolutionary hegemon — an ordering force committed to turbulence, not stability. The next two sections discuss these two dynamics, then the final two sections diagnose the two opposite temptations that we face in this situation.

A. An Inadvertent Empire

There are both cultural and material reasons for this. As I said above, other nations cannot and will not generate the will or power necessary to rival the United States in the coming decades. They are just too invested in the global order and the global economy, in which the United States plays an inescapably central role; they face challenges, economic and demographic, that will require them to rely on that order more fundamentally than attempt to change it. Culturally, for complicated reasons, many advanced industrial societies have delegitimized the very use of force, leaving the United States as the sole nation willing to consider it. Materially and culturally, then, the rest of the world has largely ceded the playing field of power politics to the United States. Describing and explaining this fact is our task here.

The basic story here is simple. During the Cold War the United States led a worldwide alliance against a generally agreed-upon threat — international communism. After the collapse of that threat in the late 1980s and early 1990s, against predictions that the Western alliance would break into rival, squabbling centers of power (think Japan and the European Union [EU] as rivals to the United States), other nations effectively surrendered any pretensions toward or capacity for great power politics, leaving the United States uncontested. While this may sound good for the United States, in fact it creates manifold problems for both America and the world.

Consider Europe. Some think the EU will develop into a superpower counterweight to the United States, albeit one more committed, for reasons of governance structure and values, to a gentler and more generous vision of international politics than America's. But the evidence suggests otherwise. What Larry Siedentorp has called "bureaucratic-managerial elitism," the bureaucratic sclerosis and nonresponsiveness of the EU and its constituent nation-states, cripples the ability to centralize and organize power in needful ways. Europe's economy is notoriously sclerotic and unlikely to improve substantially. Furthermore, changes in its values undercut its ambitions to wield the power it cannot in any event acquire. At the beginning of the twentieth century, the "sick man of Europe" was the Ottoman Empire. Today, at the beginning of the twenty-first, the "sick man of Europe" is, well, Europe.

The problem of demographics and especially declining European birthrates may be the decisive factor here. Europe's birthrates have dropped well below the replacement rate of 2.1 children for each woman of childbearing age. For western Europe as a whole, the rate is 1.5 — so increasingly there are one-child families. By midcentury, including immigration, Europe's population is projected to be 13 percent smaller, with the working age population declining by 27 percent, and the median age increasing by a third, reaching fifty years. This decline is bad enough in absolute terms. But in relative terms it is even worse — for compared to much of the rest of the world, European shriveling is even more prominent. In 1950, the population of Europe accounted for about 22 percent of world population; today it is about half that, 12 percent; and by 2050, Europe's population is expected to be about half again — 7 percent of the world. By 2050, the population of Yemen — Yemen! — is expected to exceed that of Russia. (Russia's current belligerence is made partly intelligible by the fact that it recognizes it has very little wiggle room to operate in, given its looming dramatic decrease in population. It is trying to use its power as forcibly as it can now, in the recognition that it is not going to have that power in several decades, and so it must seek to get the best deal it can today, before its weakness becomes unmistakable.)

The effects will be profound. Not only will the population be smaller, it will be older. Today about one-sixth of Europe's population is sixty-five and older, but by 2030 that will be one-fourth, and by 2050 almost one-third. The cost of so many pensions on workers will be oppressive. It could be counteracted by more immigration, but that brings its own troubles. European nations are far less immigrant-friendly than the United States, and the immigrants who go there are impoverished, with fewer skills, and are far more culturally estranged from the mainstream than immigrants to the United States. (Most immigrants to the United States are from Latin America and East Asia and are largely Christian, despite the United States' self-image as a wildly pluralistic "melting pot"; furthermore, the relatively weak short-term social safety net in the United States forces them to integrate as soon as they can.) In short, within its boundaries Europe will become a continent of only children, pensioner grandparents, and immigrants who have little investment in and some resentment toward the "European" way of life.

It is not only Europe that is facing this nest of problems. Similar demographic changes are confronting other nations as well. Population decline, aging, and a concomitant weakening capacity to engage in a common global strategy are also in the future for Japan, Singapore, and South Korea. In fact, barring idiosyncratic cultural factors (and perhaps even including them), it seems that economic development is related to declining populations, and that declining populations slowly weaken the fiscal and social health of a polity. In general, the traditional allies of the United States are increasingly and inevitably losing both the material and the moral energies that enabled them to help the United States govern the world.

But it is not only America's friends who face dangers; the rest of the world faces enormous developmental strains as well. Demographic and political problems in Africa and the Middle East will make those areas a constant problem site for the developed world. The Middle East and North Africa had 78.7 million people in 1950, 305.7 million in 2000, and are expected to have a population of more than double that — 624 million — by 2050. This population explosion will lead to crises in water, food, and jobs, and all these problems in the Middle East are occurring alongside increasing global demand for Middle East oil.

Even possible rivals to the United States such as China and India face deep problems, because of looming environmental, economic, and demographic challenges. These developing nations, in the words of political scientist Mark Haas, "will grow old before becoming rich," and their pension and other economic costs will put extra strains on the international system as well. (For example, China's "surplus males" could generate high rates of crime and social disorder.) And while China's development and wealth explosion will no doubt affect the world in the coming decades, it is so far behind the United States as to require implausibly high growth rates — much higher than it's already experiencing — to catch up. (Given China's GDP of roughly $3 trillion, if it grows at the [overheated] rate it experienced in the first eight years of the twenty-first century — roughly 7 percent annually — by 2028 its GDP will be about $13 trillion, which is slightly less than what the U.S. GDP is *today*.) Many pundits suggest that the rise of China will "return" us to the premodern world situation, where China (or "Asia" more broadly) was preeminent. But this is deeply mistaken, for the premodern world system did not incorporate the Western Hemisphere: in that era, China was "superior" in a system that included only Asia, Europe, and Africa. So that says nothing about the new, truly global world-system we now inhabit. China will not supplant the United States' world leadership; if anything, its rise will only reinforce the necessity of it, as others weigh the merits of a U.S.-centric world compared to a China-centric one.

Nor, finally, will the United Nations replace the United States. To assume that the U.N. could do so misunderstands the U.N.'s nature and purpose. The U.N. was not designed as a world government, a kind of a supersovereign who can adjudicate and decide between rival nations' claims; it is a site for nations to air their interests and negotiate their differences on their own. It cannot "evolve" from its current structure into a world government, for to do so it would have to become something fundamentally different. (The veto-wielding power of permanent members of the Security Council would have to be jettisoned, for one, and that will not happen.) All "democratizing" reforms can do is make it structurally *more* sclerotic. Furthermore, there is no thought given in the U.N. charter to nonstate actors, and very little to the way a state treats its own citizens; the U.N. is a pervasively state-centric institution, whose primary concern — enshrined in Article 2(4) of the U.N. charter — is aggression by one state against another, not what happens within states. Efforts to incorporate intrastate issues have been repeatedly twisted to the cynical purposes of states; for example, the U.N. Human Rights Council, created in 2006 to replace the widely discredited U.N. Commission on Human Rights, has been a disaster, focusing its ire almost entirely on human rights abuses in Israel, seeking to abolish special oversight of countries such as Cuba, Myanmar, Belarus, and North Korea, ignoring human rights abuses in China, Russia, Saudi Arabia, Egypt (indeed, throughout the Islamic world), and seeking to legitimate the curtailment of freedom of speech for religious purposes. It is widely recognized by human rights groups themselves as a cynical charade commandeered by governments with no interest in human rights whatsoever. The U.N., in short, is an institution designed for a world of autonomous states, a world paradigmatically imagined by and designed in the Treaty of Westphalia in 1648 and enshrined in international law ever since, a world where states have absolute sovereignty within their own territory. The U.N. is a forum for such states to work out their differences among themselves, not the prototype of an institution to govern them.

Yet the main challenges for the foreseeable future involve situations where the U.N.'s Westphalian logic is either irrelevant or counterproductive — as was the case, in the 1990s, in Sierra Leone, the former Yugoslavia, Rwanda, Congo, and Afghanistan, and as is the case in Darfur today. The U.N. has a hard time finding peacemakers for the missions it already has under way, and there is no evidence that taking on further missions would lead nations to give it more support. Finally, the "legitimacy" granted by the U.N. seems imperfectly understood. For example, compare NATO's intervention in Kosovo with the invasion of Iraq by the United States and its allies. In fact, the Iraq invasion was much more legitimate than Kosovo, in terms of the U.N., because of the various U.N. resolutions regarding Iraq. The blithe indifference to this fact by elites bespeaks either a shocking ignorance of the U.N.'s actual resolutions or an insouciant disregard for them that simply proves the point. It is not that the United States does not need to demonstrate a decent respect for the opinions of mankind; it is rather that due attention to those opinions is not a replacement for a distinct U.S. foreign policy.

So it has come to pass that the United States currently fields the mightiest army in the history of the world for a very modest fraction of its gross national product. Furthermore, no viable alternative to the United States — not the United Nations, nor any rival nation or consort of nations — exists or is likely to emerge; there are no candidates for major U.S. "rivals" who will not be required, in coming years, to confront internal problems that will hinder, and in all likelihood cripple, their ability to rival the United States in economic or military ways. Nor is there a great deal of danger of so-called "imperial overstretch." American hegemony is secured in crucial part because of what other countries have *not* done — specifically, continue to invest, ideologically and materially, in the ability and willingness to make war to achieve their aims — and because of forces peculiar to the major alternative potential sources of world power in Europe and Asia. The United States will remain the indispensable nation, the sheriff of the global commons; it will stand alone, it will stand firmly, it will do so for the foreseeable future, and it will do so on the cheap.

The problem is that this hegemony may not be sufficient to solve the problems it faces. The crises of the twenty-first century will be profound: civil wars, due to ethnic conflict and scarce or especially valuable resources, and the challenge of establishing reliable state structures in the wake (or in the midst) of "failed states" — these and manifold other realities will be the "events" of which Harold Macmillan spoke. They will be real challenges, they will be pressing, and they will demand action. Who will meet these challenges?

The demographic changes enumerated above will weaken the "developed" world's capacity to project power — both military power and other forms of social wealth. It is already clear in military terms. There is at present an enormous deficit in the amount of deployable military force in the world. The developed world's expeditionary military capital is now pretty much invested in fighting the fires that are there. In 2006, it was almost impossible to get the European members of NATO to muster a peacekeeping force in Afghanistan of approximately 20,000 soldiers (and many of those are restricted from combat duties by their national governments). NATO cannot establish a rapid-reaction force because there are simply not enough troops. But for an alliance with more than 2 million soldiers, it is curious to "max out" with a commitment of less than 50,000 troops in Afghanistan and Kosovo. And India and China, the other possible future sources of support for international order, will be facing social (and cultural) challenges of their own, which make them even more unlikely to help. Many people worry about "American empire." Most worry that it is, or will be, too powerful. But the opposite worry is perhaps more realistic — that it will not be powerful enough.

We are going to experience what Mark Haas has called a "geriatric peace." In Haas's view, "[w]hile the United States will be even more secure from great power rivalry than it is today, it (and its allies) will be less able to realize other key international objectives," such as securing international development and peace in turbulent parts of the world. "Global aging," Haas argues, "is likely to result in a great power 'geriatric peace,' but this same phenomenon may threaten other important U.S. international interests, including by facilitating international conflict in non-great power relations." Aging will force other nations to focus not so much on "butter" versus "guns" — the classic economic trade-off for states — as on "pensions" versus "guns." This geriatric peace will of necessity "likely increase the United States' unilateral foreign policy tendencies," as other states have fewer and fewer resources to contribute to international policing; on the other hand, "neo-isolationist foreign policy strategies are likely to become more compelling for U.S. leaders in coming decades," both because of growing popular resentment in the United States for the apparent "free ride" other states are getting at the cost of American money and lives, and because of the increasing costs to the United States, as it faces its own, albeit much more mild, problems with an aging population.

None of this should be very comforting to those who think that U.S. power will secure a happy and prosperous future. But things are made worse by the internal tensions, and perhaps even contradictions, at the heart of America's understanding of its relations with the rest of the world. After all, hegemons never simply choose ex nihilo the path they pursue; they step into the future with a trajectory and momentum determined by the past. And in the United States' case, that trajectory and momentum complicate things enormously, both for the nation and for the world.

B. A Revolutionary Empire

"America did not change on September 11; it only became more itself." So Robert Kagan summarized the nature of American power after 9/11.

It is not simply that external events conspired to place naive Americans with massive firepower all over the world. There are also powerful internal motivating dynamics deep in American culture toward hegemony. It is important to understand those internal forces, and in particular the peculiar brand of American messianism, that lead America to be the odd kind of "revolutionary empire" it turns out to be.

The United States is in many ways a new kind of entity in the geopolitical bestiary: a destabilizing hegemon, a revolutionary empire. The idea of a "revolutionary empire" can sound like a contradiction in terms. Fundamentally, empires seem conservative forces, committed above all to stability. As Lord Salisbury, a nineteenth-century British prime minister, said of his nation's policies at the time, "Whatever happens will be for the worse, and therefore it is in our interest that as little should happen as possible." The United States' behavior ill-fits this model. It is revolutionary in its rhetoric and self-understanding, and often in its actions. Whereas during the Cold War those tendencies were kept in check by (and for) its allies, since 9/11 it has changed from being a defensive and status quo hegemon to an offensive and revolutionary one. These changes are not simply a matter of a nation seizing an opportune moment; they are rooted in deep millennial tendencies in American culture — due as much to institutional and structural forces as to the decisions of elected officials. In sum, the issue is this: what others could regard as stability or a (barely) tolerable hegemony is not enough for the United States. It cannot imagine itself as an oppressive empire, but only as a revolution enabler. Thus it becomes a *revolutionary empire* — and the tension between its condition as revolutionary and its condition as empire is key. Why is it this way? And what are the consequences for its citizens and others?

On one level, much of this is due to America's self-perceived "exceptionalism." The geographic isolation of the colonies and then the early Republic was a clear and recognized blessing from the beginning — the nascent United States was isolated from the wicked ways of the old world and able to exercise its republican virtues in mastering a continent. And it has remained so; the United States has historically been an "offshore balancer," a strategy that entails that it does not need to dominate the world directly, but only to ensure that no one else does — that crucial areas do not fall under the control of a hostile great power. Yet America's apartness was not most fundamentally geographical but psychological, perhaps even theological. It is tied up in a sense of selection, even election, of separateness and superiority — a sense that, in some basic way, all other nations are not fully legitimate (at least in the eyes of America), that they lack some foundational voluntary affirmation on the part of their citizenry. They are not intentional creations, but merely accidents of history, this myth says; it is America, and only America, that is truly an *intended* nation — the destiny for which the rest of the world, and previous history, are all nothing but rough drafts.

Here we see the peculiarly apocalyptic cast of America's self-understanding. For particularly potent strands of messianism and millenarianism have flourished in America almost since its founding. From the beginning, American religion was quite worldly; as Josef Joffe points out, American Protestantism is Calvinist, whereas European Protestantism (outside of the U.K. and the Netherlands) is Lutheran. Calvinism is much more pro–civic engagement, and much more involved with the Old Testament and its meditations about the complexities of worldly governance, than is Lutheranism. But by the Revolution — and in some ways because of it — American Christianity was becoming even more messianic. The motto on the Great Seal says *Novus Ordo Seclorum;* this is from Vergil's Fourth Eclogue, long interpreted as pagan prophecy of Christ's appearance, and while the Founders were not equating the United States with the second coming, they were not fully eschewing the theological energies behind the saying. After the Revolution this religiosity deepened, as was manifest especially in the tumult leading to the Civil War and also in the nation's belief in its manifest destiny — first to conquer the continent, and then to save the world. It is also intertwined with the profound role that novelty, opportunity, and hope have always played in American culture. America believes in the fantasy of second chances, a fantasy not altogether different from the Christian idea of redemption, and of the new. The two differ in whether humans can do this for themselves — whether humans can undertake this revolution on their own, can "hasten the messiah." Heresies are always undertaken by true believers. And America is nothing if not a matter of true — almost desperate — belief.

A comparison will bring this out. America and France are often identified as the originally "modern" nation-states. But no French person would imagine that the rest of the world could ever be French. (The French may be cynical narcissists, but they are not naive megalomaniacs.) To traffic in stereotypes, what the French want is for everyone else to recognize French superiority, while staying in their inferior state. The terror of Americans' genuinely welcoming attitude is precisely that we can imagine no reason that the rest of the world would not want to be like America — and we are going to help them, by God, even if they don't want our help. The roots of this belief go back at least to the founding of the Republic; as Thomas Jefferson put it in his last letter: "May it [July 4] be to the world, what I believe it will be, (to some parts sooner, to others later, but finally to all), the signal of arousing men to burst the chains under which monkish ignorance and superstition had persuaded them to bind themselves, and to assume the blessings and security of self-government. . . . All eyes are opened, or opening, to the rights of man." Such beliefs are still quite contemporary; as Colonel Pogue in *Full Metal Jacket* said, "we are here to help the Vietnamese, because inside every gook there is an American trying to get out." (Think of how painfully well suited that vision has been to American foreign policy in Iraq.) It is very easy for Americans to think that "what's good for America is good for the world." Americans have a powerful belief in the "win-win" worldview, in which there are no sacrifices, no losers; when things are otherwise, woe betide those who try to point out to us the reality.

The reasons for this have crucially to do with the conditions of America's creation. America's destiny has always seemed to its inhabitants both singularly precarious and singularly messianic. As the philosopher Stanley Cavell saw, America has had a unique experience of history. Other countries remembered a time before their current political configurations, but before America as a political entity there was only the abyss:

before there was Russia, there was Russia; before there was France and England, there was France and England; but before there was America there was no America. America was *discovered*, and what was discovered was not a place, one among others, but a setting, the backdrop of a destiny. . . . its present is continuously ridiculed by the fantastic promise of its origin and its possibility, and because it has never been assured that it will survive. Since it had a birth it may die. It feels mortal. And it wishes proof not merely of its continuance but of its existence, a fact it has never been able to take for granted. Therefore its need for love is insatiable.

Alone, it seems, among the nations of the world, the United States always remembers a time when it was not. Accompanying this terrible memory, as its reverse side, is the ineradicable knowledge that everything could change in an instant: the United States, once "made," could be unmade. Unlike the nations of Europe, such as France, with historical sensibilities that antedate their governments and civic institutions, America manifests few such pretensions of endurance. The nation *is* its ideals; without the one, many Americans believe, the other will not endure. This is why these ideals are so commonly held with quasi-religious fervor, and why the very idea of America's destiny has often been expressed messianically.

The messianism here is important, for America is justified only if the nation's ideals turn out to be valid, and they turn out to be valid only if they spread across the globe. As another important American political thinker — Bob Dylan — put it, "he not busy being born is busy dying." America is not, and cannot be, a status quo power. It must be loved, and that love is manifest in history going its way. A dissatisfaction with the way things are is worked deep into the nation's DNA. It is always itching to change things.

This exceptionalism reinforces America's curious schizophrenia about war — its ability to forget its militarism, but when it deems it necessary to wage wars of annihilation — and paradoxically gives the United States both its curiously moralized vision of war and its habit of pursuing absolute conquest as a general war aim. The nation never possessed any civic vocabulary or narrative within which war could be normalized or limited; for America, all wars are existential wars, and its history bears that out.

America's fundamentally sanguine experience with military power, and its experience of exercising that power since Vietnam, keep it a martial nation. In this situation the danger for the United States is not "imperial overstretch," but rather something like the opposite — that, feeling the cost of military power to be relatively light, Americans will increasingly become confident that military solutions are increasingly attractive. (The Iraq war will not change this fact; this attitude will return soon enough.)

Until 1941, this militant moralism was only intermittently and obliquely part of the United States' self-understanding as a geopolitical actor. But these long-term realities of U.S. culture have been accentuated in recent decades by accidents of history. Famously, the nation's inability to sustain this self-image after World War I was one of the major precipitating causes of World War II. After that latter world war, U.S. leaders worked to ensure no retreat from the world stage (against powerful resistance). They won that struggle, and over the course of the Cold War America's citizenry became comfortable with its historically unprecedented involvement in world affairs; its self-image as the "leader of the free world" became institutionalized and central to the American psyche.

If the Cold War psychologically made comfortable the nation's involvement with other nations, the enormous expansion of the consumer economy, and its wholesale integration with the rest of the world's economies, make that enmeshment inescapable. It cannot but be central to the functioning of the global economy, just as the global economy is central to it. This is not simply true as regards "foreign oil" or consumer goods; even American consumers' very ability to *spend* is itself sustained by foreign banks. In fact, the central banks of a few nations in East Asia have financed much of the United States' borrowing; today, the central banks of Japan and China together hold more than $1 trillion in dollar-denominated securities. (In fact, foreign central banks and governments held more than $2.5 trillion in U.S. Treasury securities in 2008.)

The nation's investment with the rest of the world has been warped, or infected, in some troublesome ways. For example, the past few decades' substantial investments in military funding, alongside stagnation or decline in the budget of the State Department, have led to what some have called the dramatic "militarization" of U.S. foreign policy. The military simply overwhelms the nonmilitary international relations efforts of the remainder of the federal government. In 2008, the budget difference between the Department of Defense and the State Department and USAID combined, stood at roughly 24 to 1 — roughly $750 billion to $31 billion. There are more members of military bands than foreign service officers in the State Department. Since the 1986 Goldwater-Nichols Defense Reorganization Act — which was the most revolutionary defense change since the rise of the Cold War military in the late 1940s — the military leaders of the various operational theaters that organized the world have gained unprecedented clout. These theater commanders have vast resources, substantial staffs, and the ability to act across national borders, dealing as they do with an entire "theater"; they are often compared to Roman proconsuls in their authority, both in the regions of their commands and in the decision-making process of the U.S. government back home. Today more than ever before, the U.S. government's face to the world wears a uniform.

From 11/9 to 9/11 the United States did not recognize the confluence of these changes, nor did the rest of the world, and did not have a way of responding to it (they amount to the same thing). After 9/11 the revolution of 11/9 took on new and self-conscious form: in the words of Christina V. Balis, "America may be said to have found an empire and consequently to have lost its role in the world." Most immediately there have been two large changes. The first change is one in the United States' strategic vision of the world — away from nations and toward regions, and especially the Middle East, central Asia, and Africa. After 9/11 the United States realized that the dangers confronting it did not all stem from the acts of powerful opposing states; the United States and the world order are threatened as well by groups independent of all nation-states, and indeed operating most fully in those territories where legitimate state power was lacking. Suddenly failed states were no longer broken weapons, harmless to American security; now they were "swamps" in which dangerous pestilences could fester before they swarmed over their boundaries.

This change in strategic vision is related to the second change: structurally and materially, the United States has changed from a defensive and conservative posture to an offensive and revolutionary one. No longer is the status quo acceptable, and the military is currently being restructured accordingly. The army is transforming itself to be able to put a combat-capable brigade anywhere in the world within 96 hours, a full division in 120 hours, and five divisions on the ground within thirty days. (Five divisions is almost the equivalent of two Iraq wars — that's like going from zero to sixty in under a second, in military terms.) Alongside this restructuring of military forces, the Pentagon has begun a major redesign and repositioning of overseas bases. Future U.S. military forces will be positioned along an "arc of instability" that runs through the Caribbean, Africa, the Middle East, the Caucasus, central Asia, and southern Asia. It is in these parts of the world — generally poor, insular, and unstable — that military planners see the major future threats to U.S. interests, and it is in them that the U.S. military is already engaged in a series of low-level, open-ended counterinsurgencies against local insurgents and international terrorists. Furthermore, these will not be the massive and permanent bases that marked America's Cold War military presence, whether in Germany, Japan, Korea, or Cam Ranh Bay; instead, there will be a large number of small, flexible bases — "lilypads" — from which forces may strike quickly at remote hot spots. The U.S. military presence in these areas also could act as a stabilizing factor, preventing them from becoming hot spots in the first place. The creation of "Africa Command" in early 2007 is only the most dramatic structural example of this; whereas previously Africa was divided between the "European Command" and the "Central Command," now the continent has a U.S. military structure designed to focus on its needs.

The restructuring of the military command structure and operational units; the "forward basing" of air and sea power able to skirt national boundaries and political sensitivities; the prepositioning of large, off-shore stocks of tanks, armored vehicles, weapons, and other heavy military equipment for air-lifted troops — the effect of all this is less focused on specific troop deployments than on extending broad military capabilities. These changes make it easier to use military force, in large part because the executive branch of the government is less answerable to others regarding its use. Furthermore, the character of U.S. military power makes it not simply easier to work without allies, but increasingly difficult to work with them; so alliances become increasingly costly on purely military grounds, demanding ever-more serious extramilitary reasons to care what other nations think. Furthermore, the fact that U.S. military power is currently self-standing — a "force in being" rather than one needing to be mobilized from the citizenry — makes the use of force less answerable to the U.S. populace as a whole. When then-commander of the Joint Chiefs of Staff Gen. Creighton Abrams designed the all-volunteer military after 1973, he did so in such a way as to deny the possibility of using the military without calling up the reserves, thereby forcing the executive branch to get permission from the whole nation before a war — as happened before the Gulf War of 1991. Since 9/11, the transformation to offense and expeditionary force deployments has reduced the need for such accountability — in fact, it seems partially designed to eschew it.

Since 9/11 the changes to America's mode of being in the world, and to how it engages with others, have been dramatic. What kinds of challenges does this new situation present to the world? How will the world reply? And how should Christians — those who are citizens of the United States and those who are not — respond? That is what the remainder of this chapter is about.

III. The Last Refuge of Scoundrels

Many see aspects of the changes enumerated above. But they either trumpet them as the triumph of the new American century or decry them as evidence that the world remains under the boot heel of the wicked United States. Civically and religiously, both responses are wrongheaded. Speaking civically, they give succor to attitudes their overt critiques would make us think they should oppose; they reflect, that is, a bad kind of hostility, and an equally hazardous kind of attachment, to nations' claims on our loyalty. Speaking religiously, both are forms of idolatry — in this case, mistaking a proximate and immanent reality for an ultimate one. Whether demonizing or deifying, neither response really sees either the breadth or the depth of the challenges faith faces today. We must do better than either.

Patriotism, Dr. Johnson said, is "the last refuge of scoundrels." By this he meant that, especially when displayed like a peacock's plumage, patriotism is typically a shield or deflector: "I may have done wrong, but at least I love my country, and I did it for my country," therefore all is excusable. What Johnson identified with scoundrels is true of all of us, much of the time. For us, typically, patriotism is a refuge from reality itself — from the complexities that reality presents to us. It serves as a lens through which we see the world in such a way as to filter out troublesome facets of reality — facts that do not well fit the story we are trying to tell ourselves. When we say we love our country, what we often mean is that we find our country absolutely lovable, and so refuse to believe that it could do the kinds of things that would make it unworthy of love — for example, deliberately killing innocent civilians in a war, or enslaving others, or things of that sort — and we filter out all evidence to the contrary. (This is not simply a temptation in politics; Christians who deny the role of Christianity in anti-Semitism and the Holocaust often make a distinction between "the essence of Christianity," which cannot be anti-Semitic [because Christianity is, by definition, against all bad things], and "bad [that is, anti-Semitic] Christians" — a version of the sort of filtering of which I am speaking here.) This function is a defensive screening function — it makes it hard for us to see the crimes we have done, and so means we are not really responsible for them.

Second, patriotism can be a way of elevating one's own standard by disparaging or attacking some other group. When I was in college, I spent a summer in Germany with a bunch of other American students. It was a wonderful time. But we amused ourselves sometimes by walking around the center of our beautiful, ancient university town (Trier) muttering under our breath — so that it would be heard only by our countrymen walking with us — "Marshall Plan, Marshall Plan." As disparaging things go, it wasn't a great crime. (The Marshall Plan really was a good thing for Europe, and Germany in particular.) But what it did for us was put our experience in Trier in a setting where, our words were suggesting, it was essentially a U.S. federally funded park, where everyone should still be thanking us for being Americans. But Trier is an ancient city, at one time the capital of the Western Roman Empire, old in Augustine's time (and mentioned in his *Confessions*). Our little joke about the Marshall Plan was effectively a way for us to avoid thinking about the depth of history and the enormous richness of the city. It was a way for us to trivialize it, and thus not, I guess, be confronted and threatened — that is, humbled — by the magnificence of its history and the power of its perduring presence. In such settings, "patriotism" is reactionary and preemptively protectionist — a way of attacking others so that we do not feel any need to change, a way of not seeing, a way of avoiding confronting others.

So one danger of patriotism is in how it enables an escapist refusal to see the whole story, but to choose instead to be covertly selective of what you recognize, in the service of triumphalism. In such cases patriotism is a means of avoidance of reality — which means, by and large, of complexity. It is antirealist, in that it closes us off from the whole story. This reduces to slothful self-congratulation, with no impetus to change, develop, or move. As such it is a desire to evade complexity, to escape. This is the patriotism of the hermit crab, smugly complacent in its shell. This avoidance is a major problem in politics today because it has damaging effects on our ability to appreciate the world and what we should do in it. Patriotism of this sort actually damages both true patriotism and true faith, because it hurts our identity, our ability to be honest, our connection to the full and rich range of sources that has nourished us. Ultimately it is a matter of bad faith, dishonest because unrealistic.

This is equally true for patriotism's opposite — the demonization of a particular nation, one's own or another's. Certainly there is enough of that going around. Reactionary hostility to a nation can be as damaging as reactionary support of one. Both idolatry and demonization replace genuine vision and thought with empty ideology and suspicion. Such demonization is increasingly occurring as regards the United States, and with manifold deleterious effects. Anti-Americanism is an expression of antipathy and animus not most fundamentally at what the United States does, but at what it is perceived to be, or at least perceived to represent. It leads to the demonization of the United States as *the* problem in the world, rather than as part of the problem but also a potential tool for solutions.

The experience of limited power changes one's apprehension of the world. Europeans make a virtue of necessity; having disinvested in its military, Europe is willing to accept a degree of danger that the United States is not. (As French political analyst Nicole Bacharan said in 2004, in a rather revealing phrase, "Europeans have a deep desire not to feel threatened.") The U.S. Defense Department's budget request for research and development for 2009 was $79.6 billion; the entire defense budget for the United Kingdom, NATO's next largest spender, for 2009 was $55.5 billion. The United States today spends more than $40 billion on military retirement — making the U.S. military pension fund tied with Japan for the sixth-largest military budget in the world. Few Europeans see the exercise of force outside of immediate self-defense as imaginable, and Europe is "turning inward," changing from NATO-centered to EU-centered; it is absenting itself from the world stage as it focuses upon the project of creating the EU. At the same time, extremist views — nativist extremists, anti-American extremists, and immigrant extremists — are on the rise, while moderates seem unable to muster much energy. In Europe, the best lack all conviction, while the worst are full of passionate intensity. Ironically, the United States' hegemony *is* related to the anti-Americanism so common across the world today, but the anti-Americanism — or what that anti-Americanism represents — creates the hegemony, as much as the hegemony creates the anti-Americanism.

In other words, the United States' hegemony and its demonization by others are two sides of the same coin. Again, the reality of weakness makes a virtue of necessity. The core of Robert Kagan's claim is true — namely, that the United States and Europe are moving apart in the way they view the world, and their own interests therein, and that the main engine of this change is not the surface changes in U.S. administrations, but structural facts about the different interests of the two continents.

For tubby U.S. chauvinists, this may sound humorous, confirmation of the disparaging term "Euro-weenies." But that's way too simplistic. (You go to a bar in Marseille and call a French Foreign Legionnaire a "weenie," and see if the gentleman responds with a quote from Kant and an appeal to Brussels.) Anyone who has seen European forces engaged in peacekeeping — and in some of the more muscular acts of violence that "peacekeeping" paradoxically involves — will agree that any weakening of these forces is quite worrisome for the future of the international order as a whole. The fundament of the Western alliance has always been the commonality of strategic interests, but with Europe's changes this communality is in danger of disappearing.

Political scientist Francis Fukuyama was right when he noted that the collapse of the Soviet Union also meant the collapse of the great ideological debate on how to organize economic and political life. The clash between socialism and capitalism created political debates and shaped political parties and their agendas across the world for more than a century. Capitalism's victory left the world without an "ideology of discontent," a systematic set of ideas that is critical of the world as it exists. Today anti-Americanism fills the void as a protective shield to sustain one's belief in the local conditions of one's "world," which is threatened by American economic dynamism. Yet this anti-Americanism has no real content, no vision. It is not a genuine political position, as the political scientist Ivan Krastev notes, but instead is a tempting fantasy, for "[t]he power of anti-Americanism lies in its very emptiness." It represents the failure of political intelligence, and the replacement of real political deliberation with what Krastev calls a "postideological and postutopian politics," in which "people are against America because they are against everything — or because they do not know exactly what they are against."

Bad it may be, but it has become a powerful and inevitable trend in international politics today. U.S. hegemony, particularly when wielded (as it usually is) in brutal, clumsy, and self-centered ways, will typically generate enough well-warranted ill will on its own. But a world that reacts instinctively against the United States will be less peaceful, less cooperative, less prosperous, less open, and less stable. In this vacuum, with America seeming to be the only visible political actor in the world, it is easy to gain popularity by opposing it. As Krastev put it, "Elites in search of legitimacy and a new generation looking for a cause are the two most visible faces of the new European anti-Americanism." More than this, however, anti-Americanism is used in the service of some deeply antidemocratic ends. Again and again since 2001, the United States has been a campaign issue in elections around the world; in all these cases opposing U.S. power won votes; and in some of them, the votes were used for deeply antidemocratic forces. Across the world nationalism is coming to be seen as identical with anti-Americanism: Can you stand up to the hyperpower? (Much of the attraction, at home and abroad, of various tyrannical leaders such as Putin, Ahmadinejad, and Chavez is precisely because they are perceived as tweaking America.)

None of this is to say that criticism of America, by anyone at all, is essentially or inevitably a form of "anti-Americanism." This must be made very clear: everyone has a right to criticize America, if only because everyone is affected by its actions. (Few complain about French or Dutch perfidy, and that's largely because their acts have little impact.) Furthermore, anyone who cares about the United States should welcome such criticism, for without it America's many faults will go unnoticed, continue to fester, and grow worse.

This is not an attempt, that is to say, to insulate the United States from any criticism. But it is an attempt to render more of this criticism *more real* — to make it really about the United States and its many problems, rather than a certain ideological fantasy that is taped over the realities of the United States. The problem with anti-Americanism is not that it is hostile to America, but that it uses that hostility to generate excuses not to engage the realities of America — not to undertake the difficult task of judgment, of a criticism grounded in a full vision of the many strengths and foibles that constitute America. The danger of anti-Americanism, that is, is — again — the way it encourages the fundamental (after the fall, anyway) human urge toward escapism.

A case can be made that such a view can be extended, that in fact much or perhaps most political discourse today has been seduced by this evasive tactic of being centrally *against* something rather than for it. The two other powerful political forces in the world today are antiterrorism and antiglobalization. In effect, these "anti"-isms are being used in ways hostile to true political life — to suppress democracy, violate civil rights, and thereby avoid the annoying necessity actually to listen to a regime's opponents, or members of a "loyal opposition," and to pretend to organize your life as if you didn't need to listen to those around you for what they think. This is effectively an escapist way of undertaking a parody of "politics," while avoiding the real challenge of facing our political problems, and engaging in deliberating about collective solutions to them with those who do not agree with us.

This condition puts diverse pressures on the psychologies of other nations' citizens, toward demonizing or idolizing the United States, sometimes simultaneously. Indeed, the most common response has been resentment, based on recognition of the benefits of U.S. power combined with envy of it — what chapter 2 called "ambi-Americanism." As Kurt M. Campbell attributes to an unnamed "Asian Ambassador in Washington": "The current analogy between U.S. global dominance and Microsoft's commanding market share is very compelling. Like Microsoft, we want to see U.S. power weakened, but at the same time we use and appreciate the operating system it provides."

While appreciation of the United States is mostly tacit or unconscious, the hostility is overt, even at times exaggerated as a defense mechanism. That the negativity is used as a defense mechanism is revealing. For it highlights how the negative assessment is functionally employed, not to get at the truth, but to enable hostile persons to amplify their criticisms and thereby obscure, and hence avoid confronting, their actual, more ambivalent relation to the United States and its power.

The effect of both jingoistic patriotism and demonizing anti-Americanism, then, is to smother the felt ambivalence that is the immediate experience of a minimally reflective person in our world. Both putatively political emotions are in fact essentially *antipolitical*, because both give us the illusion that we don't have to live *with*, but can only live *nearby*, those with whom we have profound disagreements. Both of these putatively "political" emotions in fact function to convince us to oppose and avoid political life. This is a general fact about our lives today: too much of the time, political discourse resists the apprehension of ambiguity and the acknowledgment of ambivalence. Today the very language of "moral clarity" is typically used to mobilize one-sided visions of a situation, and to denigrate opposing positions.

The effect of all this on our apprehension of the world, and on our self-knowledge, is unsurprisingly bad. Real moral clarity, real faith, teaches us a deep appreciation for the breadth of the relevant facts about the world, the standing of any nation in it, and our own standing vis-à-vis those nations; that appreciation would produce in us a deep and complicated ambivalence. But where can such vision be found?

IV. My Country, Right *and* Wrong

So neither smugly stupid triumphalist American idolatry nor paranoiac anti-American demonization is a genuinely fruitful way of genuinely living politically or faithfully in our world. Augustinians will see that both approaches fail because each has tendencies toward escapism. This escapism is especially pernicious on Christian grounds, because of the damage it does to believers' faith in the sovereign Lord of all creation. So now we must ask, how should we live in the world today in a way that avoids all such escapisms? To recall the line of Reinhold Niebuhr's that I used early in this book, how can we "do justice to the distinctions of good and evil in history and to the possibilities and obligations of realizing the good in history" while yet subordinating "all these relative judgments and achievements to the final truth about life and history which is proclaimed in the Gospel"? How can we be faithful, and civically engaged, in an era of nation-states, when nation-states themselves are under challenge in all sorts of ways, and where one nation-state possesses a quasi-imperial hegemony?

More bluntly: Is it right to love your country? Recall Commissioner Decatur's toast: "Right or wrong, our country!" What should a Christian citizen have done with that toast? How can we be civically faithful, given our deeper faith commitments? Patriotism seems to many today to be nothing but crass and unthinking jingoism. To others, this very hostility to patriotism suggests a smug and delusory unrealism sustainable only through the unconscious willingness to spill one's fellow citizens' blood in defense of oneself. Lost in both extremes are some real and genuine worries about unthinking national attachments, and some real and genuine reasons to affirm such attachment when it is thoughtful and good.

One part of a broad answer may be found in the tension between two registers in Decatur's toast — the political (our country) and the ethical (right or wrong). (That the tension is real is evidenced by the toast being remembered this long.) We should keep the tension alive, even deepen it as much as we can. How we can do that will vary among political contexts; for U.S. citizens, they can generate a genuine patriotism by recognizing and exploiting the tension between ideals of republic and of empire, liberty and glory, freedom and domination that pervades U.S. political history and culture. These two languages developed in opposition to one another domestically (though republicans were often self-consciously imperial and expansionist abroad). Yet there is a theme in U.S. political thought, right now underplayed, that the United States should be *less* than the sum of its parts — that, in an argument stretching forward from Jefferson's worries about Hamilton's desire to build a strong federal government, the polity would be favoring "greatness" or sheer magnitude over "goodness" or moral virtuousness. For Madisonians, there is some real commitment to the United States as an instrument of moral uplift, but it cannot congeal into the idolatry of empire building. The outward magnificence of nations is not necessarily determinative of their inner health, and when, as it may well do, the United States loses its empire, it cannot be *too* attached to it, lest the identity of the nation be too tied up with it.

But a moral critique will finally be inadequate here. A vigorous critique should be properly theological and iconoclastic, rooted in a critique of idolatry. Theologically we can see the problems here as problems of bad faith, of idolatry and demonization. That is to say, patriotism itself is not a stand-alone emotion or commitment; it is one dimension or fact of our fundamental orientation to the world, one aspect of our apprehension of it and commitment to it. Patriotism is just our working out of our fundamental faith vis-à-vis some political community or other. If we are faithful to God, our commitment to our political community will be derivative of that faith, in the sense that it is an outworking of faithful existence, a modulation of it, a kind of commitment to a particular, local, history. If we are not faithful to God, our political commitment stands a good chance of taking God's place as the center of value for us; after all, throughout history political absolutism has been a very popular form of idolatry.

To criticize blind patriotism as bad faith is not simply to label it with a naughty theological term: it identifies a functional maladaption of our commitment to the world. For both idolatry and demonization are avoidance mechanisms. Augustine knew this: he faced the complacency of the idolatry of the *imperium,* exemplified both by the false *pietas* of pagan Rome and by the cosmopolitan-Eusebian attitudes of the Christian elites of his day (recall Jerome's rather campy panic at the news of the fall of Rome). He faced also the contrary temptations toward demonization, coded into the Christian Scriptures (especially the book of Revelation) and carried forward in various sectarian and nativist movements like Manicheism, Donatism, and arguably Pelagianism. He always worked against both temptations. In all his writings on these subjects, Augustine's goal was always the same: to refuse the mythology of the state, both its original mythology as salvific and its counter-mythology as demonic. In a way, Augustine *secularized* Rome; as he saw it, Rome was not directly part of salvation history, neither divine nor demonic, but indirectly it was used by God for God's own purposes. Political entities are fundamentally secular realities, this-worldly, and are useful in securing us space and occasion to signify our gratitude to God and praise of God's glory.

Given our contemporary challenges, Augustinians urge on us an attitude of resistance to both poles. We need to refuse the mythology of the state and to remember, when we are tempted to idolize American geopolitical power, that force is not ultimately the divine will, but is always at best a tragic stopgap that can be employed only in the knowledge that one becomes answerable for all the consequences of its exercise. Augustinians will also remind those tempted to demonize American power (and idolize something like the international community) that some force is necessary, that the world is not and will never be the stable and rational place we wish it were, but stands in dire and urgent need of redemption. And this redemption is not continuous with the secular faith in "progress," nor is it brought about by the United States Marine Corps.

We can and should detach these tendencies from the national frames in which they are frequently embedded. For, again, the most basic danger from an Augustinian standpoint is not geopolitical problems — as disastrous as they may be — but the social-psychological forces that can lead to those geopolitical problems. The real problem is the way that both groups attempt improperly to have worldly realities bear the weight of divinity — and thereby alter their vision of reality and their understanding of history, in order to render less incredible their various reactionary idolatries. The *libido dominandi* is a knife that cuts both ways, for the lust to dominate all too easily becomes the dominating lust, and the mournful warrior all too easily becomes one who really enjoys his day job, who cannot imagine another way of life — and so becomes subject to the logic of subjugation in a way more profound than those he subjugates.

We can do this by changing our attitude to the political order we inhabit, first of all by learning to see that order as a mix of blessings and curses. Instead of either demonizing (or idolizing) some representatives of this system, or demonizing the system itself, we should find another way to inhabit it, giving ultimately provisional allegiance to some nations while still vividly acknowledging their faults. This is not to counsel a turn away from the world, but toward real vision of it, as a world *in via*, on the way to something else.

How do we do this? The first step is a realistic and savvy understanding of the nation-state as a political entity. Over the past few decades, many thinkers have come to a deep and rich understanding of the strengths and weaknesses of the nation-state. The nation-state is neither divine nor demonic, it is rather simply a tool we can use; after all, we should remember that nation-states, for all the flack they get, are really quite marvelous devices for political engagement. They are small enough to be coherent sites for rich and rewarding lives in modernity, but large enough to be normally effective in ensuring that all the dimensions of human life are brought under the political control of the nation. There are good reasons for why nation-states have been so successful and popular in modernity. Today, however, many say that the nation-state is both too small and weak and too large and clumsy to answer many of the challenges facing it — the macrochallenges of globalization and the microchallenges to authentic existence by the heretical imperative, consumerism, and ironism. Because of this, nation-states, and the promise of institutional-civic accountability they embody, are under threat by larger patterns of globalization and significant transformations in international relations — especially the enormous reach of U.S. hegemony, but also the past two decades' expansion of the EU (and especially the EU elite's latent hostility to democracy and politics), and now the rise of China. But that does not mean that we should abandon them as political forms; they remain indispensable political instruments for us, in inhabiting our world.

Yet the nation-state has challenges to faith that we should acknowledge. Most interestingly, scholars have emphasized the role of collective memory, and especially a collective sense of a shared history, in generating the kind of deep emotional commitment that nations need, and that they seek to inculcate in their citizens. This history is as importantly an erasure as an affirmation: as Ernst Renan — a pioneering nineteenth-century scholar of nationalism, and a philosopher and religious thinker — said, if "the essential element of a nation is that all its individuals must have many things in common," they "must also have forgotten many things." After all, patriotism is in significant ways about remembering a certain history. Contests about patriotism are overwhelmingly about how and what to remember. (Think, in recent years, of the most bitter fights about patriotism; they have often involved the meaning of certain events, captured in symbols — *Enola Gay*, reparations for African Americans' enslavement, the treatment of Native Americans, the treatment of Japanese Americans during World War II, the meaning of the Vietnam War, etc.) The histories we learn in school are often highly artificial artifacts, meant to instill a relatively unified moral message about who we are and from whence we come.

In addressing both those excessively in love with and those excessively hostile to a nation, Augustinians will try to get them to remember their histories less selectively, because history is the register of faith for Augustine. They urge this more comprehensive memory in order to induce both sides to reform their too-tidy and too-easy perceptions of reality, to confess with humility to a faith in a Lord of history whose true face remains crucially hidden, and to acknowledge that we remain pilgrims still on the way, in a story whose author we are not. We may need force to secure order, but we shall never in this dispensation proclaim "Mission Accomplished!" And we should end every day praying, with the psalmist, to be delivered of our necessities.

In these ways we see that part of what it means to have a realistic political vision is to have a realistic sense of history, and that means an untidy picture of history. We must not think of history as *symphonic*, organized around a central theme, with repeated variations and reiterations of that theme. Instead, we should think of history as *fugal* — an enormously intricate musical structure of subtle and repeating patterns, one nested inside another, with complexity mounting upon complexity, obscure allusion adjoining obscure allusion, and with the final resolution eschatologically deferred.

Speaking more concretely, for different people, this entails different acts of remembering, all of which are in the service of remembering less selectively. For those moments when we are prone to idolize a nation, remembering some of the darker moments may well serve to remind us of the whole complexity of the inheritance. For the United States, this means U.S. citizens can't forget 9/10 and all before — the ugly history of the misuse of force, and the domination that has marked much of America's behavior with other, typically weaker nations. (It helps here to remember that the *other* 9/11 was September 11, 1973, the date of the military coup in Chile that threw out a democratically elected government and installed an oppressive and bloody dictatorship in its place.) If, on the other hand, we are prone to despair of a nation ever being good or decent, again a turn to history will help disenthrall us of our pessimism. For those prone to locate the United States as the source of all evil in the world, it helps to remember 11/8 and all before — the way that the United States has, for more than sixty years, spilled its citizens' blood, and spent their money — not to mention the blood of many others — to not only serve as a stabilizing force for the "free world," but to have done so in a way that no other nation could be imagined to have. (If you don't believe that, imagine that the United States and China had changed places — or the United States and Russia, or the United States and France.) This is not to deny the grim record of U.S. stupidity and malfeasance, in Vietnam, in Iraq, and elsewhere; it is simply to say that the United States' actions have been mixed, but have contributed to the creation of a better world in a way that the twentieth century's analogously powerful nations — the USSR, the People's Republic of China, the Third Reich — did not. It is not with a love of triumphant self-congratulation, but with something closer to a grim irony, that we can say that the twentieth century was quite fortunate to have the United States as its most powerful nation.

The sort of deeper exploration of history and memory here encouraged will lead to deeper appreciation of our need of God, and a deeper sense of our helplessness in history unless we have an anchor *in* history to something *outside* of it. Outside some such narrative anchor from which we can tell the story, the events of history remain merely chronicle — one damned thing after another. If, however, the events have shape as parts of a larger story, however imperfectly apprehended, then a larger purpose can emerge from them. This is how the Christian churches offer a richer and more fruitful perspective, by telling the story of God's dealings with humanity from alpha to omega, from Israel through the story of Christ. And yet this is not escapist, because God is going to redeem *all* of history, not just a selective part of it — and God is going to redeem history through the work of the churches.

This leads into Augustine's richer and more complicated account of the theological meaning of history, its sacramentality, if you will. Questions about the theological meaning of history are perennial for Christians: Can God be present in history *through* nations? Can nations be sacramental? How is history significant for God? On Augustinian terms, history most definitely has meaning: it is the bearer of God's work of salvation, the medium God uses to tell God's story of the love of creation. But it is only eschatologically finalized. History is a register of faith; you have faith in the God of Abraham, Isaac, and Jacob, Jesus and the apostles. You have faith that God's actions in history tell a secret story, that they are like a spinal cord, around which all of history's events are organized. But your apprehension of it in this life will remain perennially incomplete. We cannot be sure what will be significant and how it will be so — so we must live without blinders, resisting ideological lenses.

More specifically in political terms, it means that politics, as a historical reality, is under God's governance, God's rule, and to be under God's rule means to be under God's judgment, God's vision of what we truly mean. And this judgment itself works in history. That is to say that the United States cannot be seen as itself messianic, but only as, like Rome, a device God uses. And God's judgment on all political entities entails both condemnation of our idolatries and recognition of the truth of our honest faith. On this reading, hegemony is dangerous because of what it does to our psychology, to our understanding of ourselves and our understanding of others.

Here is where the all-too-frequent Orwellian language of "moral clarity" can come in. True "moral clarity" doesn't make things clearer, but rather more vividly ambiguous and complicated. In this it opposes the vicious, ruthless, simplifying energies of our own ego. A true "hermeneutics of charity" slows you down, resists too-easy judgment. What

Christianity as Augustine sees it offers is *moral obscurity*, moral difficulty. Life, after all, is not easy, and the closer we approach to a true vision of the world, the more clouded, mottled, and murky does our assessment of it become.

Furthermore, this renewed perception of the ambiguities of history may lead to a renewed appreciation for the urgency and messiness of international politics — in short, to a recovery of the genuine realities of politics in this world as a way of people coming to confront the many differences and semidivergences that challenge their communion, and trying to manage them as best they can together. This is not simply a matter of the pragmatic negotiation of interests. It is deeper than that; it is a sharing of hopes and fears, a conversation about whether we can have common objects of love. The key for policy comity, after all, is a common perception of aspirations and threats; if people see they seek the same goals and face the same problems, they will collaborate on a solution. So the point is really more directly engagement with one another's perceptions than an immediate urging on all of a common positive program. Let them see the rationale of the program by convincing them of the shape of the threat. As a corollary, you should permit your perception of the world to be modified — reoriented, softened in some ways, sharpened in others, overall "matured" — by your neighbors' perception. Most direct consultation is about perceptions. If you share a vision of the world — and that means here a vision of the dangers in the world — the policies to be enacted emerge naturally therefrom.

This process of real politics — of exposing your fears, and hearing others, and letting your own fears be reshaped by that exposure — is disturbing and disquieting. But that's what negotiations are. The word "negotiation" actually comes from the Latin *nec-otium*, "unquiet." It's supposed to upset you. But the management of one's own upset, not the absence of it, is part of what it means to be a grown-up, part of what it means to live in a political world — which we manifestly do.

Conclusion

In the end, the reality of 11/9 will not be evaded. Like it or not, the United States will be the "support system" for globalization, and the international order, for the coming decades; that is what its hegemony is for. We should never imagine that the hegemony is good in itself — it is only good so long as it secures a good and just order, at home and abroad. As citizens, whether of the United States or of other nations, and as fellow members of a world community, we all should ask ourselves and one another questions about how well this hegemony is being carried out internationally (these are, as it were, "liberal internationalist" worries); those of us who are citizens of the United States should ask also about what the exercise of this hegemony is doing to U.S. civic life (these are, as it were, "civic republican" worries).

But beyond these questions, Christians in particular also must ask a third set of questions: about what life within this political order does to Christians' ability to cultivate the kind of faith we are called on to have. As we have seen, these challenges revolve around worries about idolatry. A proper understanding of how to be faithful in our political world will confront the dangers of idolatry to our identity, and qualify and orient our commitment to our polity, with perpetually renewed attention to the condition in which we find ourselves.

Augustinians, then, should support the United States conditionally; their support should be contingent upon its delivering proper order. If this is so, what does it mean to revisit such commitment? The next chapter identifies issues where this hegemony — or rather, the cultural forces it typically promotes — may need to be quite radically resisted, by Americans and non-Americans alike.

CHAPTER 4

Love in the Age of Millennial Capitalism

⌒⅄⌒

A re we happier today than we have been before? Is our age more conducive to happiness than earlier ages were? Few questions are more
fundamental. And answers to it stand behind a great many of the debates
raging today — about globalization, about moral character, about many
things. The evidence on both sides of this question is substantial. Some
point out that we have achieved a level of affluence unrivaled in the history of the world, and our appetites and desires have been domesticated in
healthy ways — we have a hard time imagining going to war over honor,
or killing another due to a humiliating slight or because of another's dif-
fering religious beliefs. In the past several centuries, those societies that
have moved toward becoming commercial societies have seen declines in
violence and increasing marks of self-discipline and order. And the end of
the Cold War seemed to promise real and substantial changes in people's
lives, some of which have been borne out; in the past fifteen years alone,
the worldwide malnourishment rate declined from 17 percent (in 1992) to
14 percent (in 2004), at the same time that population has increased by
900 million people — from 5.5 to 6.4 billion. Do not get me wrong: that is
still far, far too many people going desperately hungry worldwide — one
would be too many — but it is real progress. At the same time, others suggest that there are costs as well, harder to measure but no less real — generally describable as a decline in our capacity to live morally rich lives.
Many speak of living after virtue, having survived the death of character,
facing a dark age ahead. And, to be frank, there is evidence on their side as
well.

How should we negotiate these disputes? Beyond the variety of answers it allows, the question is amenable to challenge in several different ways. First of all, one could ask, who is "we"? Does a picture of happiness that fixates on the wealthy white people of the first world simply ignore those, near and far, whose labor and suffering are essential to "our" amusements? And if it includes them — as it surely should — should they be understood as trapped in immiseration, or simply "following behind" on the stairway to an ever-greater happiness? Second, we could ask, what is "happier"? Many would suggest that what we take for "happiness" is actually a shallow and bestial trivialization of a truly flourishing life. After all, depression levels rose significantly in the twentieth century. Others respond that depression levels have not risen nearly so much as (to choose one example) infant mortality rates have dropped, and they suggest that the exchange is very much in our favor.

This debate seems interminable. And it is not at all clear how to bring this issue properly into view. The worries are all pretty woolly, and they are often couched in impressionistic terms. And they may just be episodes in the perennial human practice of grousing about how things are today and longing for the good old days. Cultural criticism is hard to keep honest. But I think they do point to a real and interesting worry. And that is this: today our capacity to be creatures who love — who have long-standing and deep attachments that are irreducible to sheer animalistic appetites — is threatened, left to atrophy, by the consumerist mode of life we inhabit.

What does it mean to say that our mode of life challenges our capacity to love? It means that we are increasingly encouraged to think about desire and longing in ways detrimental to long-term commitments. Consider: I can get anything I want. But do I know what I actually "want" at all? Our world is awash in accessible consumer goods and pluriform forms of life, but this flood of consumables has seemed to go hand in hand with a growing sense of skepticism and even indifference to any good in particular. At the same moment when the good life, in multiple flavors, is being offered to us, we seem increasingly incapable of wanting any particular form of it for more than an instant. We live in an economic culture of immediacy and consumption, in which the idea of patience or waiting has no home to rest its head. Consumer culture "takes the waiting out of wanting," encouraging us toward a kind of constant appetitive channel surfing, as one fickle appetite follows quickly upon another. This condition does not so much directly reshape us as indirectly mislead us: for it tells us, or sells us, a story about ourselves, and through that story seduces us into believing the illusory promise of immediate satisfaction. This promise is a powerful one; if we come to believe in it, we come to see ourselves as being the kinds of creatures who have only the sorts of short-term desires that consumer culture can satiate. Scholars have recently come round to worrying about the problem of excessive choice in our world. This is a strange problem to have. And yet it is real, pressing, and momentous. Exploring it is this chapter's task.

The challenges to hope presented by the War on Terror, and to faith by the massive and enduring fact of American hegemony, are not the only challenges Christians face today. Both are in some ways fairly superficial, essentially "political" challenges. Without the discrete events of 9/11 or 11/9, these challenges would not possess the pressing intensity they have for us. But there is a broader, deeper, and more fundamentally "cultural" set of challenges to human flourishing, challenges to the shape of our love. These challenges are not dependent on the course of political events but are more fundamental to our condition today.

I designate this third, cultural, set of challenges as what Walter Russell Mead has called "millennial capitalism." By this phrase I mean to identify the (possibly self-contradictory) slew of forces — economic, cultural, social — reshaping our world in fundamental ways, by reshaping the nature of our desires, our loves. "Millennial capitalism" is the right name for it, because it is equally, and equally basically, religious and economic. It is fundamentally the encroachment of the market on all aspects of human life, and the social and psychological agitation that is generally, and with good reason, associated with that encroachment. The trajectory of this "economization" puts noneconomic aspects of our lives increasingly under pressure to be redescribed as "essentially" market choices. This process has been going on for some time, but what make its most recent stages "millennial" are both the absolute comprehensiveness of the changes currently occurring and the apocalyptic conviction held by many that such a consumerism embodies, as it were, the end of history. Of all three challenges, this one is the most broadly, profoundly, and intimately felt across the world — so intimately felt, in fact, that sometimes it seems like the "natural" way for things to be. From "coca-colonization" in Europe to the fear of the decay of traditional cultures in the Middle East and Asia, this is the condition that Benjamin Barber has called the "McWorld," to which the reactionaries in all cultures respond with variations on "jihad" — and quite apocalyptic jihad at that.

This raises many and diverse worries. For our purposes, we are most concerned with the challenge that our ever-more economized world poses to our understanding of love, and through that, to our understanding of the kinds of creatures we aspire to be. These consequences are profound. Perhaps the easiest way to describe them is that, in the current dispensation, we are *pursuing* happiness but can never *achieve* it; we are caught on a treadmill of purely momentary satiation, of naturalized dissatisfaction. (The menace of this is nicely caught in the German word for pursuit — *nachjagen,* "to hunt after.") We shall never achieve happiness itself. We shall be endlessly pursuing happiness in materialistic terms as long as the system can maintain itself — gaining in affluence but never satisfied. We are so caught because we have a bad understanding of desire, a bad understanding of our deepest longings, of what and how and *why* we want — a misconstrual, in short, of love.

This is not to deny that the pursuit of happiness has not had good consequences. Again, as I said above, the level of material wealth in modern societies, even among those not relatively well-off, is astounding. I do not want to demonize materialism; I want, rather, to suggest that we typically today rely on a misapprehension of what makes us happy, a misapprehension that traps us in a series of conundrums that we would be wise to avoid. To do better, we need an account of the human person (and especially of human agency, of the nature of human action), and a political psychology undergirding it, that is built not around our capacity to consume but around our capacity to love.

While I think the best such account we have available is one derived from an Augustinian psychology, others will have different accounts that may appeal equally, or more plausibly, to them. My aim in this chapter is not to suggest that an Augustinian account offers the only viable approach, but only one viable approach. It is exemplary, not obviously supreme.

To get to this conclusion, the chapter explores the nature of the challenges we face, and suggests how we should resist them, in an argument of four large steps. Part I details the language Augustine offers us to think about persons, in order to argue that it can frame our worries in a suitably capacious and appropriately profound way. Part II uses that language to characterize the nature of our new economic-cultural condition, and explores the challenges to existence posed by living in a culture of hyper-abundance. Part III charts the ways in which our existence in this culture always tempts us to deform our lives. And finally, part IV suggests some strategies for confronting the forces encouraging our deformation, and resisting them.

I. *Libido Dominandi*

Worries about people being fundamentally misshapen in ways that they themselves cannot easily recognize are not a modern invention. Augustine formulated them quite perspicaciously in his simple phrase *libido dominandi*, the "dominating lust": the lust to dominate that is also the lust *that* dominates. This is our desire to master others that, in an act of psychological jujitsu as neat as the ambiguity of the English (and Latin) phrase suggests, quickly takes hold of us and comes to dominate all our behavior in the world. Augustine did not invent the idea, but he realized its descriptive and diagnostic value and made it central to his analysis of Roman society, and through that analysis to human society bereft of God in general, in an innovative and powerful way.

This desire for domination begins in the presumption, both arrogant and despairing, that we do not depend on one another, and finally on an ultimate other — namely, God. In this presumption, we anxiously obscure our dependence and try to replace our need to trust one another (and God) with the guarantee of mastery by force. What Augustine shows about the early history of Rome is a truth that history teaches us again and again: security sought through sheer violence gives a peace bought only at the price of a bottomless paranoia.

But violence is only the most unsubtle form of the *libido dominandi*. The overwhelming majority of people eschew its crudities, whether out of cowardice or a more refined form of self-unknowing. For us, yet more gentle techniques of attempted domination insinuate themselves in our dealings with one another. It suffuses human life, in the temptations to instrumentalize other people, or other things, for our own exclusive benefit — out of a pattern of seduction that eventually becomes a desire for it. The French writer and philosopher Albert Camus well described this in his novel *The Fall* (the most Augustinian work of this dissident Augustinian author), when the narrator of the novel, Jean-Baptiste Clamence, talks about how the habit of seduction eventually becomes enslavement to it, so that eventually you take what you do not want: "believe me, monsieur, in some situations there is nothing harder than not taking what you do not desire."

Once we go down the road of domination, it is endless. It does not end in happiness, because it does not end. No amount of power will ever make us happy, because no amount of power will get us what we in our sin seek — namely, to control everything, to have complete mastery, to be God. It is not properly intelligible. It is bottomless; its questions have no answers, indeed cannot be answered at all. Ultimately the whole project ends up making all our pleasures hollow, for they serve us only as momentary pauses in the endless drama of manipulation we undertake with the world. We indulge in them finally not for themselves, but only for the respite and diversion they provide from the increasingly wearying task of struggling to overmaster the cosmos. Experience becomes wholly a matter of evasion, of avoiding the facts of our life, of escape. As Augustine suggests in a sermon, such a life makes even sexual activity finally a matter of evasion and boredom, simply of staving off contemplating the emptiness of our lives: "Such is the weakness of the flesh, such is the irksome nature of this life, that everything, however wonderful, ends in boredom." And he himself describes his own pursuit of such a goal in the *Confessions* as a process whereby he ended up making of himself a *regio egestasis*, a "desolate region," a desert. To seek to make a God of oneself is to end by making a wasteland of the world.

The project of *libido dominandi* relies on a radical misconception of our end, rooted in a radical misconception of our place in the world. In one way it is based upon presumption, in another way upon despair. We presume that humans can achieve this level of divine mastery over the universe, and act accordingly. But we presume this because we despair of believing in a God who could be as good as we need God to be; it is only because we do not trust God as we should that we decide to seize the role of satiating our desires for ourselves. In a way, we become committed to the *libido dominandi* because we fear that God is not truly in charge — because we refuse to hope.

So the *libido dominandi* is a way to talk about the debasing enslavement of the self to a bad understanding of what happiness is, and how we go about getting it. Augustine offers us this model in order to show us how false this picture of ourselves truly is, to explain to us why we act like this, and as a prelude to offering a better way. Can we still use this language today? I think we can. We will see how, next.

II. Creative Destruction

It will help if we get a good grip on the nature of the economic and cultural world in which we live. This world is relatively unique in human history, though our inhabitation of it makes it hard for us to see its peculiarity. Yet peculiar it is: it is so pervaded by market relations that it afflicts its inhabitants with a kind of radical existential turbulence, a turbulence that upsets our self-understanding in ways that force us out of any relatively stable sense of self. The triumph of the market is not the triumph of the self, but its demise.

Throughout this section I talk about "market relations" and "the triumph of the market." But what exactly do I mean by "the market," and in what does its triumph consist? By "market" I mean the sphere of life wherein goods and services are exchanged in an exhaustively monetary fashion, so that all "products" — whether physical widgets, immaterial advice, or the right to wear someone's photo on your T-shirt — are translatable into a single register of monetary value. This suggests that all products are interchangeable with a certain amount of money. Note, though, that my complaint is not about "capitalism" in itself, but about consumerism, a certain kind of overreaching capitalism that damages the souls of its inhabitants.

The triumph of consumerism consists in the fact that the logic of market capitalism is ever-more universal, in several senses. First of all, the market encompasses the globe. There is no place that is "outside" to the market, nowhere untouched by it. Certainly there may be places that opt out of the market for reasons unintelligible, strictly speaking, to the logic of the market — North Korea and the Vatican come to mind — and there may be places that have simply been, in proper apocalyptic argot, "left behind" by the millennium, like much of sub-Saharan Africa, but generally everyone else is part of the matrix. Second, the logic of the market increasingly infiltrates all aspects of human life, so that relations that were once governed by other criteria — family loyalty, religious fealty, a set of shared political or ethical commitments — are reimagined in the radically stripped-down logic of sheer economic cost-benefit analysis. Not just careers and skill sets, but bodies and personalities are becoming increasingly the object of commodification in the market; we undergo repeated "reengineering" and rebranding (through pharmacology, training, or physical alteration) in order to remain a "hot property." Reproduction and the family are increasingly economized as well: think of the "market" for adoptions. Even government is increasingly supplanted by economic logics, whether self-imposed (think of gated communities as privatized ministates, run for profit) or as part of a larger economizing of our public imagination (as citizens are treated as consumers, not cosovereigns of their polities but customers of a governmental bureaucratic-managerial elite).

Along with its universality, the market is enormously dynamic, excessively so. The perpetual turbulence of the market keeps people in permanent motion around the world. We are undergoing what the contemporary social theorist David Harvey calls "time/space compression": a change in our experience of time and our experience of place, in a way that makes us less attached to either, and more portable. In this situation we are induced to view our location in place and time — the location that normally gives us most of what we think of as the attributes of our identity — as something fundamentally accidental to our more "punctual," true, "inner" selves. Furthermore, even the language whereby we typically understand these transformations is harmful for us. The explicit picture within which we imagine our relationships with each other shapes us decisively, as Iris Murdoch has said: "[m]an is a creature who makes pictures of himself and then comes to resemble the picture." In several ways, that is, our societies and our selves are being redescribed and re-created by the surging forces of economic rationality.

To see this in more detail, it will help us to see specifically some of the material changes already under way — changes that are vast, tectonic movements in the shape of human social life, occurring at such a fundamental level, and in a timescale just beyond that of a single human lifetime, that they are easy to miss for those living amidst them. Perhaps the most fundamental, though often unnoticed, fact of this new dispensation is urbanization. Sometime in October 2006, for the first time in human history, the majority of human beings lived in an urban environment. It is hard to overestimate how dramatic this change is. Throughout human history, villages have been the home to a very large majority (about 85 to 95 percent) of human beings; the survival of villages was what allowed cities and states to regenerate after local disasters such as plague and famine. Even in 1950, roughly 70 percent of the human population lived in rural settings. These new cities are by no means small: in 2000, there were 411 cities with over a million in population, and the biggest are larger than some countries. And this is a third world urbanization: over the next three decades, urban areas in less developed regions are expected to double in size, growing from 2 billion today to 4 billion by 2030, at the same time that birthrates are dropping — so that effectively the population is not so much expanding as concentrating in the cities. Urbanization makes children less useful than they would be on farms; hence people in cities have fewer children.

Historically, city life has been seen as enriching but perilous. Civilization is classically an affair of cities; think of words like "civilized" and "urbane." Those we imagine as the cultural elites do not live on ranches or in vast palatial country manors; they live in cities. The experiences of city life — of substantial human pluralism, of the increased speed of human interaction and human life in general, of living in a radically human-constructed environment, and of the simultaneous feelings of solitude, even isolation, and of subsumption into a mass community identity — make for a powerful shaping force. Taken on its own, city life is a rich and complicating thing.

But contemporary patterns of urbanization fall well short of the best models of city life. The best example of this bad individualism is the increasing spatial separation of the polity along class lines, exemplified in the accelerating "suburbanization" of the United States in the past century. A new Tocqueville would look to the suburbs and exurbs to understand the future of American democracy, for suburbanization at its worst combines the insularity often imputed to good country people with the shallow interactions, isolation, and commercial mind-set associated with "city folk." In the past century, suburbanization has been the functional analogue (in America's culture and political economy) of the nineteenth-century frontier movement that Tocqueville saw as generating good social dynamics for the nation. Joel Kotkin argues that the suburbs have moved community and family out of the city, possibly undermining the city's moral order. The virtues of communal living are not simply moved to the country; according to a census bureau report in 2003, about 7 million American households (over 6 percent of the total) live in gated communities, and for new houses in California the proportion is 40 percent. The rise of "new urbanism" and the like seems to counter this trend, though whether it will have a significant impact is unclear at present; furthermore, it may well simply be suburbanizing the city as well, by transferring some expectations for isolation and lack of community back into the city from the suburbs.

Alongside this global urbanization (and suburbanization), the human race as a whole is aging. In the twenty-first century humanity will change, for the first time in history, from a relatively youthful species to a middle-aged one. Before 2000, the young outnumbered the elderly, or even the middle-aged; since 2000, old people have outnumbered young people, and will continue to do so into the foreseeable future. Modern medicine, changes in lifestyle, and improved nutrition will lower mortality rates and lengthen life spans. This will affect the whole world: the percent of people sixty-five years or older is expected to more than double over the next five decades, increasing from 7 percent to 16 percent.

The effect of this on the developed countries of the first world (and in China and India, both of whose population-control policies have had real success over the past several decades) will be quite profound. As we saw in the last chapter, it will have geopolitical repercussions, because over the next several decades it will also produce a geopolitical generation gap, as an increasingly middle-aged first world confronts a still-young third world. It will have fiscal repercussions, for as workers age and retire, they will not be replaced by an increasing number of workers but with, at best, a working population of the same size, which will have to take care of a great many more retirees than the generation currently working must do. An aging population hence puts great strains on the pension and health care safety nets that are the basis of a good deal of modern welfare. It also has cultural repercussions, as cultures shift from having their cultural center of gravity anchored in the interests and concerns of young people (and especially young families) to the interests of people in their fifties. Will the typical middle-aged person be a respectable and wise citizen, suitably weathered by life, prudentially able to govern his or her passions and judicious in balancing public and private good? It seems more likely that the passions and interests of the adolescent will be cultivated and deepened by our advertising culture, and that the middle-aged person will be more akin to a fickle spoiled child, controlled by his or her desires and unable to envision, let alone act upon, any long-term goods. It is a change that can be caricatured, but only slightly, in the change of aging voters' concerns from good school districts to low taxes and good health care. Retirees' well-known opposition to taxation for schools, and the rise of pharmacological advertising directed largely at the middle-aged and elderly, seem to support this.

The above changes are profound in themselves. But they also lead to enormous turbulence in populations, as people move with increasing frequency, and velocity, from place to place, driven by the exigencies of the market. Migration is now a common occurrence for an increasing percentage of the world's population, within and between nations. China currently is engaged in the greatest migration in the history of the world, from the countryside to the cities — far faster and vaster than the migration of Europeans to North America in the nineteenth and early twentieth centuries. Even in the developed West, the velocity of job changing has increased many times over in the past few decades, so that the idea of spending one's life in the employ of one company is now increasingly considered quaint.

Different names have been offered for this phenomenon; to my mind, the best one is "creative destruction." The idea here is that the ruthlessly competitive environment of the marketplace makes endless demands for novelty and so encourages the perpetual upheaval of human life in search of the Next Big Thing. Here destruction is not the accidental consequence of the creativity, but rather its precondition. Increasingly, time and space are not barriers to what I want; I can get my "authentic" Civil War reenactor's costume delivered to me, wherever I am in the world, by overnight delivery. As I said earlier, eschatology has been replaced by next-day air: we have removed the waiting from wanting, in ways that make our experience of time nothing more than an annoying delay. Whatever we name it, this phenomenon is increasingly dominating our imagination, and particularly our moral imagination — the stories we tell about why and how we care about what we care about.

The upshot of all this is radical existential turbulence: the decline of selfhood as permanent and stable, and in its place the rise of evanescent, fungible, and "liquid" forms of agency. This turbulence is relentless and vehemently antihuman, privileging monetary abstractions over real people. It favors "capital flows" — the vast sums of money that banks, companies, and fund managers control for investments — over humans, and so forces real humans into Faustian bargains with supranational (and thus seemingly suprapolitical, apparently "natural" and irresistible) economic forces: economic well-being, or at least the momentary experience of economic well-being, in exchange for acquiescence to the reductionist logic of the market.

Yet religious metaphors seem oddly out of place here, for in such a total market nothing is holy. I mean that quite literally: the globalized market is moving toward creating individual choosers, agents, with no absolute ties, no "sacred" at all, people for whom all is up for negotiation. It offers no opportunities for piety, and no plausible space for the sacred, for what is nonnegotiable, nontradable, for what cannot be captured in the terms of commodity value. In short, if we understand the "sacred" to be that which a culture or some person understands to be set apart and marked out as incommensurable with the profane workings of life, millennial capitalism recognizes no sacredness in existence at all; everything is ultimately for sale. The modern market system makes all values fungible, so that value is abstracted from objects and persons, "flowing" from one container to another with no essential attachment to any.

I doubt that such a world, a world without absolute values, is ultimately achievable. But it would take another book to make my skepticism heard over the trumpeting triumphalisms and jeremiads of market millennialists and catastrophists today, let alone intelligible to them. Fortunately we don't need to do that. All we need to do is note that, though the worldview of millennial capitalism doesn't recognize it, it *does* in fact have sacred votives today, or at least one sacred votive, and that is the god of Choice. Millennial capitalism can imagine no greater good than the fundamental good of "individual choice" (which it treats as a black box, not to be interrogated). Choice is the absolute standard that is not questioned; in its faith system, it goes without saying that *more choice is always good, and exercising more choice is good*. The rhetoric of "choice" to which we have reduced our agential and creative energies has become the ultimate necessity. And this choice is as it were an imperative — indeed, the *only* imperative we can properly feel. We have, as it were, no choice about choice.

Let me be very clear. Of course, I think choice is a good, and a very important good. There is no doubt that the market world we live in brings us benefits and blessings unimagined by our ancestors. Our material lives are richer by far than any age before us; your typical working-class person in the first world lives amid more material comforts than did nineteenth-century royalty. (It is an astonishing fact that increasingly across the developed world, the central emerging medical problem confronting the lower-income population is obesity.) And even as the scope for human agency has expanded, and continues to expand, at breathtaking pace, still for many people in the world too much choice is hardly a looming danger. None of this can be denied, nor should anyone take seriously complaints about this situation that suggest a belief that it would be better for humanity, on the whole, to go back to the way we lived two or three centuries ago. Certainly individuals are free to "simplify" their lives if they so wish, but it must be noted that even such decisions are just that — free choices, enabled as such by life in our world. And few who talk about going "back to the land" are really able to do so without relying on modern medicine, government, and education.

But these facts should not induce in us any Pollyannaish placidity. Despite the intoxicated exuberances of market zealots, this world poses real dangers for its inhabitants. The blessings of our lives come with enormous and complicated challenges. Most fundamentally we face the prospect that integral, coherent, and deep lives, lives of the sort that humanity has talked about trying to live for most of its time on this earth, may be increasingly difficult to inhabit. And this danger is compounded by the fact that many people think that our newfound choices are simply and solely good. That is not true. Living as we are in the midst of perpetual "creative destruction" means that we live without explicit recognition of absolutes; we live in a way that makes all up for grabs; we live in the midst of radical existential turbulence.

But is choice *the* good? That is going too far. The logic that would make it so can be questioned: Would it be good for you to *choose* each breath you take? To *choose* each step? The self-conscious exercise of agency cannot be the ultimate good, lest it run into multiple incoherencies. The truth is that a worldview of absolute choice, however superior it may seem to us when we compare it with what we imagine of previous worldviews, is complexly tyrannical. It misshapes us, so that we come to care less *what* we choose and more *that* we choose. But surely some of the things we "choose" are not really "choices" on our part at all. Most superficially, our hobbies are not simply chosen; there is something about model trains, or baseball, or antique cars, or Celtic folk music, or weaving, or whatever that resonates with you in a more fundamental way than the language of "choice" can capture. Similarly, for those of us who feel our professions as vocations — literally, "callings" — it is not true to our lives to think that we "chose" them. Most profoundly, I cannot speak of "choosing" to love my daughter or my son or my wife without misdescribing the experience I have of being drawn to them, transfixed by them, *just because* of them — because of who they are.

We see this, and can be brought to acknowledge it, when we are argumentatively cornered, as it were, but our languages of agency, in the broadest sense of "language," make it very hard to express it in any vivid or realistic way. This growing inability to express our cares outside of a language of choice — which inevitably misexpresses them — is part of what Friedrich Nietzsche named "nihilism." Eventually, if none of the objects of our choices matter outside of the fact of our choosing them, then we are choosing between meaningless goods, and eventually the choices themselves become meaningless as well. Ultimately we seem to be tending toward a vortex where all our choices are understood nihilistically, as signifying nothing in themselves or beyond themselves — a vortex in which value and meaning are found simply in what Iris Murdoch described as "the quick flash of the choosing will," not in the thing it chooses.

These worries are not unique to Christians, or even expressed only by adherents of other traditional religions. Many wholly secular people — "liberals" and otherwise — recognize and worry, lucidly and vociferously, about them. Christians can form pragmatic alliances with such critics, agreeing with them that the monochromatic economization of our understanding of agency is deplorable, and that a properly reflective voluntariness can be a good to be pursued, even as we differ metaphysically (though significantly) about the ultimate thoroughness of that voluntariness.

That said, Christians will offer their own positive prescription about what to do. Over the past few centuries many thinkers have worried about these changes, and they have developed several different vocabularies in which to anatomize them, and diagnose the dangers they present to flourishing human life. Nietzsche's talk about nihilism, mentioned above, was one such vocabulary. Others, such as Durkheim, Freud, and Weber, have offered other ones, of "anomie," repression, and pathology, or of disenchantment and bureaucratic rationalization. Most powerfully, Tocqueville described the fundamental worry as a rising "individualism" that encourages an isolation and anomie among citizens, and a lessening of the human capacities for true greatness and excellence. He worried that prosperity leads to wealth, and people use wealth to purchase security, in many different forms. The ease and relaxation of security create the appearance of the naturalness of such security, which in turn creates a sense of entitlement to such security, and even to comfort. This luxury gives us the opportunity only to be concerned with ourselves, which is what Tocqueville meant by "individualism."

But Tocqueville missed something. We are confronted in our lives by certain ineliminable challenges to security. Most obvious here is the fact of death, but more broadly we can speak of the challenges associated with the simple reality of human finitude. When people delude themselves that their lives are immune from the dangers attendant upon such finitude, this view argues, they lose contact with a recognizably human form of life. This is a powerful worry, even if framed in a fairly misanthropic way. But it does not seem to capture the problem properly. It is not that people are weak and need to "suck it up," so to speak, in order to get tough; it is rather that they use luxury and comfort to hide their real and permanent weaknesses from themselves. Our destiny is not to become iron statues, too tough to suffer, but to become vulnerable in the right ways — vulnerable to each other, and ultimately fully vulnerable to God.

So Tocqueville's language of "individualism" needs to be supplemented. It is not that Tocqueville was wrong in worrying about individualism, but this language does not fully capture the real depth of the challenge. We redescribe the problem he identifies in terms of the properly Augustinian concept of *escapism*. For, as Tocqueville saw, the material riches we enjoy do not make us significantly better, but rather give us many new opportunities for avoidance — avoiding one another, avoiding ourselves, avoiding reality itself — and ultimately, on Christian terms, avoiding God. We are likely to use luxury, prosperity, and abundance not to inhabit life, but rather to avoid it. We use our abundance in the service of escapism.

This is not a jeremiad; I am not interested in absolute condemnation, but in diagnosing the most powerful temptations to which we are prone. The next section details the ways in which this temptation toward escapism is manifest in different aspects of our lives.

III. Our Crisis of Abundance

Today the reign of scarcity as the fundamental problem of social existence is over. Humanity's basic needs are largely met. As the economist Amartya Sen has spent his career arguing, famine is not an ecological or environmental problem, but always a political one. This is not a triumphalistic claim, though it is a triumph; if you are reading this, I doubt you have real grounds to fear that your children and grandchildren will not always have enough to eat. Yet there are vices attendant upon our good fortune that must be faced. What kind of agents best suit this Brave New World? We must compare what our faith wants us to become as agents with what the culture as a whole urges upon us. We suffer from these distortions in several spheres of our life — in morality, religion, civic commitment, and the like. As I suggested above, what they all point to, I think, is a cultural tendency toward escapism, a refusal to engage. My point is not finally that living in this culture, with its tendencies toward consumerism, expressivism, the therapeutic, and subjectivism, inevitably makes us as Max Weber once described us, specialists without spirit, sensualists without heart; it is rather that these forces are urging us to experience and understand ourselves in ways that for Augustinians deeply distort our attempts to inhabit love, the root of our soul, and that over time can seriously hinder our proper formation.

"Creative destruction" is sometimes identified with America, but that's not quite accurate. Rather, the process is tangled up with a debate about the meaning of certain terms deeply associated with "America" — terms like "liberty," "freedom," and "choice." These terms have in effect been hijacked by contemporary libertarians and marketeers, and attached to agendas from which earlier defenders of liberty would (and did) recoil. The debate is really about what kinds of creatures we imagine ourselves to be. The issue is then an ideological battle about the proper understanding of freedom and agency, what we are seeking when we aim to be "free." Narrow libertarian construals of terms like "freedom" fixate, as I earlier argued, on the bare act of autonomous choice. Of course, choice is important. But we need a better language to understand our cares and commitments, one that can acknowledge that and how our relations to the world are a two-way street, with realities in the world "gripping" us at least as much as we "bestow" value or importance on them. But how can we do better?

We can begin to construct such a language by attending to our dissatisfactions with current understandings of freedom, dissatisfactions that typically get attached to "consumerism." Many people complain about consumerism, but few offer more than vague condemnations. For our purposes consumer society is one organized economically and culturally around the satisfaction of consumers' desires for nonnecessary products, goods, and services — and which also necessarily works, intentionally and substantially, to cultivate and shape consumers' desires in ways most beneficial to the continuing flux of the economy. The mark of a consumer society, then, is the amount of energy and wealth dedicated intentionally and substantially to shaping desire, by product design and above all by advertising. Diagnosing what we find unsatisfactory about consumerism may help us think more usefully about it.

Interestingly, we should note how pervasive dissatisfaction is in consumer societies. To prosper, these societies require constant cultivation of dissatisfaction in consumers — the "warranted obsolescence" not only of the products we buy, but of our satisfaction with those products themselves. Such dissatisfaction would be intolerable without some overarching acceptance of such dissatisfaction as, curiously, satisfactory; you need some way to survive a life lived fundamentally in the experience of lack. So this lifestyle entails a therapeutic project of ensuring a minimally positive outlook on life, irrespective of whether such an outlook is warranted by reality. The goal is feeling good, having the subjective feeling of self-worth and accomplishment. But feeling good has only the most superficial relationship with being morally good; we aim to be "nice," not good — socially acceptable and civically inoffensive. Such psychological cosmetology need be little more than skin-deep to succeed, and so it is. Self-knowledge and moral rectitude are sacrificed on the altar of happiness.

The picture of reality that this account assumes is quite shallow. Nothing can *really* matter — matter so much that its loss can mean a real change in who we are. Reality is fungible, wholly replaceable, bit by bit. Our longing for a frictionless existence means that it is in our best interest, in this worldview, to refuse to recognize that anything has intrinsic importance, to suggest that the loss of something is or can be an inconsolable or irreparable loss. Instead, an attachment to fundamentally subjective happiness means that one "good" can be straightforwardly replaced by another with equivalent monetary worth — with no tears. Tragic choices become unthinkable. When we have had enough we still want more, and we have continued to dedicate our energies to economic activities for want, it seems, of imagining that there might be other pleasures worth pursuing. Ultimately this moves us toward anomie and what Jonathan Rauch has termed "apatheism," the condition, not so much of disbelieving in God, as (far worse) of disbelieving that belief in God could matter much one way or the other.

The picture of the human person that this account implies is flimsy as well. It is visible most especially in the language of agency that most of our culture provides us. As agency language increasingly moves toward a model built around shopping, our belief that choices have irreversible significance becomes increasingly hard to keep in focus. A pair of shoes, a book, a marriage — they can all be returned (so long, of course, as we keep the receipt). This language is not just wrong in the sense that it misdescribes reality; insofar as we come to believe it, we become misshapen ourselves. Again, recall Iris Murdoch: "man is a creature who makes pictures of himself and then comes to resemble the picture." And as our choices begin to seem arbitrary, agency comes increasingly to be seen as meaningless — a language we use, Augustinians think, in order to avoid encountering ourselves, to avoid coming to terms with the terrible reality of the urgent sincerity of our cares. For the truth of the matter, of course, tells another story: we want things to be reversible, but this absolute fickleness makes us less happy; as Edward Rosenthal points out, psychological studies suggest that "people who are able to change their minds end up *less* satisfied with their picks than those who have to stick with their choices!" If choice is all about following our whims, we just float from one appetite to another, along the model of addicts, slaves to their desires; but we're worse than that because we're so flighty. At least addicts have the sham virtue of integrity, of sincerely wanting *something*.

Typically at this point, complaints like this recommend a "return to traditional values." Perhaps this might be a useful strategy, if it could be pursued. But there are two problems with it. First of all, it threatens to become nostalgia. What such Jeremiahs have in mind for a "return" is typically a return to the 1950s, not the 1250s. And while there were many good things about the 1950s, those years were by no means free of the tendencies enumerated above; furthermore, they had their own moral and religious challenges, most visibly in the United States around a far more pervasive and overt racism and sexism. These Jeremiahs fail to recognize their own ambivalence, and try to bury it in a sea of apocalyptic hostility.

The second problem with this strategy is that what such jeremiadists understand to be the repositories of such traditional values are really not very "traditional" at all. Most of U.S. religiosity, conservative and liberal, is just as affected by these patterns as any New Age witch collective. Sociologists such as James Davison Hunter and Christian Smith have identified the ways in which putatively "traditional" religious groups are actually deeply shaped by modernist currents. Smith describes the dominant religion of the United States, shared by conservatives and liberals alike, in the cutting phrase "moralistic therapeutic deism." On this picture, God is little more than the vaporous affirmation by the universe — there when we need it, and not intrusive otherwise.

Even conservative evangelical churches are becoming more postmaterialist. Witness the enormous appeal of the megachurch minister Rick Warren and his book *The Purpose-Driven Life*. Warren is speaking directly to individual exploration and personal happiness in ways that would have seemed bizarre to evangelical preachers a century ago. Joel Osteen, another megachurch leader, has written a book, *Your Best Life Now: 7 Steps to Living at Your Full Potential*, which is as traditionally Christian in its content as *Who Moved My Cheese?* All in all, in American religion, conservative and liberal, what William Galston says is true: "The Gospel of personal salvation trumps the social gospel."

These patterns are much older than modern consumerism; as H. Richard Niebuhr described the upshot of late-nineteenth- and early-twentieth-century American liberal Christianity: "A God without wrath brought men without sin into a kingdom without judgment through the ministrations of a Christ without a cross." But the forces driving contemporary faith in this direction are increasingly agitated. It was a sign of some vestigial health and residual piety in the American Christianity

of Niebuhr's day that his judgment on the churches was felt as powerfully as it was. I suspect that not a few Christians today would think of
Niebuhr's judgment as a description of an *ideal* Christianity for them, a
theological goal toward which to strive.

The civic consequences are just as profound as the religious ones.
There is a decline in civic engagement, caused by a general rise of an attitude of spectatorial entertainment about civic life. As political life has
become increasingly centralized, with more and more essentially political decisions made by specialists (in the legislature, bureaucracy, or judiciary), ordinary citizens have grown increasingly alienated from and
averse to political engagement even in their local political settings. In
the United States, for example, national association groups a generation
ago genuinely involved their members in civic projects at the local,
state, and national level, but in the last generation they have become, in
the words of Theda Skocpol, "advocates without members," groups
more interested in lobbying the center of power in Washington, D.C.,
than in organizing their constituents to do anything, or anything more
than writing them a check once a year.

This is just one example of a larger transformation under way today
in the nature of politics. This is usefully described as a change in a populace's general values from "materialist" to "postmaterialist" values — a
change in the kinds of things people worry about. In an age centered on
materialist values, the basic concerns are physically existential, issues,
quite literally, of bread and butter: Where will I get my food? Can I af-
ford a house? Who will protect me? For more and more people today,
these material needs are no longer the primary objects of concern. People today care about what are rather unhelpfully called "postmaterial"
matters — matters that express what they believe in, moral and religious abstractions, often representing whole worldviews, things we can
put scare quotes around: "human rights," "international order," "American primacy," "the culture of life," "a pro-choice nation," "environmental
decency." People are concerned about the environment because they
have the *luxury* of being concerned about the environment. Many of
these certainly have some connection to material concerns — American primacy has much to do with security, and "environmental decency" can be explained as sheer self-interest — but most fundamentally these commitments are *expressions* of what we care about,
communicating something about what we believe, who we are or think

we want to be, more deeply than they are strategies of securing the world so that we can flourish. The truth is, our flourishing — or the outward conditions for it, anyway — is pretty much guaranteed today; that's why we can turn to other, more "immaterial" interests.

As politics has become more postmaterial, we have witnessed what some have called "the great sorting out," the ideological organization of political parties, wherein both align around very narrow languages in which to frame their purposes. (This seems aggravated by actual geographic sorting, where places become more ideologically monochromatic, so that locales polarize too.) Those who identify with each party have different interests and different views of the place of government in society. The candidates from each party respond to their party constituents and pursue policies that reflect their electoral base. Each party's voters are more favorable toward their own candidate and more disdainful of opponents, but leaders have less flexibility to handle the various challenges they face, for they are held to higher standards for ideological consistency by voters. Increasingly, the center in American political life is not, in Arthur Schlesinger's terms, a "vital center," one that hews to a common public philosophy and that shares a common cultural sensibility; it is increasingly becoming, in the words of James Davison Hunter, merely a "statistical phenomenon." Politics is made simpler because of all of this, but civic life — which politics is supposed to serve — is made harder. When the two sides polarize, politics becomes all about one side winning. What gets lost is John Stuart Mill's idea that neither holds a monopoly on truth, that truth is what is found in their mutual encounter and struggle.

This polarization is aggravated by the political language people increasingly use today. Americans especially increasingly cram all social problems into language of rights, and have civil rights as their fundamental imagination. (This is why the abortion debate is framed as one between those supporting the "right to life" and those supporting the "right to choice.") All movements of progress are framed as necessary for undoing someone's irrational oppression — and thereby opponents of such movements immediately become oppressors. This is a zero-sum game. We would be wiser and more honest to use much broader and more local programs — experiment locally, and find other and better languages than rights — framing ideas perhaps as opportunities, possible routes for flourishing lives that we want to consider.

But postmaterial politics are not simply expressivist politics; they are also a genuine pragmatic attempt to get some control, or at least influence, over real challenges facing the world today. This is evidenced by the rise of so-called identity politics. It is precisely the slipperiness and evanescence of our experience of the world today — a slipperiness at least significantly enabled, if not directly caused by, consumer culture — that make a politics based around the fantasy of fixed identities so profoundly attractive for so many.

Identity politics happens when people mobilize together to assert a fairly monochromatic identity in order to achieve a certain kind of recognition and legitimacy in the political order. But such identity politics function largely in defensive ways, ways meant to protect them from other groups. Thus relationships between groups are established only on grounds of the most narrow self-interest, of what is in it for the group — whose success becomes the ultimate goal of politics as a whole for group members. Identity politics, ironically enough, is not so much a positive way to gain an identity as it is a way to secure *one* fairly narrow identity against the multiple incursions of our other characteristic affiliations and allegiances. Identity politics has at its heart a defensive understanding of selfhood, and pragmatically reduces most often to a way to avoid encountering others unlike oneself, and a way to avoid confronting those parts of oneself that do not toe the line of the identity the group wishes you to affirm.

Along with the damage this causes to civic life and to real political community, the ideological sorting of politics and public life into rival teams misshapes our lives well beyond the explicitly political sphere. This is especially visible as regards concerns about identity. On the one hand, the velocity of change in contemporary society, saturated by and defining all in terms of market relations, makes traditional sorts of identity very hard to sustain. Identity is, after all, sticky, a way to say some things are more fundamental to who we are than other things. But the problem with our commodifying society (though here the connections between explicit commercialization, political culture, and the broader cultural values in general become very hazy) is that such stickiness is not at all rewarded, but instead is penalized in various ways — overtly or, more insidiously, covertly. When you decide to stay in a certain town to raise children there, economically your rejection of mobility will cost you job opportunities. The triumph of a choice-centric worldview has gone hand in hand with a significant rise in a kind of individualism that is structurally hostile to traditional institutions and the constraints they put on our lives — constraints that are, normally, not felt as "constraining" at all but as enabling, orienting our lives and giving us a meaningful external frame in terms of which we can evaluate and understand our lives. Furthermore, the rise of genuine values pluralism has forced us to construct ways of dealing with quite radical, indeed unprecedented, religious, moral, and cultural diversity. But we have done this poorly. After all, when one refuses to make moral judgments about ways of life out of a hesitation to "judge" others, one weakens one's ability to understand one's own life in moral terms. In this way, the language of toleration can insidiously destroy your moral vocabulary. Both material conditions and cultural challenges, then, make identity hard to secure.

But we want identity to be secure; in fact, there's a good case to be made that we need it to be secure, that we need the appearance of a firm identity as part of what it means to be human. And the fact that such identities are increasingly hard to secure in contemporary life is not going to make us surrender that need. For just as in one way the sociocultural conditions of contemporary life make it ever more difficult to be a self, in another way the economic energies of our culture make it all too easy to become one. Prefabricated identities are available to us through consumerism; all you need do is buy the requisite equipment (clothes, music, books, technology, hairstyle) and, presto, you're a member of the team. The brands we buy, the restaurants we eat at, the coffee we drink — all these become ways of announcing our identity to the world, and also to our own anxious selves.

The problems I have sketched here are not so much problems with reality as problems with the languages we use to understand reality — languages that in turn shape us in certain ways. No one who witnessed the immediate response to 9/11 or the Indian Ocean tsunami can seriously doubt that people all around the world care about each other and that they are willing to help each other in palpable emergencies. But our language makes it difficult for us to articulate and therefore intelligently analyze and intentionally cultivate those immediate responses — to train them into rich dispositions across the whole of our lives.

This is what Charles Taylor has called "the ethics of inarticulacy": we increasingly inhabit a language in which we cannot explain our deepest commitments, and we cannot explain why we *do* and not only *should* love each other. What goes missing in all this is not directly our selves, but rather our experience of our cares — those things to which we are ultimately answerable, those things that we don't choose to love but rather simply *find* as lovable. It becomes increasingly hard to understand ourselves as really inhabiting the world, fundamentally responsive to the goods we encounter therein, ergo capable of receiving anything, especially anything so fundamental as joy. Just as we increasingly, in an age of millennial capitalism, have the means to avoid each other and even ourselves, we increasingly are able to avoid any real confrontation with our values, our God.

A picture of agency built around such often experiences a quite different vision of who we are called to be through the one we find subtly insinuated (or not-so-subtly insinuated) by our consumer society. The next and final section explains how.

IV. Pursuing Happiness, or Surprised by Joy?

We need a better account of what it means to be a person, and that means we need a better account of what it means to be an agent, to be pursuing goods. I cannot offer a complete such account here. But I can identify some things that need to be in such a picture.

Perhaps the simplest and most immediately psychologically satisfying strategy would be straightforwardly to condemn "choice" and offer up a rival picture of the self. But that is only partially satisfactory, and in some ways incoherent, for we would be urging ourselves to *choose* to reject choice. Instead, I would like to urge a reevaluation of the whole picture of how we value, and how we act on our values. I would propose, that is, that we change our picture of agency from a picture of striving to overcome limits to one where the fundamental act of the agent is to work, largely indirectly and over long periods of time, to change our orientation toward the world, or what it is we value, and why. But to get there we should begin with a dissection of our current picture of agency.

The root problem is misconceptualization of the human's end in a too-narrow and shallow account of "happiness," built upon an absolutization of choice and instrumentalization of "end." "Happiness" on its own is a vague term, an empty term. Different people find quite different things conducive to their different happinesses. But by and large, people understand happiness in consumeristic terms, in terms of having appetites satisfied by discrete goods. We increasingly inhabit what Tibor Skitovsky has called a *joyless* economy, one built structurally and intellectually upon an inability to imagine that humanity has longings that are not collapsible back into some thin account of momentary and monetary satiation. We imagine love as a particular kind of self-focused satisfaction, based on what Wendell Berry calls our "fundamentally ungenerous way of life," our captivity to a theology of endless (in several senses) acquisition. We imagine "joy" in terms of *more*: more of what we want, and an infinite supply of equally disposable, perhaps interchangeable goods and pleasures. This fixation on more offers no space to challenge our desires themselves — to ask whether those desires will ever be satisfied on the terms they propose; it simply assumes that more is better.

But things are worse than this. Theologically, the logic of "pursuing happiness" is dangerous in several ways; as Robert Wuthnow argues, the contemporary belief in the "gospel of happiness" creates a religious situation that is deeply inimical to the proper apprehension of the Christian message. The problem lies in the picture of agency implied therein. It assumes that we are all *pursuing* happiness, that we are the primary agents. The instrumentalization latent in the word "pursuit" makes it hard for us genuinely to inhabit the world, to live *in* it; instead we are constantly trying to get things *out* of it.

Agency taken as ex nihilo always gets us in a game of endless escalation with the universe, of trying to tell the universe that I am setting the terms of my engagement with it, that I am my own cause, my own end, my own God. And this is a futile quest: Augustine urged us to recognize that all our attempts to orient ourselves toward fundamentally mundane and immanent ends inevitably end up with us being prodigally misspent in the wastelands of empty desires. Choice as a human ideal is perhaps seductive to us, but ultimately it remains a Promethean fantasy — an instrumental good for other goods, but not an ultimate good in itself.

As an alternative to this picture of agency, Augustine offered another and better way, which we can develop as well. We can begin by noting that in asking about choices all the time, we never ask about how *we* are chosen, by God. We never think about ourselves as receiving grace, receiving the gift of being itself. We never think about a model of agency built around joy. For Augustine, the fullest picture of good human agency is human agency as it will be exercised in the eschaton. He characterized that agency in a famous Latin phrase, *non posse peccare*, when humans will find it "not possible to sin." For him, true, fully achieved human agency was not one where "choice" played any role at all, but rather was a kind of full voluntary exercise of one's being, where one is wholly and willingly engaged — but where one seems to have no choice about this. This does not require compulsion of any dangerous sort; after all, it is "involuntary" in much the same way that one has no choice about laughing at a funny movie, but one laughs, at times (if it is *really* funny) with more than one's voice — with one's whole being. For this to happen we must be liberated from the slavery to sin to which we are all manifestly, for Augustine, captive. It is that enslavement that divides or splits our will and so sunders our integrity. Here is a picture of idealized agency where the center of the picture is not a wide range of options, but no options at all — a picture of human agency whose flourishing lies wholly in the complete and unimpeded engagement of the whole person in the dynamic joy of paradise.

This is an entirely different picture of agency, one that highlights humans' capacities of participation, receptivity, and particularly love: aspects of agency that subvert a picture of the human as fundamentally active. Love is the "root" of the soul, and so we are in a way composed by our cares: we do not make things valuable, the things that we value "make" us — or better, reveal who we truly are. When the soul is properly oriented in the love that is *caritas*, it is a unifying force, equally for our own self-integrity, our relationship with God, and our relationship with our neighbor. But love is not only an affective orientation toward things we care about, it is also intelligent, an articulate cognition of our situation, an attempt at assessing the true value of the world and the things within it. So when Augustine (in)famously says "love and do what you will," he does not mean do what *you* will, insofar as the you is the you that you were before you felt God's love; rather, that love has so transformed you that you now will to do love.

On this picture, joy is what we receive, a gift. We do not pursue it; we are always surprised by it. And what we do is bear it to others; it is by nature communicative. In loving, you become an instrument of God, and a vehicle for God's love of the world. Hence *caritas* is politically unifying: as this energy has been directed toward the conversion of the self back to God, so it in turn energizes the self to seek communion with others. This is not a form of violence; we love others in friendship and treat them as would God.

This understanding of freedom entails a particular picture of the nature of human agency, one that sees such agency, at its core, as a matter of response to God's action upon it, not as a matter of simply self-starting willy-nilly into the world. Furthermore, it is fundamentally responsive to a longing that is primordial to its being, the longing for God, so that all our acts are to be understood as forms of seeking our true home in God, a seeking that is also a beseeching, a pleading to God to come to us. As such it is both active and passive, with the passivity taking the lead. The primordial act of our agency, that is, is to respond to the eliciting call of God — to listen, or hear, or attend, or — most properly — *wait on* God. In doing this, we should see ourselves not as desiring but as desired, as objects of love before we are agents of love. Our destiny is not primarily to do something, but first and foremost to be loved.

Such joy is always only begun, always only inaugurated for us (not by us), and so we must learn to begin again. This is a harder lesson than it may at first appear. We must learn to see our life in the world, its sufferings and joys, as an ongoing process of resurrection. So for Augustine proper love, when inhabited, understands itself as in important ways training in longing, not in simply enjoying but in complicatedly enduring the conflicts, contradictions, frictions, and tensions of our existence in time.

We must do this, in significant part, because we exist in what Augustine calls the *distensio* — the "stretched-outedness" — of time. We live in both the "now" and the "not yet," having accomplished some of our goals yet seeking to accomplish still more, always partially dwelling in the past in our memory and straining toward the future in our hope, therefore never fully in the present moment. This is why we cannot, as the bumper sticker has it, simply "be here now." This is not meant as a complaint about how we are currently living, at least I do not mean that this way of living is for Augustine anything but our inevitable lot in this life, after the fall. There is no special technique for escaping this condition, as ancient questions and many contemporary writers (and bumper stickers) try to convince us; this is our life. Most of the time, most people spend their psychic and intellectual energy trying to deny or avoid the fact that they live in this "stretched-out" manner; they never question whether it is possible that their lives require time's endless deferrals to be healed and that such healing is unavailable in this life. That is what Augustine wants us to do. In living in this *distensio,* we confess we presently inhabit an experience of tantalizing incompleteness, yet proclaim we will be healed in the eschaton — and we must recognize both our own incompleteness and the way it tantalizes us. There is real joy, real happiness in this life; but it is a joy "borrowed" from the end of time, from our eschatological consummation.

What could such a life look like? Something, perhaps, like what Saint Paul is describing in his second letter to the Corinthians. After earlier explaining that "anyone who is in Christ is a new creation" (2 Cor. 5:17), which paradoxically suggested both rupture and continuity (for how can you be wholly new creation and yet still be in any way connected to the person you were before?), Paul now says, "now is the day of salvation!" In this he emphasizes the tension between redemption and the ordinary experience of today (*today* is the day of salvation? you can imagine people asking, as they look around the room). And he goes on to explain what he takes living in these paradoxes to mean — a way of life that is, naturally, rich with paradoxes:

> through great endurance in afflictions, hardships, calamities, beatings, imprisonments, riots, labors, sleepless nights, hunger; by purity, knowledge, patience, kindness, holiness of spirit, genuine love, truthful speech, and the power of God; with the weapons of righteousness for the right hand and for the left; in honor and dishonor, in ill repute and good repute. We are treated as impostors yet true; as unknown, yet well known; as dying, and behold — we are alive; as punished yet not killed; as sorrowful yet always rejoicing; as poor yet making many rich; as having nothing yet possessing everything. (2 Cor. 6:4-10)

All these things, in their stubborn contradictoriness to each other, are true, for Paul. It is to live into this tension that we are called. Life in this tension *is* distended. But it is a life that is more honest for how it recognizes the way both poles are true, or at least getting at something significant.

140

I readily admit that the question of how to offer this model today in a way that is not simply apocalyptically condemnatory is a large task, but I take that to mean that we better begin work on understanding it immediately. Where could we so begin?

Such an understanding of agency requires us to reconfigure received understandings of the nature of virtue. "Virtue" has traditionally had dangerously agonistic and heroic connotations, and it seems gravitationally attracted toward understanding moral improvement as an achievement of the agent. Augustinians see this traditional understanding as undergirding and motivating the Pelagian temptation to imagine that we are able to be good on our own — which they see more deeply still as reflecting a deep unbelief that God could actually be as good as Augustinians understand the Gospels to make God out to be — to seek us out and help us, in what looks like (to ancient eyes) an undignified manner deeply unfitting to the Ruler of the Universe. But, Augustinians affirm, only grace can save us — and so we must change our perception of ourselves from Promethean to Adamic.

Insofar as we want to use the language of virtue, then, we must do so with profound care. The basic way we should use it is to transform it from a gymnastic language of achievement to a medical language of suffering, of being willing to be shaped (not to shape ourselves) by the medicine of a gracious God. Such an ascetic transformation of the virtues implies an ecclesiology as well, for this ascesis involves the working of a whole community on all of its members, singly and collectively. The church is a hospital of virtue, and the virtues are the medicine provided by God. Concomitantly, we should try to inhabit the virtues not (as in ancient ethics) by achieving a morally heroic character, but rather by rendering ourselves more fully vulnerable to the action of God in our lives.

One way to understand this transformation is to appreciate the radical change at the heart of the Christian transformation of cultural heroes from the picture of the hero as *doing something* to the picture of the martyr as *one who suffers*. This is a quite radical revision of the received Roman model of the admirable human. It suggests that we should change our understanding of the paradigmatic exercise of agency from one manifest best in extreme situations or extremities of effort to one manifest best in an extraordinary depth of compassion and capacity to suffer, and especially to suffer the reception of grace. At its uttermost, the extremity of Christian heroism is to die, to be a martyr. This makes a language of passion and compassion the central moral language; on this picture, the fundamental moral task is not to achieve, but to suffer aright, to endure. Furthermore, this suffering must be public, and in a way *for* the public, for others. Ancient heroes are gloriously, emphatically narcissistic; even their self-sacrifice is done out of the aim of their own glory. But martyrs and saints are not heroic; they are for the people, not for themselves. They do not stand out from us; they are for us, as our teachers. In fact, they are teachers in the sense of showing us the way we must follow — for finally we all become like the saints, sanctified. And they show us the way as much in their failures, foibles, and weaknesses as in their successes; from Paul through Augustine and beyond, this tradition places a premium on one's openness and frankness as regards one's own weaknesses — it is publicity of our frailty. Also, publicity, outwardness, paradoxically helps us in our inwardness as well — by exhibiting our faults to others, it is harder for us to hide them from ourselves.

This understanding of action and virtue entails an irreducibly communal dimension to individual agency and moral achievement. Just as the martyrs die for others, so Christians achieve the virtues and thereby "flourish" as a community, not finally as individuals. This has scriptural precedent; consider Paul's message to the Corinthians, and his reflection on the benefits (not to mention the inevitability) of diverse gifts in any community of the faithful. "There are varieties of gifts, but the same Spirit; and there are varieties of service, but the same Lord; and there are varieties of working, but it is the same God who inspires them all in everyone," he avows (1 Cor. 12:4-6). What does this mean? It means that the community as a whole is the object of God's concern, that the community as a whole is more than the sum of its individual members — and that by joining together, they become more than what they would be apart. "If one member suffers, all suffer together; if one member is honored, all rejoice together" (1 Cor. 12:26). No one is a self-enclosed and self-sufficient agent; each one has gifts that, collectively, make the whole more than the sum of the parts.

Is this a totalitarian vision, wherein the individual is subjugated to and absorbed by the mass? Not so; for Paul, the diversity of gifts and vocations is necessary for the unity of the whole. "If the whole body were an eye, where would be the hearing?" he asks (1 Cor. 12:17). There is real diversity, real difference, even as that difference is understood as part of a larger whole. But that "whole" is not necessarily immediately present in the here and now of the current community. The ecclesial body that is imagined as our true community is crucially incomplete until the resurrection of the dead in the eschaton, when the full membership will take its places at the name of Jesus.

In the interim, we begin to move toward this community not by fundamentally sacrificing our self-interest to the community (though such sacrifices will be necessary at times), but more primordially by coming to see a real if only partly achievable harmony between us and the whole. We, self-interested as we are, and the community as we have it, will never in this life be wholly harmonious, and efforts to force a premature unity will be disastrously totalitarian and apocalyptic. But some fundamental longing for unity keeps us seeking such harmony, just as a clear-minded apprehension of how sin distorts all our longings keeps us from placing too much confidence in the appearance of any realized harmony. That is the glory and tension of Christian societies, and it is not very different from the vision of "liberal" societies. It is a glory and a tension that it is our fate to inhabit, in this life.

Conclusion

The struggle for love is struggle for the other — for community. But the struggle for love today is beset by many dangers. I have tried to enumerate them here, and suggest some routes for overcoming them. For this is a crucial struggle: without doing better at gaining some real community, we are in danger of continuing to have a politics of polarization, and trivia and evasion, a failed politics, doing ever more damage to our world. And we are in danger of becoming empty vessels, hollow cymbals. Both pragmatically and ecclesiologically, then, this struggle is one about which everyone should care, because it is a struggle to make the future world more fit for flourishing human life than it presently is.

For Christians this especially matters because this struggle is central to the cultivation of Christian life. Without love, faith and hope are empty, unreal, merely parodies of what they are supposed to be. To begin to learn to love is to begin to come to grips with our destiny as citizens of the kingdom of God.

Now we have sketched the full range of challenges and struggles that lies before the Christian in seeking a flourishing religious life in the contemporary world. But the question remains, why should these virtues be so central to our concern? The answer has come to us in pieces throughout these chapters, where from time to time we have glimpsed a larger picture of the whole shape of Christian life as lived in public — a picture of Christian citizenship in the whole. In asking about the nature of proper Christian citizenship, we will see that we need to elaborate these virtues more than we have so far done. So we must ask about the general contours of this vision as modeling Christian citizenship. We do that next.

PART II

LOOKING LIKE CHRISTIANS

CHAPTER 5

Love and Political Responsibility

⌒✑⌒

You shall love your crooked neighbor
with your crooked heart.

W. H. Auden

S o far I have been talking about how Christians should *see* the world
— about how they should understand the full scope of today's challenges, in order to become more fully what they want to be. Now, with
this chapter, I will turn the lens around, so to speak, and ask how those
interested in this project will present themselves in the world, to the
world. Here, that is, I ask how Christians should *be seen* by others. Such
presentation is not just a matter of superficial appearance; it is about
how they really should be, deep down inside, in order properly to cultivate the virtues. It is about how they should manifest in their lives, at all
times and in all places, certain dispositions, attitudes, and practices
(what goes into the "virtues") both for their own deepening faith and as
a way of witnessing to the rest of the world (not to "the world," mind
you) what it is that God has done in Christ.

In undertaking this exposition, these last three chapters reverse the
order of the previous three, in order to see something new about the
way the virtues interlock. This chapter begins this project by reflecting
on the virtue of love and its role in Christian citizenship. Given what
the previous chapter detailed as the complex challenges of inhabiting
love in a world dominated by an ideal of "choice," we can now ask more

particularly about politics: What role is there for love in the civic realm? Politics is often ugly and violent; can love be usefully *political?* Can love energize, orient, and even restrain political engagement?

The Augustinian tradition suggests that it can, that love can actually eventuate in proper political action, that love is a crucial element in politics, especially around the inevitable exercise of political authority. For one of the tasks of citizenship is accepting responsibility for authority. Such authority is a basic component of democratic republican citizenship, for being a citizen just means being a cosovereign in government, being one of the authorities that authorize government (that is why the Constitution begins, "We, the people . . ."). But there are also more discrete instances wherein we accept authority in some particular political role. How should Christians accept, and inhabit, such authority? They should inhabit it, the tradition says, lovingly. Explicating what that means is what this chapter is all about.

To explain this, I look to that dimension of politics most apparently remote from love, namely, the use of force. As the twentieth-century Augustinian Christian ethicist Paul Ramsey put it, "the justice of sometimes resorting to armed conflict originated in the interior of the ethics of Christian love." For Augustine, then, political action, held to account by God and the neighbor, can authentically explain itself in terms of love — even unto the use of force.

Some Christians will blanch at this. Jesus was about love, nonviolent, self-sacrificial love, even unto death. And no one will argue that nonresistant love was what led Jesus to the cross, and through it to humanity's redemption. Love and bloodshed are part of two separate orders of being.

But such readings of Christian social ethics are a bit too simplistic. After all, Paul tells Christians in Romans 12 to feed their enemies, and then in Romans 13 he authorizes Christians to kill their enemies for a just cause — a juxtaposition that can produce exegetical whiplash in an attentive audience. Perhaps one can say that Paul is not as authentically "Christian" as Jesus (by which one means the Gospels, which after all were not written by Jesus, but about him, and written down after Paul wrote his letters). But then one must face two facts: Jesus does command his disciples to wear swords, and he does drive the money changers from the temple with a whip, and it is pretty unlikely he didn't draw blood with the whip he used.

The tension between these two passages is considerably reduced if you understand the distinct roles in which Paul is addressing his audience: first, as members of a religious community, and second, as members of a religious community who are also part of a this-worldly political community. And the tension that yet remains is put to productive use in Paul's understanding of the idea of authority. This understanding, as we will see, is grounded in a certain understanding of God's activity as loving judge of the world. So love can indeed be manifest in the use of force.

This chapter explains how love can guide politics, only by making once again intelligible, and indeed inescapable, the concept of political authority — that is, of proper political judgment and action. Parts I and II try to display the profundity of the problem of authority, and our anxious befuddlement before it, through a discussion of the quintessential and inescapable political act of judging. Part III analyzes what Augustine understands to be the general nature of political authority and unpacks his proposal for how it is to be inhabited. Part IV discusses the most pointed political issue that can eventuate from the exercise of political authority, namely, the use of force. It asks: How can slaying an aggressor be an act of charity, however alien? Finally, the conclusion attempts to place this practice of political authority in light of our eschatological destiny as judged by God, as called to hear God's judgment on us.

I. Authority and Its Discontents

What is the purpose of government? I begin from the premise that the fundamental task of government is judgment. This is a deeper insight than it may at first appear. Beneath or within all legislation, all attempts at securing order and stability, all efforts to form more perfect unions — beneath or within all of these lurks the fundamental political activity, the discernment of what is to be done in a particular case in a particular setting. (And "politics" as we typically understand it is actually only one subregion of the realm of such discernment.) How is such discernment to be undertaken, and by whom? There needs to be, as it were, a decider — someone or some body beyond whom there is no further procedural appeal, someone on whose desk, as it were, the buck stops. However hedged-about these decisions are — however richly funded by expert advice, wise counsel, properly sober procedural deliberation, reflective assessment and analysis of the alternatives — ultimately, someone has to decide. From the parking enforcement officer through the school board to the president, politics is crucially about decisions, and those who make the decisions are the people we call the authorities. Politics, properly understood, has at its center, then, the idea of right authority.

Today, the presence of authority in our lives is more central than ever before. In fact, it is quite likely that everyone reading this book is an authority of some sort or other. I do not mean that in the charming populist sense of "every man a king" or the priesthood of all believers, though that latter at least has something going for it. No, I mean that quite literally every reader is, or soon will be, a duly licensed authority of some sort or other. You may be teachers, managers, ministers, coaches, craftsmen, doctors, parents. You have or will have special competencies, capacities, and perhaps gifts, which you will attempt to exercise, usually in the midst of, and often upon, other people. As authorities, we are put in situations of grave responsibility — responsibility over other people's education, over their lives, over their beliefs, perhaps over their souls.

If you have been following my argument attentively, and if I have not radically misjudged my readers, you will now feel at least a small kernel of nervousness deep down inside you. How many of us think of ourselves as authorities? If, like me, you teach, you probably go out of your way to demystify your role in the classroom. No hierarchy for us! If you are clergy in a church, you may well do what I have seen so many ministers do, which is labor mightily to be seen as "human," which of course makes everyone else wonder what else they could be in the first place. It is one of the marks of our nervousness about authority, even one of the distinctive marks of authority in our age, that we are constantly trying to convince ourselves, by convincing others, that we do not actually possess it. In our world, authority is the social reality that dare not speak its name.

Authority is a fraught term today, a dirty word. It provokes skepticism and suspicion in most people. All claims to authority, simply by being put in the form of such a claim, are likely to be met with skepticism and cynicism. These reveal the deepest anxiety we feel about authority — the worry that claims to such authority always and everywhere inexhaustibly reduce themselves to nothing but masks for power.

And power, without authority, is nothing but brute, inhuman force — in short, it is authoritarianism. Yet how can the exercise of power, manifest in judgment, be legitimately cloaked in the mantle of authority, and indeed loving authority? How can it avoid being the brute manifestation of authoritarianism?

We should recognize and respect the simple fact that elicits much of those suspicions: authority, and the power it can authorize, is an awesome and terrible thing. It claims to act on others and on the world as a whole legitimately — that is, in a way that cannot be rebuked merely for its exercise. But this action has as its uttermost extension the fact of compulsion. Authority is finally the claim that someone can rightfully compel others to do what he or she judges to be right. Thus our common anxiety is not simply an irrational fear, but a genuine positive apprehension of the real otherness of the others we presume to have authority over — their real difference from us — and so a salutary hesitancy about presuming to be better positioned than they to know what is good for them.

This hesitancy is salutary only if we apprehend it a bit more self-consciously than we usually do. For authority, and the capacity to judge that it always entails, is a terrible and fearsome burden, and our ambivalence about it should not be silenced with a triumphant reaffirmation of our authoritativeness. Instead that ambivalence should be recognized for what it is, a distant reflection of our fallenness, and God's refusal to take our fallenness as the last word in our relationship with God. Even as it is necessary in our world, the question is how well will we understand its presence in our lives, and to what ends should we use it.

I want to suggest that a clue is found in the idea that love is basic to the human being — that an account of the human that is built around *love* can offer a viable understanding of authority. On this view, proper action, done out of love, is always done out of loving acknowledgment of authority. A loving exercise of political power, even one that uses force, is properly authorized — enacted by one in a proper situation to exercise it, and one who will be held to account by the source of one's authority. It is what we may call "distantly paternalistic," and understands itself to derive from a transcendent source of authority — namely, from the triune God.

But this salutary hesitancy is turned into skeptical, cynical paralysis by some real confusions about its meaning and concerns about its practice. Here I want to try to explain how our common suspicions and anxieties about authority — suspicion of those who claim to exercise authority and anxiety when we realize that we exercise authority — are finally rooted in confusions about the kind of creatures we are. To begin to show this, I want to lay out three different ways in which our cultural, intellectual, and theological inheritances make us suspicious of claims to authority and squeamish about claiming it when we should.

What, after all, does "authority" mean? It has two distinct components. First, as is apprehended in its connection with the word "author," it can refer to the principle, instigator, and agent of organization — the master patterner — who directs the action and to whom all participants therein are accountable. Second, it can also mean the fact of that organization itself, the structure within which we are accountable. There is no authority without a licit structure, and any licit structure implies accountability to a principle of ordering. Responsibility and authority are implicated in one another, and unintelligible, at least formally, without recourse to one another. We fulfill our responsibilities on this model when we fulfill our duties to the authority, and we do that by *obeying* the authorities. One way some of us obey the authorities is by being an authority. But how do we do that?

Such legitimate authority is what kings, potentates, and other rulers have claimed throughout history. And one may think that in a democratic and egalitarian age every such claim to legitimacy and rationales for compulsion has been shown to be vacuous — that any and every such authority is defunct, that no such compulsion is necessary, that everything works out of the consent of autonomous individuals. But some little reflection tells us this is not so: authority has been dispersed, but it has not been dissolved. If my city votes to lower the speeding limit on our streets, and I disagree, and vote against it, and I lose, I must still obey the law that I did not approve, and if I do not obey, the police will compel me to do so. Certainly such compulsion has its constraints, as constitutional government gives its citizens certain inalienable rights, but the nature and application of those rights can be contested, and in those settings judges often decide, and then I still must obey or be punished. (Think of the legal doctrine of eminent domain, or of the state's right to judge, in wartime drafts, whether your claim to be a conscientious objector is valid.) Even speaking directly of politics, the difference between an age of kings and a democratic age is not the difference between authority and autonomy; the difference is that in democratic republics each fully mature agent has a say in political authority. We are no longer subjects, we are citizens. You and I make war; you and I execute convicts; you and I disburse government aid, or refuse to do so. You and I are the sovereign, the "We" in "We the people."

That is a very significant difference between democratic and monarchic cultures, and we will explore it later. But it does not eliminate the question of the ultimate propriety of authority. What little reflection we give to it is largely negative, concerned not so much to establish its legitimacy as to mark the outer limits of its propriety — that is, we talk most about its *il*legitimacy, passing over the implied *legitimate* exercise of authority in silence. We seem left with two choices: either to be unremittingly hostile to such claims to authority or to silence and ignore these worries and celebrate authority in a way that makes it dangerously close to authoritarianism. In our sin we pursue power not often out of positive desire for it, but because we fear someone else getting it first and using it over us. (So even our desire for power is often merely preemptive.)

Authority seems invisible to us because it is so pervasive in our world. In fact, pretty much the entire discipline of sociology is built on this puzzle. How is it, sociologists ask, that human society, which is so profoundly complex, essentially involving the voluntary consent and synchronization of so many millions, and now billions, of people — how is it that society works so smoothly? (Sociologists spend a good bit of their time studying deviance, but that's really an avoidance mechanism for them; the real mystery at the heart of sociology is not that there are some people who break the rules, but that there are so very many who do not.) Clearly, society works as well as it does because people obey. They order their lives according to some fairly sophisticated, if rarely articulated, rules. You don't swerve across yellow dividing lines on roads, at least most of the time. You don't just cut across the lawn any which way — most of the time you follow the pavement, or the well-worn path that everyone takes. You go to college to find out what you want to do, and if you still don't know what you want to do when you leave college, it seems, you go to law school. If you have conflicts with other people, you do not kill them, you take them to court. People today complain about the increasing litigiousness of our society, but social scientists point out that over the past four or five centuries our increasing recourse to legal restitution has gone hand in hand with a remarkable decline in violence. Despite what you might think about the repressive and totalitarian past, or the licentious and libidinous present, people before modernity were in fact less rule-bound and more wild in their behavior than we are at present. We may have orgies and bacchanals, but they are orgies with decorum, and our bacchanals have their own distinct and delicate etiquettes. (Anyone acquainted with the mating rituals of undergraduates in our universities will know what I mean.) We have more experts, for more aspects of our lives, than ever before, and we listen to them more avidly than we ever have. (Think of this strange phrase, "life coaches.") Scholars like Michel Foucault have shown this in relation to changing notions of what is "reasonable" or sane behavior in public, and scholars like Norbert Elias have shown this in relation to changing notions of what is acceptable behavior at the dinner table, but they all agree on this: humanity today, for all our talk about individuality, is a remarkably docile, obedient, and rule-bound species. Authority is all the more powerful for being so thoroughly imperceptible. Its ultimate triumph lies in how it is embedded in our psyches: we obey authority when we think we *ought* to do something. The sociological discussion of authority begins from the fact of the pervasiveness of obedience and conformity.

In this formal sense, authority is simply our accepted basic framework of orientation, our primordial means of depicting the world to ourselves. How do you describe to yourself and to others your deliberative process? How, that is, do you give an account of what you do, and why? How do you decide to act? What "final vocabulary" do you use in such moments — on what vocabulary is your spade turned? What, in the end, makes sense of you? Of what community are you most fundamentally a member? The things you rely upon in such accounts reveal your authorities.

An example will help here. Imagine two people, Kate and Ken, who are both involved in providing medical care for people in a refugee camp. (I bet you imagine that camp to be in sub-Saharan Africa, but I'm actually thinking of one in northeast Texas, after Hurricane Katrina flooded New Orleans.) They work together as equals in the triage unit. Their job is to assess patients when they first arrive, treat minor injuries, and assign more serious cases to doctors in order of urgency. At the most basic level they are doing the same thing — and they could be doing it anywhere in the world. (Others all over the world are doing effectively identical tasks every day.) But we find what they are doing different, I wager, because they are doing it in a refugee camp. Very well, then; their work in a refugee camp gives their actions a distinct tinge. Now add another layer: Ken is doing this out of a firm belief that all humans deserve dignity and a basic level of decency, simply on account of their being human, and he thinks that those in better-off settings should willingly forgo their comforts until this base level of human dignity is met. Ken is in this job for the long haul. We would know that just from looking at him; he is fifty years old.

Kate, on the other hand, is twenty-five. She is working here as part of a Christian vocation program, out of a general conviction that all humans are God's children and bear the *imago Dei*, which can be seen no matter how dimly, in all. But part of her work is intentionally meant to shape her vision, the better to see this *imago Dei* in all people. She has been at this camp for two weeks, and she's never seen anything like it before. Her understanding of the world is that suffering will never be ended, in this dispensation, and so she does not act out of a desire to see all suffering eliminated, though she devoutly, in her sin, wishes that she could accomplish that; she acts out of a conviction that everyone who walks through that door is Jesus Christ, seeking relief.

Now, after we add this last layer of description, these two people are not, I would argue, doing the same thing. Certainly there are levels of description on which their actions are not divergent, but a full picture of what they are doing would certainly describe them differently. What makes the difference? The values to which they understand themselves to be committed, and the different worlds those values enable them to experience. Were you to take away those values, those convictions, Kate and Ken would not simply be confused, they would be *disoriented* — ignorant of where they were or where they were headed — unable to see the varying significances of the world, so unable really to inhabit a "world" at all. They would lack something essential to their proper functioning as humans; they would lack what their values are — their authorities.

When we try to think about authority in any helpful way, we are hampered by our world's self-congratulatory belief that it has no authorities on which it relies. We seem intellectually incapable of recognizing authority's inescapable presence in our lives in the form of our unthinking obedience to norms. But this sort of sociological explanation of why authority is a puzzle for us leaves undisturbed a further puzzle, this one about the origins of our belief in our fundamental self-determination. Why are we so committed to the idea that we are all unique and fundamentally free individuals? (Indeed, this collective belief in our discrete individuality is one of the things that makes us moderns so alike.) What is the source, and the rationale, of this belief in individuality? This dogmatic bias against authority is rooted in beliefs we have about the nature of the human as an agent. These rely on anthropological convictions, convictions about the picture of the human agent we assume. To dislodge them, we have to tackle their philosophical fundaments directly.

The forces encouraging and reinforcing this picture of the human are complex and manifold. On the surface, the problem may seem to be linguistic. Our language of "choice" offers no way to acknowledge our participation in, or vulnerability to, one another; it assumes that we are fundamentally separate from one another. As we saw in the last chapter, we understand ourselves to be creatures marked most fundamentally by our capacity for agency, and we increasingly understand that capacity through the language of "choice." It seems incoherent, or at least improper, to attempt to wrest another's choice out of another's control; given the basis of such choice in the mysterious subjectivity of the agent ("there's no arguing with taste," as the saying goes), it seems almost a category confusion to imagine that one could exercise another's choice *for* him or her. To claim the authority to choose for another is not just, on this picture, morally to violate another's autonomy; it is ontologically to invade the other — to damage the other's sense of being himself or herself, to harm the other's authenticity.

But note here how we are already moving from problems in our language to some more fundamental philosophical presuppositions underlying that language, presuppositions about the human agent. A large part of our problem here — I do not say the whole problem, merely a large part of it — lies in the picture of human agency most of us unreflectively assume today, and in this picture's depiction of the relationship between God, humans, and creation. This picture, as the last chapter argued, assumes that human agency properly operates through radically unconstrained choice, which is modeled on the radically unconstrained, ex nihilo action of God in creation. It is, in short, a Promethean vision of the human — a vision that emphasizes the human's capacity to act while ignoring or downplaying the constraints on the human's dependency on forces and persons beyond the human. To be sure, it relies on and obeys real authorities, as we saw above, but it cannot explicitly acknowledge them *as* authorities. This ex nihilo picture cannot, that is, understand authority. It offers no way to acknowledge our enmeshment or participation in, or vulnerability to, one another; it assumes that we are fundamentally separate from one another. Here love appears as nothing but the negotiation of our individual, private happiness. Seen in this light, our perplexities about civic engagement are rooted in deeper philosophical perplexity about our self-understanding as agents, and indeed as humans: we talk, that is, as if we do not believe that love is the core of our being; as if we believe that the world is ultimately a matter of sheer power, of conflicting wills, without respite; as if we want to be left wholly alone. Beneath our latent Promethean idolatry is a deep existential despair, a sense of being alone, of being abandoned.

Many today decry this picture of who we are, and not only Christians. All I want to suggest is that our commitment to this picture goes deeper than we normally suspect, even among those who decry it, and that to replace it we must articulate an alternative and much richer picture of who we are and why we do what we do. So how should Christians understand the proper account of agency to differ from this debased one? Our hesitation about authority is due to our received anthropology, which blocks any actual appreciation of authority's pervasiveness. To do better, we need to attend to the realities of the exercise of authority, the phenomenology of it. And to do that, I argue next, is to look carefully at the act of judging.

II. Judge Not?

Our nervousness about authority is related to a similar nervousness about judging, about the propriety of making moral judgments. In fact, that is putting the connection too loosely: the strong suspicions and anxieties we feel whenever we presume to exercise whatever authority we assume ourselves to possess, are most palpably felt when we experience ourselves, or witness others, engaged in acts that fall under the broad category of "judgment." This anxiety contains two ironies. First, our worry about moral judgments is actually (and is often expressed as) a *moral* worry, itself predicated upon the moral judgment that "it is morally wrong to make moral judgments." (Such attitudes are most frequently explicitly encountered among undergraduates, but they are far from unique to that population.) Second, in fact we are all more than willing to make moral judgments on political parties, and political leaders, and political programs — that is to say, on movements and events comprised of millions of individuals, any one of which we would never feel it right to judge in this way. But somehow, when they act together, we find it easy to assess the moral propriety of the event. (I include myself in this.) So we morally condemn the act of making moral judgments, and we do not deign to judge one person morally. But hundreds, or thousands, or millions? Well, we find that easy.

Such behavior is not only self-contradictory. It also speaks to our recognition of the necessity of judgment, and of our authority to judge. This recognition is tacit, because we are nervous about it, but it is inescapable. And when it is brought to our explicit attention, the nervousness is accentuated.

I do not want to destroy that nervousness; instead, I want to nourish it, cultivate it, in a certain way, for it is part of the cruciform nature of sacramental authority, which is to say *all* authority, in this world. Hence I will not here give tips on how to be authoritative in various spheres of life, but rather on what the exercise of authority should do to you, how it can be understood as part of our ascetical training to become fit citizens of the kingdom of heaven, able gracefully to bear the weight of glory God has prepared for us. The exercise of authority should be an ascetical vocation.

Our disquiet with authority is deeper still than just the contingencies of our modern mind-set. It is funded by an ambivalence about authority in the Christian tradition itself. Our bad model of agency is reinforced by a common misreading of the New Testament's deep theological anxieties about power. The New Testament voices a good deal of suspicion about those who wield power (this accounts in part for the seductive attractiveness of accusations of "Constantinianism" among many thoughtful Christians). Power always looks like empire on this account, and "empire," as I said earlier, is fundamentally a theological concept, perhaps even a demonological one.

What are we to say to these concerns? Can they be dismissed? By no means. But they identify deformations in authority with authority itself — a classic and old mistake. We must do better than this.

The New Testament actually does do better. Paul's idea that "authority is from God" is a crucial insight to build upon. Paul and the epistle writers more generally saw Christ as the fulfillment of the promises contained in the Old Testament. So a crucial first step is to root the New Testament, with its worries, in the Old Testament narrative. This is a theological move, and one internal to the New Testament itself, for it helps you see that Christ is prophet, priest, *and king*. It is that "king" part that today we often forget. And even those who affirm it typically mean by it only that Christ is really, really powerful. But that's not the point; the point is that Christ's presence in this world is not fundamentally *otherworldly*. Christ is not just a messenger sent to this world from another one, nor fundamentally a worker within this world, healing us or reconciling us to another; this world *is* Christ's world; Christ is the sovereign and the standard, the ruler and the rule, in Greek the *pantokrator* — the ruler of all, the ordering principle governing the whole cosmos. The language of Christ as "king," however politically awkward it may be for us, serves a crucial theological function. For this is Christ's world. Understanding this shows us how judging (and the exercise of power in which it participates) may be made properly legitimate.

The question then becomes, precisely *how* may we judge? How do we participate in Christ's kingly function, and participate even now, in some distant way, in the ultimate, eschatological ordering of the world? To answer this question we must engage and critique the bad philosophical assumptions we today assume, and then see how we might find a better way to inhabit authority.

The key question is whether we can imagine power exercised legitimately, even lovingly. That sounds paradoxical. As we said, ultimately power is inevitably attached, in this life, to compulsion. But how can love compel? We can't imagine love leading to compulsion. Love seems to us not to compel, but to be passive, basically about adoration at a distance. (There is desire-love, but we do see this as oddly connected to adoration-love, I would submit.) We are tempted to set love against compulsion; we assume an "either/or" of power versus static bystander. We are tempted to believe that we must value each other *or* force one another, in an instrumental way, which merely makes the other an extension of my ego.

Practically, just as we are caught in a performative self-contradiction about judging, so we are also confused about how love can compel and be invasive. This is visible even in our ordinary uses of compulsion. Thinking about the breadth of our everyday use of words like "compulsion" can help here. For it is ordinary use of the English language to say that a book, a piece of music, or a painting is compelling. We can be compelled by things — for example, works of art we find "compelling." What does this mean? It means that we find ourselves judged by it, put in our place, commanded, made to sit up, found wanting. (Think of a poem such as Rainer Maria Rilke's "Archaic Torso of Apollo," with its famous last line, "you must change your life.") Authority need not be oppressive and destructive; it can be enabling and creative.

The larger lesson here is simple: Love is not simply self-abnegating spectatorial respect. Power is not invasive; it can be enabling and creative. The lover's gaze can change the beloved. We often disparage paternalism, but it is an inescapable part of our lives, for it speaks to this phenomenon, most frequently visible in parents, of genuinely seeing and being committed to the other's good. With parents and children, often the parents' love is as the sun, nourishing and bringing to maturation. In ordinary life we both practice paternalism and allow it to be practiced upon us. It is love, and not the power we exercise in light of love, that makes us intimate with one another. Love is ontologically a real force, not just a word used to mask our admiring manipulation of one another.

How then can authority be manifest in the properly loving way?

III. Fear and Trembling

The problem we have in thinking about authority is due, then, to depictions of human agency that assume that we are wholly self-making, radically unconstrained agents. We can call this the ex nihilo understanding of agency, to highlight how it models human agency on a particular understanding of divine action. And the key disagreements Augustinian Christians should have with such ex nihilo models can be seen by drawing out two layers of the full meaning of authority and responsibility.

First is the *moral* sense of responsibility, in which I am held responsible by others, and will be held accountable to them, called to account before them. Second, and underlying the first, is the *ontological* sense of responsibility, in which my actions are understood as fundamentally responses to actions upon me, "dialogical" in the sense that they are usefully understood as one side of a dialogue, part of an ongoing "conversation" with reality (a conversation where reality takes the lead). In neither sense can the ex nihilo account acknowledge the reality of human responsibility. First of all, it is hard for this account to make sense of how anyone else's claims upon you can be anything more than a sheer demand for you to act as that person wants you to act — or an expression of resentment at you for not acting as that person wishes. Second, the idea that our actions are responses is rendered unintelligible by the primary assumption of this account, namely, that our acts are in fact completely spontaneous, provoked by nothing beyond our own immediate will.

This difference highlights the deepest divergence between the traditional model of agency and the ex nihilo one, namely, the rival understandings of action they assume. On its deepest understanding, the traditional account of human action understands such action as only secondarily "action," in the sense of a brute, self-initiating intervention in the physical world. First of all, it is not fundamentally brutally physical but meaning-laden: it is intelligible, responsive, one moment in our ongoing intellective engagement with God, the world, and our fellow humans. In our engagements with the world, we are always involved both agentially and intellectively, asking questions about what kind of world this is, and what kind of God creates, sustains, and will redeem it. Furthermore, this inquiry is narratively structured so that our actions become what they are by finding their place in a story — we are story-formed creatures, and to know who we are, both for ourselves and for others, is to know the shape and texture of the story of who we are. The shape of our action, understood as response, reveals how we understand our world, and reveals who we are and who we hope to be in the future. In this way our actions confess how we understand ourselves to be in a "dialogue" with those around us, and with the cosmos as a whole; in short, with God.

This condition applies to all actions, but especially to certain kinds of particularly morally charged actions. So the way a country fights a war

— if it recognizes the humanity of its enemy by not carpet bombing their cities, for example — reveals much about how it understands God, the neighbor, and the way the world should run.

This may appear to be a fairly esoteric account. But it seems so only because our explicit picture of agency is so profoundly degenerate. In practice we employ something quite similar to this picture, even as we tell ourselves an altogether more self-congratulatory story about how we act. For to talk about agency at all, you must have some account of responsibility, some account, that is, of why we say this person is responsible for that act, and why the person did it — what were the person's reasons for so acting. And in seeking such reasons, as with the examples of Kate and Ken, we excavate the person's authorities.

How, then, do we behave authoritatively in a responsible manner? Here Augustine can be of some help, for he thought long and hard about the responsibilities of those in positions of authority in his own day — both their responsibilities to their cities and their responsibilities to God. One of the best, though frequently ignored, texts in which this is visible is his sermon 13, on judging, and how to exercise power — how to be an authority. It was spoken especially to political authorities in Augustine's day, but in our day, when all hold a share in political authority, it speaks to all of us.

The sermon was given in a setting that was redolent of authority, triumphant and also complexly compromised. First of all, Augustine gave it, we believe, in Carthage, at the Basilica of St. Cyprian, built on the site where Cyprian had been martyred in 258, in the Decian persecution. Cyprian had been martyred because, though he would (and did) pray for the emperor, he refused to sacrifice to him — for, he insisted, his faithfulness to God determined and defined the quality of his commitment to any worldly authority. In death he became a saint, and his shrine a particular source of salvific energies. Now, a century and a half later, the sermon may well have been preached to some of those *illustri* who held the offices once occupied by Cyprian's killers. There were still Caesars, and still an *imperium Romanum*, though now Rome was Christian. Yet no one in the service of the emperor, sitting in a chair or standing at the front of the congregation, could have missed the complex situation in which he was put by being in that place. Furthermore, Augustine now was at the height of his authority in North Africa, and stood the closest he would ever stand to the imperial government. The struggle against the Donatists had propelled him to close contact with the authorities, and they had supported his every move. Among the populace of Carthage he likely had all the glamour of a great man with none of the overfamiliarity of a prophet in his own country; Hippo was close enough for him to have been here innumerable times for important matters, yet it was far enough away that he always seemed fresh and new.

So Augustine is an authority, at his most magisterial in this setting. Yet what is surprising, perhaps, is how deeply suspicious he is of all human exercises of authority, his own included. The putative text Augustine is expositing is Psalm 2:10: "Be instructed, all you who judge the earth." He uses the text as an opportunity to inquire into what it means to exercise authority. The structure of the sermon says something as important as its explicit argument. First of all, the pattern of biblical texts cited in the sermon is unusual and significant. Augustine spends the first part of the sermon talking about the general story of sin, grace, and redemption, in which all humans play a role. In this story we are all, at best, coworkers with God in our own journey back to God, and secondary coworkers at that, for God gives us the will to do good, Augustine insists; so we are to work out our redemption, he reminds us in an explicit echo of Paul, in fear and trembling (Ps. 2:11 and Phil. 2:12), working under God's guidance, "that you might find yourself in him, as you have lost yourself in yourself." His first interpretation of the Psalms text, then, presents it in terms of humanity's common struggle with our inherited sin from Adam.

Then, and only then — fully a third of the way into the sermon — does he turn to what he calls the "everyday understanding" of the phrase, namely, the political sense. Judging of this sort does surely take place, he avers, as it must. But such judging is immediately fraught, for kings are no closer to God than anyone else; "the earth itself is judging the earth, and when earth judges earth it ought to fear God who is in heaven. It is indeed judging its own equal, a human judging a human, a mortal judging a mortal, a sinner judging a sinner." Why is this so fraught for Augustine? Because, he says, Christ tells us that only the sinless should judge. And the one sinless man who could judge — namely, Christ himself — chooses *not* to do so. That is to say, in political action we should be merciful, as Christ demonstrated in his dealings with the woman caught in adultery.

163

Why is this so? Because, for Augustine, the point of political judgment is found in crucial part in its salvific benefits, its ability to serve the redemptive purposes of God. That is to say, political judgment is part of the larger judgment of God. This is how he understands the story about Caesar's coin: "just as the image of Caesar on the coin is restored" to Caesar, Augustine says, so we should "restore to God the image of God in the human being." Certainly Augustine was "political realist" enough to know that in our fallen world the time of political authorities would largely, at best, be occupied with securing whatever modicum of a parody of true justice and peace as was allowed them by the exigencies of the day. But they can never forget that they are not just authorities, they are humans, and as humans they are called upon by God to act to help their neighbors when they can. After all, it is as humans, not as authorities, that this obligation is put on them; that is to say, the obligation does not flow from their political office but from their humanity, and it is as humans who find themselves in those offices that they should act.

For Augustine, political authorities are not motivated by the noblesse oblige of royalty who "know better" than others because of their status; instead, they see that as humans they can use their accidental occupation of an authoritative office for their neighbors' good. God puts political authorities in their offices (*officium*, "duty," is the revealing root sense of the word Augustine uses) to secure justice and be merciful in their dealings with those who are subject to their authority — as God surely is with them. And in such offices, sinful humans do not exhibit glory or splendor or authority in themselves; whatever authority they have comes from God, as vehicles of justice. One can prudently use one's authority only when one knows one's own sinfulness and one's temptations toward pride, and knows that one will, in the end, be judged for them.

So the first step toward a healthy use of authority is to realize that, insofar as people have any real authority, they have it not as their proper "right" but on loan: we borrow our authority from our social order, and ultimately from God. Ultimately, God is the only real authority, the only true judge, and we are all at best "occasions" for the exercise of authority, not ourselves instigators of it. This is perhaps most clearly visible to us in a classroom setting, where authority is inescapable. As Augustine shows through his depiction of his own education in the *Con-*

fessions, education does things to students that neither students nor teachers fully comprehend, and plants seeds that neither can control. Authority is legitimate for Augustine, only on theological grounds; because sin disorders human society and human individuals, authority can ultimately only be grounded on divine authority, and all human authority is borrowed, and should be exercised humbly and with hesitation and the constant confession of the authority's own weakness.

This is far from the kind of majesty that most leaders, in any age, have tried to claim for themselves. They have sought not authority in this sense but charisma, a kind of *idolatrous* power, hiding the leader behind the incense of magic or an aroma of godliness (as the word "charisma" comes from "divine favor"). In contrast, on Augustine's understanding, authority is transparent: you see through the leader, beyond her or him to the end that the leader serves. Wise authorities know people will want them to appear as wise and all-knowing, even though they know they are not; and so real authorities engage in a fairly delicate dance between exuding the appearance of charisma and renouncing it, being one of the "ordinary folks." That is why the first act of "judgment" must be an "inner" act for Augustine — a constant self-lacerating assessment of the reasons for one's continued acceptance of this terrible burden. Because of this, Augustine says, "judge yourself first" — you must make yourself be tortured "on the rack of your heart." Certainly authority is a powerful thing, he says; but that is precisely why it is so very dangerous.

In fact, in the sermon, it is only after exploring the presumptuousness of judging, when those in authority have come to see their fellowship with the sin of those who would stone the woman caught in adultery, and their implication in the paradoxical human condition of working out our salvation in fear and trembling — only once the authorities begin to feel in their guts the presumption of their offices — only after this last, chastising swipe at political rulers is given, does Augustine turn to the text that had already by his time become one of the most fundamental New Testament texts for Christian political understanding, namely, Romans 13 ("let every soul be subject to the higher authorities, for there is no authority except from God," etc.). Even here, however, even after all the framing given before, Augustine still resists the glorification of political authority; even here he works to make the authorities queasy. For after all, he suggests, if God has given out this authority, God will take it back, and so *all* will be judged, even those who exercise authority, and all must act in fear and trembling.

Augustine further complicates the authorities' authority by recalling his congregation's attention to where they physically are, at Cyprian's shrine — "think of the blessed man whose blood was shed on this very spot" — reminding all of how terrifically, horrendously wrong the exercise of authority can go. And then he turns directly to the authorities (one can imagine him literally turning toward them, were they in the church that day): "If, then, you don't want to exercise your authority unjustly, all you human beings who wish to have authority over human beings, well, *be instructed*, so that you avoid judging corruptly, and perishing in your soul before you manage to destroy anyone else in the flesh." He wants these worries to worm their way into the rulers' hearts, so that they will be constantly alive to their terrible presumptuousness.

Naturally, given the terrors involved in such judging, and in the exercise of authority that they entail, it is not surprising that many seek to avoid acknowledging the way they are not their own sources, but are responsible beyond themselves to another. That is why we so typically fall into presumptuousness as authorities. All such authorities, inasmuch as they attempt to grasp authority, to become self-authorized authorities, fail to grasp it. The classical (indeed, pre-Christian, perhaps simply postlapsarian) vision of stern authority, with its apparent marble confidence in the controlling hand of the master, is cunningly subverted for Augustine by God's uncanny providence.

Hence the first virtue of all exercises of authority in this life is mercy. Following Christ, who (quoting Hosea) urged us to "Go and learn what this means: 'I desire mercy, not sacrifice'" (Matt. 9:13), mercy is a crucial part of the vocation of political authority in this world. Yet this is not because of fear on the authorities' part of "blowback" from God — not, that is, because of fear of one's own judgment by God — but because this is the central truth about God's judgment of the world. God is *merciful*, first and foremost. Therefore, if authorities want their action to conform to the "author" of that authority, the actions of that authority must manifest mercy as well. This is a persistent theme in Augustine's writings: again and again, in his treatises, in his sermons, and above all in his letters to political authorities, he underscores the need to recognize the preeminence of mercy in judging. Yet at the same time Augustine is no laxist; rightly understood, punishment is itself a form of mercy. Rulers should understand their role as analogous to a loving father who "has care" of his whole family, and who uses discipline — including beatings — only when necessary for the family's whole good. Eschewing such discipline, Augustine argues, is actually a cruel form of cowardice or indifference.

The paternalism of this vision of authority, and the patriarchy of it, is inescapable. But we cannot wholly condemn it for that. First of all, family is more primordial than the state, so that the latter should be modeled on the former: love, that is, not force, should be the binding energy of the polity, and in his letters Augustine repeatedly called political authorities to unheard-of levels of forbearance, including his insistence — astonishing for any writer in the ancient world — that rulers should avoid capital punishment except when completely forced into it. Besides, he is right about the need for order and discipline in families, and mothers and fathers today still exercise it. We do not talk about this much, but the truth is that it is there. (Just try living with a six-year-old for a week to appreciate the value and necessity of authority.) Indeed, it is there in many aspects of our life, wherever there is hierarchy. Augustine is simply being realistic in recognizing this.

But his is not the cold cynicism that too often passes for "realism" today; that would be unrealistic, denying the power of love as a real force in the world. A true realism recognizes both the power of love and the inescapability of force, and insists on the reality of both, against the too-confident coherence of a bitter cynicism or a naive idealism. So the aroma of paternalism and patriarchy that lingers around Augustine's proposal of authority can be significantly decreased if we reframe it as not addressed to rulers but to citizens. Here the emphasis on humility and mercy becomes very important. Citizens wield sovereignty and grant the right to exercise it to certain elected officials (and their authorized deputies), but in doing so the granting should carry with it the citizens' own humility, their wariness of their own presumption in the exercise of power; and it should also communicate the citizens' earnest desire that that sovereignty be exercised always with an eye to human fallibility, with a will to allow humans to correct their mistakes, and with a hesitancy to pronounce absolute judgments and execute complete justice — in short, with mercy.

Indeed, all components of the sermon — where it was given, the progression of scriptural passages discussed, and the argument itself — reinforce Augustine's basic message, which is that to exercise authority is a grave, terrible, and always potentially presumptuous thing, a burden to be accepted only with fear and trembling. And once accepted, such "higher authorities" should sit uneasy in their seats. For in such offices sinful humans do not exhibit glory or splendor or authority in themselves; whatever authority they have comes from God, as vehicles of justice, and so they will "honor" themselves, and "praise" those with whom they have dealings, by recognizing the larger frame of judgment and justice that encompasses them both.

It would be easy to reinforce the point of this sermon with other texts of Augustine's, written throughout his ecclesial life. Not only in his sermons, but also in his letters as well as (most famously) in his *Confessions*, Augustine hammered home the same point: power is properly wielded as authorized service of others' goods, oriented, informed, and motivated by one's love for these others, and is finally an act of obedience for which the actor is held eschatologically responsible to God for its exercise. He himself was very uneasy in the episcopal chair. Augustine was quite consistent in delivering this message, with his lips and in his life.

So, for Augustine, proper political action is exercise of *authorized power*, which is itself a complicated idea. Proper political action flows from God's dispensing of this authority. But the legitimation of this power comes at a cost to those who wield it: authority always stands under the eschatological judgment of God, and all of us in positions of authority must recognize our implication in the violence and necessities of the world. So we should be uneasy in our authority.

A concrete example will help here. The two greatest tasks of government are instruction and protection. We saw the ambiguities of teaching discussed, briefly, above. So next I look at how this vision manifests itself in the conduct of war.

IV. The Mournful Warrior

Put bluntly: How can slaying an aggressor be an act of charity, however alien? That is what we turn to now: the exercise of this authority in war.

How does the tradition conceive of the use of force, and the nature of politics as a whole? Through the idea of *compelling necessity*. In fact, the use of force is the ultimate example of our enmeshment in the necessities of the world. (One of Augustine's favorite scriptural passages — appearing again and again when he thinks about politics — is Psalm 25:17, "From my necessities deliver me!") The past constrains and orients our action in the present and for the future. Those authorized politically are those who have been put in a situation downstream from history, as it were. And sometimes they must accept the historical necessity of the legitimate and authorized use of force for righteous ends.

The language of "necessity" stands at the basis of the well-known "just-war tradition" of Christian reflection about war. I will not get into the technical details — the "grammar" — of that tradition here, such as the criteria that help the rightly formed agent determine when it is right to go to war or what it is right to do in war. Instead here I focus on the deep theological background and worldview that motivate that tradition.

To begin with, we should recognize that the language of necessity, which Augustine uses, is theologically problematic for him as well. After all, talk about necessity is complicated by God's free providence. In Gethsemane, Jesus doesn't say that his death is necessary, but that the Father wills it. When Augustine uses the Latin *necessitas,* he does not mean inevitability or determinism, but the will of God. God's will is not subject to any helpless compulsion; God need not do this. But this is not properly understood simply as a whim of God's that can be revoked, or as a sheerly arbitrary act of God's *will.* The distinction between "being" and "will" is one that makes sense for humans, because of the conflicts and incoherencies in our fallen existence (the experience of which is quite clearly something we have); because God does not have those conflicts and incoherencies, that distinction makes no sense in God's case. What God necessitates is neither arbitrary nor inevitable. But that does not make God's will any less omnipotent, or any less the prime mover of history; it simply means that what God, in the unity of God's "being" and God's "will," has proclaimed will be the course of history. Thus "necessity" must be understood not as an impersonal brute force pushing blindly from behind the scenes of human history, but instead as the unvexable and wholly free dynamic action of God leading history through judgment to the mercy seat. Possibly the only great modern political thinker who has understood the course of history in this way is Abraham Lincoln.

But this "necessity" is consciously compelling for you only if you have a vibrant faith in God's providential ordering of the world. So we cannot restrict the reality of compulsion simply to the political sphere; it reveals God's providential governance of the whole world, including human agency. And this governance is not simply located in the fundamentally contingent peculiarities of our particular era; we are embedded also in history, in a history defined by the great drama of creation, fall, redemption, and sanctification, and we will be made to answer for this drama. So Augustine's political insight that we are responsible not just for current structures of order but for the past as well, that we have inherited guilt, is a general fact about the human condition. Humans in this world are not able to choose with total impunity; we always come to consciousness of our situation *in medias res,* with lines of filiation and obligation (and opposition and enmity) drawn before we have a chance to say yes or no. We are always constrained by the course of history, global and local. The twentieth-century political thinker Hannah Arendt put it well: "When Napoleon, seizing power in France after the Revolution, said: I shall assume the responsibility for everything France ever did from Saint Louis to the Committee of Public Safety, he was only stating somewhat emphatically one of the basic facts of political life. It means hardly more, generally speaking, than that every generation, by virtue of being born into a historical continuum, is burdened by the sins of the fathers as it is blessed with the deeds of the ancestors." Again, the picture of agency we hold is crucial for the full reach and significance of this account. We are not ex nihilo actors. Our action is part of our larger interchange, our "dialogue," with God, and through God, with the world and our neighbor — a story stretching far back behind our birth, and far forward into the future.

The implications of this picture for a proper understanding of the use of force are substantial. Those authorities legitimated to use force do not act on behalf of their own private vengeance, but always are compelled by a proper apprehension of the particular situation in which they — as the particular political agents they are — find themselves, including their own particular obligations and commitments in that situation. A useful analogy is with an individual's right to self-defense. "Right" here is almost too contingent for this reality; if someone attacks you, it is almost automatic that you will defend yourself — it is simply a reflex, not something you voluntarily or deliberately do. The ideal of political authority would be similarly automatic, reflexive, in terms of defending those with whose care the authority is charged.

Because of this, the Augustinian tradition understands the just-war mode of deliberation to be not essentially an exculpatory moral algorithm, checklist, or any sort of relatively portable set of criteria, applicable by just anybody. Instead, the tradition views such deliberation as a narratively enframed interpretive matrix that both offers a picture of the world and proposes how to live within it. It requires properly formed — morally and religiously — agents to enact it. And part of the formation of these agents is their coming to see themselves as tragically malformed in certain ways, ways that should shadow their every exercise of political power in complicated and complicating ways.

This last point is especially crucial. The failure of secular accounts of the just-war tradition is not simply a problem with their forgetting of the tradition's history; what is worse, that forgetting means they offer a more deeply flawed construal of just-war reasoning. For at its heart the just-war tradition is not exculpatory but obligatory. It does not *permit* our intervention, nor is it about *unleashing* us — "cry havoc, and let slip the dogs of war" — giving us license to indulge in what we already want to do. Rather, it *insists* that we acknowledge our prior implication in the situation and our responsibility to confront it as best as possible. As Augustine says in his famous letter to Boniface, "it ought to be necessity, and not your will, that destroys an enemy who is fighting you." As such, the just-war tradition is not a distinct and self-sustained tradition at all, but is properly intelligible only as part of a Christian theology of justice and judgment: God's justice and judgment are beginning to be worked out *in history,* the tradition insists, and we are to inhabit history as the site where and medium whereby that judgment and justice are deployed.

Central to this "working out" is an emphasis on suffering and crucifixion. Where secular applications of the tradition have generally moved at the level of policy decisions, the Christian just-war tradition is more comfortable at the level of existential soul-formation — not with the decisions but with the deciders, and those who go forth to enact the decision. It is not finally concerned with licensing the act of war in situations of necessary violence; it is rather about how we should be driven, by a proper apprehension of the situation, into terribly difficult actions. It is about putting particular moral actions within a rich theological narrative frame in order to understand properly where you stand — what necessities are forcing your hand, and what judgment you stand under. It does not excuse or whitewash the actors, nor does it simply permit and excuse; rather, it obligates. The just-war tradition depicts us as necessarily part of the world, and as such part of the awesome and horrendous unspooling of God's providential judgment on the world. Here as elsewhere, the just-war tradition is part of a larger theology of history as providential.

This may sound horrific. Isn't it enough to permit one to use violence? What is gained by making it obligatory? But in fact, the idea that one needs only permission to go to war is morally more troubling than the thought that one needs a command to do so. A "war of choice," so understood, is an avoidable war, and a war that can be reasonably and morally avoided should be. (So Augustine critiqued Moses for killing the Egyptian overseer, and Peter for cutting off the right ear of the high priest's servant, because both exhibited "hasty zeal.") Obligation is a more realistic, and ironically also more gentle, merciful, and humane, way to think about a war's rationale than via a language of "permission." This is what Paul Ramsey means when he speaks of the Christian just-war tradition originating "in the interior" of the Christian ethic of love. Here war is done out of the compulsion of love; it is not a free-standing ex nihilo act, but emerges from the recognition of prior relation and responsibility, recognition of our implication in the violence of the world. Far from absolving political agents of responsibility, this love-based account means to accentuate their sensitivity to the fraught character of their actions.

But this emphasis on love is paired with a realistic assessment of human sin. That is, just-war theory is not only based on the "Christian universalism" of egalitarianism and universal concern that lies at the basis of international law, as many point out; it is also based on that other, less palatable Christian universalism unacknowledged in international law but even more basic in international relations: the universalism of sin. Just-war theory emerges out of an account of human fallenness; without it, just warriors may delude themselves into assuming that they are ever other than significantly morally compromised. The "justice" in just-war theory should never be claimed to be more than relative justice. As Frederick Russell puts it, Augustine's own account is not so much a systematic theory as it is really "clusters of ideas grouped around the central theme of sin and punishment." Just-war theory, that is, is part of a larger theological worldview that begins from a vision of human life as tragically, irremediably corrupted, and it describes one facet of how humans should participate properly, or least improperly, in life so conceived. But it harbors no pretense of offering a tidy resolution to the problems it is designed to address, and to suggest otherwise is to court a dangerous hypocrisy. On the Christian understanding, just-war reasoning is not undertaken by people who see themselves most primordially as rulers or other political actors; it is undertaken by people who see themselves most primordially as sinners — creatures who suffer from the same basic maladies as their opponents.

For these reasons the Christian just-war tradition insists that the decision to go to war can never be a light one; if war is thinkable, that means it demands hard consideration. And that hard consideration involves realizing that one may be obligated to do something that is, in some way, potentially morally distasteful, perhaps even compromising. That force must be used, that it is obligatory, is always an occasion for moral regret, for the recognition that such evils that a war will inevitably bring are to be regretted. But much depends on the range of viable possibilities for action in this sphere. Often the tragic course and contradictions of history stymie the impatient antiseptic fantasies of utopian thinkers in ways that make it impossible to find the perfect solution of which they dream. This is why just-war reasoning always leaves space for "prudential judgments" on the part of the enactors. This may seem like a concession to human autonomy outside of divine sovereignty — as if humans at last have an autonomous role to play, a vote in the action itself. But in fact it means instead that the command of a living God cannot be captured in a neat algorithm, and that at any particular moment space must be given for those of proper discernment to discern what God is calling them to do. Discerning leaders may come to see that the fine-grained conditions "on the ground," so to speak, seem to their mind to compel them to engage in violence. That is to say, they may freely decide they are compelled. For the wise, it is hard to imagine a more painful decision, or a harder one.

In such situations regret is inevitable. But it may also be insufficient. Many thinkers about violence, in the just-war tradition and out of it, acknowledge the inevitability of regret in political action — regret that one cannot do everything one must do without harming some people;

yet this regret is also a whitewash, for it does not speak to how the harm done to those you do harm may hurt your own soul. But the tragic opacity of human life makes us go beyond regret into remorse: not only is the idea of a perfectly immaculate policy not to be had in our world; our sense of the flaws in our policy should help us cultivate a recognition of our own sinfulness, and likely complicity, in the evils we intend to stop.

So just-war reasoning, as part of a larger worldview, not only must not be an algorithmic system or checklist aimed at exculpating those who act; it must also discourage any moralistic evasions of responsibility and so, positively, encourage our recognition of our sinfulness. It must not merely make warriors, it must make mournful warriors, who recognize that their decisions have been made at real moral cost. This is not about imposing on soldiers a framework alien to their experience — as if they would not have these disturbing thoughts unless some troublesome priest inserts them into their minds — but rather giving them a way to talk about what they experience already. The frequent recognition of the import of "regret" does not go far enough, I think, in recognizing the moral state of near-despair that "just warriors" ought to cultivate.

This brings to the fore the irremediably theological context and eschatological overtones of just-war reasoning. I recognize that many of its original convictions predate Christianity, and today parts of it are embedded in wholly secular international law and the laws of war. But just-war thinking in its true richness is far more organically related to the Christian theological tradition than many allow. To imagine you can pluck just-war reasoning from its theological setting and that it will continue to flourish, encourages a dangerous distortion of just-war theory, to which all of us must be sensitive. Most secularizations of just-war theory do not acknowledge the profound moral troublingness inherent in any act of war making, no matter how just — and indeed the troublingness of human life in the world in a register more profound than many accounts, secular and religious, of human life allow. Just-war reasoning can easily be a lie we tell ourselves about the intelligibility, transparency, and rationality of the world, and often secularizations of it amount to just that. Of course, we should seek whatever clarity we can find, as diligently as possible, but the pursuit of that genuine clarity is also and simultaneously the rejection of any and every offer of spurious sanitation offered to us for purchase. Furthermore, any appropriation of the just-war tradition that lets its adherents assume that *we* are in charge of the world is, on Christian grounds, deeply flawed. This is not an idea native to the just-war tradition, but a modern accretion. The idea that authority bestows power, understood as something like unconstrained freedom to act as we will, is one of the saddest of delusions about political life, and typically one of the first surrendered by even moderately intelligent authorities when they gain office.

Alongside these problems are others. Secular variants of the just-war tradition not only fail to recognize the tragic complexity of the actual situations in which human beings find themselves when at war, but they also refuse to recognize real transcendence and eschatological idealism of the historical just-war tradition. Such secularizations clip off its lowest notes and highest aspirations. Our recognition of the tragedy of war, our sense of our moral implication in its necessity and in the particular implications of its waging, is decisively shaped by our eschatological sense that "this" — how much horror is pressed into one bland word! — is not how things should be, and it is not how things will finally be. Our moral remorse and regret are or should be in large part informed by the very disquieting idea that we will be made to answer for our complicity in these events; that we will be held to account, if not here on earth, then in some final court of justice; that justice is not forever deferred; that the blood of the innocent cries from the ground; that God will not be forever mocked.

Augustine's deepest example of how authorities should use force is found in chapter 6 of book 19 of his *City of God*. Here he is puzzling over the nature of Christians' participation in the murkiness of "worldly" affairs. He offers his proposal by discussing the hardest case he can imagine — the case of a judge who, as part of the legitimate civil authority, is compelled by "social necessity" to torture people (which was the normal practice in Roman juridical affairs) the judge does not know are guilty and may very well be innocent. Suppose, he says, someone is brought before the judge accused by another of doing wrong. The judge, upon hearing the initial evidence presented, orders the accused to undergo a "trial" by judicial torture; suppose that, for unforeseen reasons (perhaps the accused has a weak heart), the torture kills the person. By trying to learn the truth the judge kills the one person, possibly innocent, at least not obviously guilty, by whom he might have learned that truth. Because he "cannot discern the consciences of those whom they judge, the ignorance of the judge generally results in the calamity of the innocent. And what is still more greatly intolerable and deplorable . . . is that the judge, to avoid killing an innocent man, out of miserable ignorance tortures the accused, and kills him — tortured and innocent — whom he tortured in order not to kill him if he were innocent."

Augustine uses the tragically paradoxical situation of the judge as a summit from which we may view the whole expanse of the miserable necessities of human society. Human social order is a fragile thing, always vexed by miscommunication, inattention, and outright malfeasance. Securing society against dangers is a matter of at best marginally managing catastrophe, failure, and menace, a matter of resisting immanent malice with crude threats meant to cause fear, not to appeal to reason or noble desire. Hazards to society are often most effectively — or to be honest, least ineffectively — countered by threats, or acts, of brute force, and so to secure some small modicum and parody of peace, vast and awesome violence must constantly be threatened. *Ultima ratio regum* read the motto stamped on the mouths of King Louis XIV's cannons in the seventeenth century: "the ultimate argument of the king." And as the famous adage of the Supreme Court has it, finally the president of the United States has only the authority that command of the Eighty-second Airborne Division provides.

Given this, and given in our world the fact that political authority is pragmatically reducible to sheer brute force, should Christians serve in political office? In Augustine's words, "[i]n light of such darkness in our social life, should the wise judge dare to sit in judgment?" His answer is forthright:

Sit he will; for he is constrained by and drawn to his duties to human society, to desert which he regards as wicked. For he does not think it wicked to torture the innocent in others' cases, or that the accused are overcome and confess falsely and are punished, though innocent. . . . All these many evils he does not count as sins, because the wise judge does them not out of a malicious will, but out of the necessity of ignorance, and also, out of consideration of society, out of the necessity to judge. Here therefore we speak not of the maliciousness of the judge, but of the sure misery of humanity.

Yet this vivid picture of the "tragic vocation of the judge" does not simply offer a blanket affirmation for Christians' acceptance of the vocation of political authority. Such an obligation is not the end of Christian struggle, but only the beginning. A Christian occupying the judicial bench is not morally whitewashed because God wants her in that office, for she always remains under judgment. In such a situation, if the judge makes tragic though unculpable mistakes, "is it a problem if, while he [the judge] is innocent, he is yet not happy? How much more considerable and worthy is it when he acknowledges our miserable necessities, hates his part in them, and, if he is pious and wise, cries out to God, 'from my necessities deliver me!'" (Again, the allusion to Psalm 25:17.)

The exercise of political power — an exercise sometimes entailing the use of force and always relying tacitly on the threat of force — is something that should affect our souls; it should trouble, humble, even perhaps break our wills, make us wish we were other than who we are. Happy is the land that is ruled by someone who does not enjoy ruling too much; best is the war that is waged by someone who wishes earnestly that it did not have to be waged, and who fears for his or her soul because of the "necessities" involved.

It is this vision of political reality that informs Augustine's understanding of the exercise of political power, and of the nature of the authorized use of violence. So in a real way Augustine thinks that just war is pacification, and has as its end peace, true peace, the tranquillity of order. This end is not merely extrinsic to the behavior in war; it will shape the means that are suitable as well. The war must be waged with justice throughout, for the more just it is, the closer the approximation of peace it will realize in the end. "Wage war peaceably," says Augustine to Count Boniface, and the just-war tradition sees no overwhelming paradox in that phrase, much to its benefit.

It is important to notice here how unusual, and how morally demanding, even morally perfectionist, are the conditions that Augustine demands be in place for something to be genuinely a state of "peace." It is not simply the absence of overt war. A peace in which children are tortured systematically by a state is no peace, and those who insist that it is are at least indirectly culpable for those tortured children. Peace is the end of war — even the wicked, Augustine insists, seek peace. But what sort of peace? Of triumph and subjugation, or of right order? We must beware, Augustine seems to say, of seeking the peace of mere indifference, the peace of the dead. The peace Christians seek is eschatological, the peace of those who have been resurrected. For Augustine, we participate in Jesus' peace, which is Jesus Christ's union with the Father in the Holy Spirit. But we are at war with ourselves, so we do not have this peace fully; and we cannot see each other's hearts, so we do not have this union with one another.

In this way this Christian vision is not a cry of despair, but a stern consequence of the height of its "ideals" (what an inadequate word that is). Paradoxically, our sense of sin is based on our hope, and indeed the former is unintelligible without the latter. We must hope for and fear God's judgment at one and the same time, and cling not to our own righteousness — which we know to be an illusion — but to the righteousness we have as an alien gift.

Conclusion: Hearing the Word:
The Politics of Divine Recognition

The question of "just war" is not separable from the larger questions of the meaning and purpose of authority. And this understanding of authority is really an outworking of what it means to love someone. Furthermore, if we say this, we can understand better what it means to say that "God is love." For God is love in the same way that God is authority, just as all political sovereignty is simply a surrogate for God; we are simply God's agents, acting in God's name. And God's "authority" is better understood as God's judgment. In this way we always also stand under God's judgment. So love, authority, politics, and judgment are all internally related. The task of politics in general, for this tradition, is quintessentially one of *judgment* — of policing the community to secure the closest approximation of peace, the tranquillity of order.

This vision reminds us, again, that the goals of politics transcend political realization. To associate love and politics is not to denigrate the former but to realize the true depth of the latter. Politics is not simply a mundane thing; among its many motivations — getting along in the world; organizing social energies; protecting us against bad people, whether they are others or ourselves — is a curiously noninstrumental one: we long for genuine encounter with others, an encounter best described in terms of communion. Civic action also moves toward communion, genuine engagement. We want genuinely to see each other and to be seen. Yet this hope, this longing, is not finally realizable in the world as we have it; it is an eschatological hope. It is the work of this Augustinian vision to make this hope politically intelligible.

But this longing for communion is complicated and shadowed for us by our sense that we stand under judgment, that we will be condemned if anyone truly knows us. We are imperfect vessels for God's judgment — flawed, cracked, leaking — and we will be judged accordingly. And we know this. All our encounters with the other (which is what politics in this world is all about) and our longings for communion (which is what politics always aspires to be) are always shadowed by this anxiety about judgment; so all our efforts at attaining the communion of love are always fraught by an ambivalence we would be well advised to acknowledge.

This, in turn, says two things, one about God and one about us. About God, it suggests something of the character of God's being toward us. For God in Christ is judge, forgiver, and commander — all at once. We are *judged* and found wanting, in all details, with nothing not exposed; *forgiven* those transgressions, as fully and completely as they were acknowledged; and *commanded* to do a new thing, to sing a New Song. This is all not just simultaneously proclaimed, but rather all three of these proclamations are facets of a larger action of God for us and toward us; they do not happen simultaneously so much as they are the same thing. We cannot be commanded unless we are forgiven, and we cannot be forgiven unless it is clear what we have done. They express and enact the coherence of God's action, and the derivative coherence of God's creation. This gets at the fundamental question of "new creation," which signifies both a rupture with our past and a kind of continuity. (Coming to appreciate the mystery of how this happens is one way to approach appreciating the mystery of the Trinity.)

What we need to do, then, is to learn to see politics as about exposure, about vision — about recognition and acknowledgment — and about us as simultaneously fearing it and longing for it. Most fundamentally, what we must hear is the judgment that we are lovable. This is a matter of hearing it, from outside ourselves — for on the inside we cannot know whether we're lovable or not.

To hear this judgment and to be resurrected are related. In hearing God's judgment addressed to you, you hear a recognition of a relationship that is still there: you are really connected to God. (This is true more generally than just theologically — it is true about arguments with your spouse or your friends. A relationship has ended when they're not talking to you but to others, about you. A similar thing is true of God's judgment, but God always speaks the judgment to you first and foremost.) We hear judgment, then, we hear the Word, we hear that God has chosen to be in love with us. And we, in return, are called to live in faithful relation to God.

How are we to be faithful to a God whose integrity is so radically free and so fundamentally complete? That is our next question.

CHAPTER 6

Faith and Political Commitment

Democracy, while weapons were everywhere aim'd at your breast,
I saw you serenely give birth to immortal children, saw in dreams
your dilating form,
Saw you with spreading mantle covering the world.

Walt Whitman, *Leaves of Grass*

A friend of mine — a thoughtful, faithful, articulate, politically astute man — was once confronted with a question about the depth of his loyalty to God and country. Years ago at a dinner party, in conversation with another thoughtful and faithful person, he was brought up short by something the other man said. "I am an American," he said. "I've always been one. I see the world with American eyes, and I love America as much as anyone can. But I believe that my identity as an American is finally incidental to who I really am. After all, I am a Christian, a child of God, a sinner whom Christ died for, and my ultimate citizenship is in his kingdom, not any of these temporal principalities. Because of that, I ultimately don't give a damn about what happens to this nation. I mean, ultimately, I know its destiny. America is not saved by Jesus, human beings are. America will not be taken into heaven the way you and I will be taken up into the celestial choir. America will be judged and found wanting, even as some of its people are saved." My friend was struck with this, and did not know what he thought of it then; he still wonders at it now.

Whatever else you are in this world, you are almost certainly a citizen of some political community. As such, you are bound to be implicated, in some way, in your polity, and pragmatically committed to it. But how much commitment is it right to have, especially as a believer? How can we be citizens here if our true citizenship is in heaven? Do we, as citizens and as believers, owe something to the polities we inhabit? Do we in some way *belong* to these polities? How does our obligation as citizens relate to our fidelity as believers? Should we put *faith* in our politics?

"Faith" is obviously a fraught term here. But it captures both a psychological reality and a theological warning. Psychologically it captures the fact that in our world the political dimension of our identity is typically a crucial determining factor for our overall identity. The nation-state is a remarkably powerful force for telling us who we are; by education, by a culture that has been shaped along national lines, by learning from our elders, we always think of ourselves as most fundamentally defined by our national identity. But theologically that is just the problem: in Christ there is neither Jew nor Greek, and that prophetic claim qualifies our contemporary political categories' application to our lives as well. Political powers often tempt us to see ourselves exhaustively in political categories, and thereby to reenact in our lives the factitious divisions, however pragmatically valid they may be, that scar the face of the earth. Think about it — the United States gets upset when their citizens start thinking about having a passport from Canada, for God's sake; what's going to happen when the state hears that many of us also want to be known as citizens of the kingdom of God?

This could very easily become a demonizing polemic against nation-states. But I do not mean it to be. The liberal nation-state can legitimately request of citizens a genuine degree of commitment, and the Christian faith should allow, and indeed encourage, its adherents to offer that commitment. And besides, the fact that political entities *can* tempt us reveals that *we* can be tempted by them, so the sin lies more in us than in the state.

How can we be both Christians, part of a universal community, and citizens of some state or other? How can we have this sort of dual citizenship? And what does its duality mean for both communities? These are the questions driving this chapter. We will try to answer them through the language of the virtue of faith. As was the case with love, our capacity to inhabit this virtue is deeply challenged today, on two levels. First, faith faces the improper reduction of religious faith to the essentially this-worldly categories of our political world. That is, too often our faith becomes one small part of who we are, and who we are is primarily understood in terms of essentially political categories. I am more American, or more Russian, or more French-Canadian, than I am Christian, and so my Christian identity finds its place under the canopy of the larger and more essential category of that political or ethnic identity. Second, the kind of integrity and depth that faith suggests in the person — the idea that we can have real and profound convictions that move us to act — is increasingly challenged in the conditions of the contemporary economy and culture, where the kind of "stickiness" of identity that real faith assumes is undercut by the socioeconomic structures we inhabit. If the conditions of modern political life tempt us toward the idolatry of absolute national fidelity — recall "my country, right or wrong" — the conditions of modern commercial and economic life tempt us toward the nihilism of complete and utter personal dissolution into a series of random and incoherent appetites. In both situations, true faith gets lost.

What can we do to cultivate faith in the face of these challenges? First we must understand why and how faith is so important to our identity. Then we can see how developments in political thought and institutions over the last three centuries, gathered under the name of "liberalism," offer an opportunity for faith to be seriously engaged in public life, in ways that strengthen both faith and public life. Third and finally, the chapter sketches the practices of faithful commitment that this account, in our setting, enables.

I begin with an old story, but one that can still be told.

I. Politics, Identity, and Sacrifice

Gaius Plinius Caecilius Secundus, known to history as Pliny the Younger, was appointed governor of Bithynia-Pontus, on the north coast of Asia Minor, in A.D. 111. Sometime in the fall of the following year he held an audience with some inhabitants of his province, who accused others resident there of blatant immorality and impiety — in short, of being Christian. In response to these charges, he brought the accused before him and tested those who did not admit to being Christian; he asked them to invoke the gods, make offerings to Trajan's statue, and revile the name of Christ. He seems to have thought these would be escalating tests — that some Christians would invoke the gods and/or offer sacrifices to the emperor, yet still refuse to revile Christ's name. But he found that it never got that far; the Christians simply refused to invoke the names of the gods or sacrifice to the emperor. Their God was a jealous God, who would condemn them for dallying with demons. Again and again Pliny sent unrepentant Christians to their death, notifying by letter the emperor of what he had caused to be done. And the emperor replied, by return post, approving of Pliny's moderation in persecution — but also approving the executions.

For states that expect quasi-religious fidelity from their subjects, Christians are a difficult people. This fact about Christians has been recognized from the Roman Empire onward. Indeed, the pagan critics of Christianity saw, often better than did the Christians themselves, that this new faith was radically opposed to the tight association of religion and a "people" that classical religion and civic life assumed. Christians' resistance to these sorts of commitments has troubled many political thinkers since the Caesars. Even modern thinkers like Rousseau worried that Christianity poisons, subverts, and/or dissipates the civic energies necessary for the health of any civic order. Aren't Christians ultimately more committed to their God than the civic order we all share? Won't they impose their faith on everyone? Don't they inevitably try to use all this-worldly activity for their otherworldly aims? Such questions, asked by many in different ways today as always before, remind us that the state remains, after all, a jealous God, and often looks on any and all of its citizens' extrapolitical allegiances with suspicion and tacit animus.

Yet in fact, Christians are very civically engaged, and usefully so, but they are not so engaged always on the polity's own terms. Study after sociological study shows that church attendance leads to deeper civic engagement. So some thinkers today consider religion a source, perhaps the most powerful source, of civic commitment; for them religion is a good thing because of its functional value as encouraging social cohesion. Many would agree with William Galston that "[t]he greatest threat to children in modern liberal societies is not that they will believe in something too deeply, but that they will believe in nothing very deeply at all."

Many share this worry because they have come to share a sociological concern about the moral dangers of liberalism. Liberalism's typical strategy of resistance to the absolutizing tendencies of modern politics is to instill in its citizens' souls an oscillation between confidence and self-doubt. But while this oscillation helps to disrupt the confident monologue of totalitarians, it may also undermine liberal citizens' confidence in their own moral convictions, and thus enervate their own moral energies. But they need those moral energies to defend themselves and their communities against enemies both foreign (such as totalitarianism) and domestic (such as moral apathy). Hence liberal societies benefit from, and may need, strong communities of people who have languages that vigorously resist liberalism's characteristic kind of corrosive self-criticism. A wise liberal polity will recognize that it has need of communities that propagate fundamentally nonliberal (or even illiberal) forms of faith. And traditionally, liberal states have done this, through practices that insulate the churches from the state, such as the exemption of religious institutions from taxation and the historical practice of recognizing conscientious objection as fundamentally deriving from one's religious convictions. In these ways religions perform valuable service for the state, service that the state can, in some relatively direct way, acknowledge and honor.

This is one way religion can be seen as useful for civic cohesion. We might call this the "Eisenhower strategy," for its general attitude is encapsulated in President Dwight D. Eisenhower's (in)famous claim, "our government has no sense unless it is founded in a deeply felt religious faith and I don't care what it is." It has not gone away since Eisenhower; in a poll conducted in January 2001, of those who wanted religion to have a more influential role in the United States, 76 percent didn't care which religion it was.

Such enthusiasm aside, the state remains, I submit, structurally suspicious of Christian political engagement. (The fact that in the U.S. setting churches get along so well with the state system is not evidence to the contrary, but rather evidence of certain failures of the American churches, and certain proper kinds of restraint on the part of the U.S. state and other liberal states, as I will explain later in this chapter.) After all, Christians claim to be citizens of another polity, and their care about politics seems to have roots that run to other sources of nourishment than the rich soil of the state or motherland. Jason Bivins has coined the term "political illegibility" to describe the problem with some Christian political activity; on his reading, such activity may seem not intelligible within the received political categories, hence menacingly opaque for those working with the received political vocabulary. And states tend not to look fondly on what they cannot comprehend.

On the other side, those communities will often, precisely because of the strength of their moral commitments, never be wholly comfortable with the liberal condition. Their sheer existence reminds the polity that the liberal state's claim on them is not the highest claim that a human can feel. They will exist in an unsettled but relatively stable truce with the liberal condition of society as a whole. Perhaps thinkers like Rousseau are right: an ineliminable tension, sometimes outright conflict, exists between Christian faith and totalizing civic commitment of the sort that is the gravitational tendency of political states. Neither readily allows its demands to be subordinated to the other.

Recall the definition of faith we gave earlier: to have faith means to be *determined,* in two senses: as regards one's convictions — to be confident and persevering in them — and as regards one's identity — in the sense of moving from an indeterminate and amorphous sense of self to a more definite, determinate sense. Our "faith" defines us, gives us a determinate identity, which is manifest in the confidence with which we hold and express our convictions.

To talk about faith is to use a language of the self and its "god," to what or whom the self sacrifices. In an explicitly political register, it refers to that thing to which you organize your values and in terms of which you understand your relations with other people. Recall the discussion of authority in the previous chapter: What are you willing to kill for, or die for — what, in fact, would be a kind of death for you if you lost it? In answering this question you uncover your deepest authorities. Analogously, to talk about your faith is to begin to talk about whom or what you worship — what it is you sacrifice to. For sacrifice, of some sort, is always at the heart of faith. "Sacrifice" means, first of all, to lose something, to accept a cost for some other good, to suggest that that cost was worth it. But it is more than that — for the etymological root of sacrifice is "to make a sacred offering," to consecrate something for a holy end. Sacrifice reveals not only what you are willing to give up, but also, because of the end implied, what you are *not* willing to give up. That is what Pliny, and his Christian interlocutors, dimly comprehended, and why both of them agreed that the issue was a matter of life or death. Emperor or God: How can you have two masters? Your faith must be with one or the other, ultimately — mustn't it?

Faith is so basic to us, in short, because of the kind of creatures we are, and sacrifice, properly understood, is intrinsic to the idea of faith itself. One of our deepest characteristics as humans is our desire for self-understanding, for identity — here meaning the story we tell others and ourselves about who we are. And we want that identity to be stable and secure; it cannot be constantly in need of reconstruction, for it is the foundation on which we act in our larger projects of building a life. Our identity is not ever fixed, and one of the most characteristic truths about a life is that many "outward" projects — childhood, education, career, family — are also "inward" projects, a series of testable hypotheses about who I am, and experiments in living in a certain way to see if indeed I am that person — if I can live as, or at least with, the "me" so constructed. Yet even at this level of existential experimentation, not everything is up for grabs: everyone assumes, in some sense, a "me" that is there to be "discovered" or "invented" (at this level the vocabularies amount to pretty much the same thing), and more fundamentally still, the idea of a project of self-determination is also assumed. So, curiously, the project of self-understanding itself is never an all-encompassing investigation without remainder, so to speak. For that project to get under way and be sustained, we need to hold certain truths self-evident, as it were, at least to ourselves. And we will sacrifice other things, and aspects of ourselves, on the altar of those self-evident truths.

Yet there is a problem: no such stability is available. There is no clear sense of a final, authentic self we find in this world. Or rather, there *is* such a self, but it is multiple and plastic. We "find" our authentic selves many times over the course of life: in marriage (perhaps, today, even multiple marriages), in careers (can you feel different "vocations" at different stages of your life?), certainly in friends and family (we talk of "outgrowing" our friends, or of once being "too young" to appreciate the wisdom of many of our elders). Any final self — any stable self at all — is only achieved by including some things and excluding others. It is, in a way, a technology of control, and often a very narrowing technology — eliding much of reality to tell a narrow story. The experience of contemporary life is increasingly volatile and turbulent. Both in our personal relations with others as friends, lovers, spouses, or neighbors and in our work life, where we are likely to change not just jobs but careers several times in our life, the way we live puts new pressures upon our sense of stable selfhood. We may not recognize this, or we may try to ignore it, but that is partly because the language of authenticity is a jealous God, and will not let us (or better: we will not let ourselves) see that earlier movements of our lives "felt right" in the same way that this one does. An existential amnesia about previous versions of ourselves is the compliment that our vice of apocalyptic presumption pays to the virtue of sincerity.

Some people take this instability to reveal the illusory nature of a search for an authentic or "true" self. After all, if each of these is authentic, what evidence do we have that they are progressively *more* authentic? (And what would "progressively more authentic" mean here in any event?) Furthermore, what evidence do we have that alternative choices would have been less authentic had we made them? We have no evidence for either of these beliefs, say proponents of this view, and so we should jettison the register of authenticity altogether. Who we are is one damn thing after another, and the idea that we are in quest of our true selves is a project of fiction, not fact. The mild (and, such voices say, temporary) disorientation that accepting this truth entails is, for its proponents, well worth the benefits that come with forgoing the need to wring our hands incessantly over our authenticity, like some wildly bearded anarchist in a nineteenth-century Russian novel, silly and profound in equal measure.

I assume that most readers of this book can feel — probably have felt — the attractions of this view. But if you're reading this book, I assume you have also so far managed to avoid succumbing to it. That is a good thing. For in fact, its advocates are better marketers than therapists. Their proposal asks us to forgo something that is quite hard to forgo, namely, our desire to make sense out of the shape of our life — to tell an intelligible story about it. In fact, I would argue that this desire is impossible to jettison, and those who urge us to jettison it invariably indulge in just the sort of autobiographical orientation that their views disavow as bad faith.

Yet the view does recognize an important truth, which is: no such story will be acceptable to us, because every such story is one told *in via*, as we ourselves are still *in via*, and the voyage we are on does not end before death, at least. Those who hold the above view wish us to focus on the impossibility of completing this task, and then to use our recognition of that impossibility to warrant tossing the whole project overboard. That seems hasty, to say the least. The fact that completion of this project is impossible does not at all undermine our sense of urgency in going about it. That not everyone, and practically no one, can play the cello like Pablo Casals speaks not at all to each cellist's obligation, felt or otherwise, to practice daily. Futility does not subvert obligation. "Cannot" does not imply "ought not."

The critics are so vehement about this for a good reason: they have seen the damage that bad identities can do, to individuals, groups, nations, and even the world. For we are profoundly tempted to silence the instabilities of the self — to close ourselves off to the idea that we may one day be different from who we are at present, and no less ourselves. We obscure that fact with stories about ourselves that deny our indeterminacy. And more often than not, among those truths are ones with an origin in our political communities. Politics gives us identity — it is orienting, a way of seeing the world; faith gives us a world and a self.

Our political identity is only a part of our identity, and often it is itself composed of a complex of subidentities. We can have multiple political identities; I can be an American and a Southerner, a Californian and a Native American, an African American and a New Yorker. A citizen of Belgium may feel simultaneously a Walloon, Belgian, and European. A Canadian may be any number of things. All these identities are complex. *But they matter to us,* in a way matched by none of the other communities of which we are members — the companies we work for, the sports teams we play on, the circle of friends we have, even the churches in which we worship. At their narrowest, such political identities serve as the ultimate end of our political activities. They make their own security and self-promotion into the ultimate aim to be politically advanced; they make us into their servants, rather than the other way around. Our identity today is crucially composed by political realities.

Because any such identity involves a series of sacrifices, to have one identity is to close off others. Insofar as an identity determines us, it does so in crucial ways by forbidding us the characteristics available in other identities. To define is to delimit, to restrict — to reduce an indeterminate self to a determinate but quite lessened self. Furthermore, the identities our polities offer us are contrastive, requiring some other identity to explain itself. If there is an "us," there must be a "them."

In fact, what is true about identity-formation in general is even more true about political identity-formation: political identity needs others, and those others are easily seen as enemies. Because of this, these political identities are importantly false (and encourage self-deception), reactionary, and essentially estranging. Our political identities are altogether too much about who we are *not* — about our *not* being something else. The desire for purity in one's identity generally comes down to a resistance to allowing or acknowledging certain commonalities or affinities with some other group or groups. In this sense, all politics is identity politics, a practice meant to tell us who we are by telling us who we are *not*. (That this tells us little in the way of a positive identity is just the cost we are willing to bear, to be able to believe that we know who we are.)

Recall that I defined faith earlier as being determined toward some end. But as I hope is now clear, such "determination" has its own dangers. There can be multiple versions of ourselves, and our determination as one person in particular, with one configuration of a social or political identity, inevitably reduces the self, causes the loss of parts of us that have, to all appearances, just as good a claim on being "truly" us as the parts that we affirm. What is worse, the reduced self can ossify into the apocalyptic determination of presumptuousness — a conviction that we know already who we will fully and finally be, who we will ultimately become. More precisely, here I think the sin lies in our own warped desire to be a certain kind of thing — to have a certain kind of identity, a final, definitive, and *apocalyptic* identity, one that will render us — at last! — impervious to the imperative of history to keep changing, to never be the same. Yet this is not just a fantasized understanding of identity, but a reactionary one, for not only is it not what we are at present, it is not even an accurate picture of what we will be; rather, it is just another form of resentment, our resentment at the fact that we want to rival God and cannot do so. The problem of political idolatry, then, is part of the larger problem of idolatry, which in turn is the problem of our apocalyptic impatience to *be* the people we will be only at the end of days. We feel this temptation, and we feel it *as* a temptation, because we know we are incomplete, and we feel that our incompletion is bad, imperfect, a vacuum that needs filling; much of our manic activity is driven by our panicked recognition that we need to do something to be a self. Bad faith is a form of false closure, a pseudoresolution of our inescapable human openness, in this life.

Given this picture of the relationship between identity, faith, and politics, and the temptations toward bad faith that inevitably beset us in this life, what advice can Christianity offer?

II. Rendering unto Caesar

Return to this chapter's inaugural question: Do we owe something to the polities we inhabit? Christian thinkers today typically offer two bad positions, a too-simple collaboration or a too-facile opposition. Both are tempting, but both are deeply flawed.

One group answers yes, we do: our civic identity is as fundamental to us as our religious identity; we are created to worship God and to live in political society, and this latter facet of our lives underwrites our obligation to the polities we inhabit. For such thinkers the two identities are essentially complementary, each needing the other for its own fulfillment. The other group answers no, we do not: the state is a demonic entity that cannot but rival God, and sets itself up as a Power in institutionally direct opposition to God. For such thinkers "Christian" is an identity that contests exactly the same space — politically, psychologically, and existentially — as "Canadian" or "American." Like Reverend Mapple in Melville's *Moby Dick*, these thinkers say the true Christian "acknowledges no law or lord, but the Lord his God, and is only a patriot to heaven." We cannot serve two masters, so inevitably and ultimately we must choose between these two.

Obviously both sides have strong arguments and solid evidence from both Scripture and tradition to support them. But both affirm half-truths, so neither is fully adequate.

Those who offer an unqualified yes, who recognize that our world needs ordering, focus on continuities. For them, God works through the found conditions of our world to govern our world as best it can be governed. But they make two missteps. First, they threaten to naturalize the given political structures — an act that always stands in danger of baptizing the status quo as God's ultimate will. That is, they do not sufficiently recognize that such forces and institutions are not simply superficially inflected with sin; in this world political states inevitably participate in the entropy of self-love and come to expect to be worshiped. Furthermore, they make a theological error in assuming states were part of God's prelapsarian order — so that, had Adam and Eve not sinned, mankind would yet have developed states. This allows too little seriousness to the moral calamity of the fall and the distance between where we are, religiously and morally speaking, and where we were meant to be. For such thinkers sin complicates life, makes it more difficult, but life itself remains largely continuous with what it was meant to be. Here the fall is essentially a consoling doctrine — we have screwed up, to be sure, but that works mostly to excuse our mistakes. The cosmos as a whole is not radically flawed, and our received patterns of thought and behavior can proceed without too radical transformation. They ignore the lesson of Scripture, tacit in Genesis, that it was Cain who built the first city, after murdering his brother Abel (Gen. 4:17).

Those who offer an unqualified no certainly recognize the moral calamity of the fall. For them the state — perhaps the world itself, at least as we find it — is intrinsically demonic. They wisely see that a world ruled by violence is in some fundamental way in opposition to God's will, and that the fall has had a devastating effect not just on our individual agency, but on our relationships with one another and on the whole human world wherein we live, move, and have our being. But they go too far, and yet again ironically render the fall a kind of consolation. For they preemptively conclude from this that any and every collusion with such forces of violence can serve no other end than the further rebellion of humanity — that there is no way in which humans or God can use this system for other, more wholesome ends. If those in the first camp offer a consolation based in complacency, partisans of this latter camp suggest a consolation based in despair. The world as a whole is just wrong, and any involvement in it that colludes in its existence is quite literally bad faith.

I can imagine someone asking: What's wrong with these views being consoling? What's wrong with consolation? I mean something quite precise. They are consoling in the sense that they imply that we needn't worry that our understanding of our world or ourselves will be radically challenged and may well significantly change.

For example, both proposals are consoling insofar as they accept credulously the received opinion that something relatively autonomous called "the church" eternally stands in some sort of complicated relationship (either opposing it or informing it) with something relatively distinct from that church, something we designate as "the world." But this distinction is a subeschatological one, as it were — not so much a perpetual structure of reality as a defining characteristic of the era we inhabit, before the eschaton. That is to say, the church/world divide is a factical one, contingent upon the accidental configurations of our fallen world, not an ultimate, theological division. What we call "the church" is destined to be creation itself, and so it does not need the category of "the world" as its conceptual alternative; that would be to define itself against a passing phenomenon, and to grant that phenomenon altogether too much theological significance.

This theological failing has manifest practical effects. Because both sides accept this absolutization of the categories of "church" and "world," neither can recognize the dynamic and tension-laden gap between the way the world (both "church" *and* what they call "world") presently is and the eschatological kingdom of God. Because of this, neither of these accounts demands of the faithful the kind of alertness to the texture of our changing context, and sensitivity to its ever-modulating demands on us, that we ought to inhabit. This is consoling because it tells us that we need not *look and see* what is going on. Nor do either of these admit that in any real way believers may well change their understanding of the meaning of their faith. Both indulge our sinful presumption that we understand fully, and finally, what we say we believe, and so have reached a certain kind of conclusion. We do not admit to ourselves that we live in history, and are thus ourselves bound to change. We ignore John Henry Newman's famous adage, that "In a higher world it is otherwise, but here below to live is to change and to be perfect is to have changed often."

Instead of such escapist, consoling views, we should affirm something like the following: we do owe something to the polities we inhabit. But the conditions under which Christian faith warrants this political fidelity are qualified, as chapter 3 tried to make clear. These qualifications will leave the secular authorities unsatisfied and possibly a bit nervous, and they will leave believers with a considerable amount of work to do, to determine what sort of support and service a particular polity warrants. But it is the proper stance for Christians to take.

Polities exist to provide order, or to restrain disorder. Part of order, internally essential to it, is justice. What is justice? Justice is the condition in which all get their due — what we may call, at least in part, respect. But this respect is *not* the indifference of mere "toleration." True respect is more a matter of challenging others than simply consenting to their views without contesting them. We participate in God's work by supporting the goals of order and justice, primarily (though not exclusively) *through* the polities we inhabit. Yet we do this not on the terms or for the reasons that the polity asks us to. Our account depicts the polity as serving God's purposes, not its own ends. The polity is not its own final cause. So Christians' civic fidelity is anchored in religious fidelity; it is not a matter of separate sources of legitimacy, such as God's "natural" will to create and sustain and God's "supernatural" will to redeem and sanctify. They seek the welfare of their cities, so to speak, out of fidelity to God.

Jesus offers us something of an account of this with the story of Caesar's coin. When Jesus replies to the Pharisees, "Render to Caesar the things that are Caesar's, and to God the things that are God's" (Matt. 22:21), one can understand this statement as, in part, challenging the terms on which the question is put. It is crucial to keep in mind, Jesus seems to be saying, the distinction between what is rightfully Caesar's and what is rightfully God's. This may at first sound impious, as if they are on the same level; but then, second, Jesus implies that they cannot be; so Caesar is and always will be subservient to God (and it was because the Christians believed that, and acted on it, that the Romans persecuted them). Yet it is Caesar's face upon the coin, hence we should allow some secondary and subsidiary voice wherein Caesar may make claims on us, within a certain realm, if Caesar is willing to inhabit that realm, and no other. The key here is Caesar's *relative* autonomy and legitimacy, an autonomy and a relativity expressed by the framing of the two obligations in one sentence. As Oliver O'Donovan puts it, the story means to reject "the view that Jesus assigned Roman government a certain uncontested sphere of secular right." Any claim to authority that Caesar puts forward, that is, is open to skeptical challenge. Jesus' saying injects instability into politics; the rule is, that there is no rule, no fixed maxim, no settled percentage to be doled out to each. The relationship between them, so clear in theory, must be continually readdressed and reconfronted in practice.

Extending, hopefully not too far, this reading of Jesus' words, we may say that while the state may be a tacit rival to God, such claims as it makes on our fidelity can be resisted and the state can be a force for good, for order and decency — at least for a restraining justice, and occasionally for the more constructive purpose of promoting some good.

It took a few centuries for this vision of politics to become visible for Christians. The New Testament writers, it seems, were caught up with apocalyptic expectations and were almost exclusively concerned with cultivating the eschatological community of believers; their attitude toward the state was either a quietist acquiescence (as in Romans 13 and 1 Timothy 2:1-2, which commands Christians to pray for government, "that we may live a quiet and peaceful life") or apocalyptically renunciatory, even resentful (Revelation). Here, the New Testament writers seemed to be saying, we have no lasting city, so we should look for the city to come; more reflection on the details of this passing age, they imagined, was just a waste of what little time they had left. Only when these apocalyptic expectations began to recede did thinkers reincorporate the Old Testament's vision of sojourning in a foreign land, and seeking the welfare of the city, in a new vision of Christian citizenship that became most articulate with Augustine. This deepening Christian political vision was part of a wider appreciation of the goodness of God's creation and a recognition of our obligations for its sustenance. Christians accept the call to love God without reserve, and in loving God they are to love the world.

This reading of this passage is contestable, of course. And the kind of commitment it suggests can sound tepid, and inadequate both politically and theologically. Does this provide a political community's members with sufficient motivation to fight, kill, and die for their polity? Don't you need more vehement, more absolute, forms of commitment than this allows? Many political thinkers would agree. And to be sure, in earlier ages political rulers may have been unquestionably right, by their own lights, to be disappointed with Christianity's merely provisional granting of authority to them. Fortunately for us, however, on its own self-understanding, the modern liberal-democratic state can properly ask for no more than this. It is the purpose of the next section to explain why.

III. The Distinction of Church and State

The lesson of the above is simple. Political communities are inevitably possessed by pretensions toward thinking of themselves as the ultimate homes of, and the defining frames for, their inhabitants, implicitly expecting those inhabitants to see their individual good as inextricably associated with, then indistinguishable from, and finally subservient to, the good of the "larger" institutional order. This is an old lesson in political life — as old as the Israelite prophets (think of Nathan before David) and the Greek tragedians (think of *Antigone*). So far we may say, no surprises: there is nothing new under the sun.

But perhaps, once in a long while, there is something new. And if modernity has a claim for genuine novelty, it lies not in technological progress but here, in its political innovations: for over the past few centuries, first in Europe and then beyond, institutional forms have arisen that resist, in important ways, the pretensions gripping previous political structures. We name these institutional forms "liberal democracy." Liberal democracy develops the crucial claim that the individual is in important ways superior to the state, and creates a viable political environment for this view to flourish. An appreciation of the institutional structures, and the politico-moral cultural ecology of liberal democracy, helps Christians think politically in a more dialectical and ambivalent fashion, beyond simplistic stances of unadulterated affirmation or blanket condemnation.

Now, in talking about "liberalism" in this way, I appreciate that I am taking sides in a very long and ugly battle, and employing a word commonly used in diverse — indeed, incompatible — ways. Some think "liberalism" is structurally and essentially hostile to human flourishing. Others think everyone should be liberals, as it is the inevitable destiny of all mankind. I tend to agree with thinkers such as Lionel Trilling and the John Stuart Mill of the essays on Bentham and Coleridge (and perhaps of *On Liberty*), who recognize that what they call "liberalism" can be a good thing, but that it cannot, even on its own terms, be allowed a complete and uncontested imaginative and psychological sovereignty over our souls. I suggest that, while we may accept liberalism as a political reality, with its own blessings (and challenges), it cannot become our sole cultural reality.

There is a complicated story to tell about the intermingled rise of liberal-democratic theories and vocabularies, on the one hand, and the institutional emergence of the modern nation-state, on the other; I will not try to tell it here. The modern nation-state is a remarkably powerful and unprecedented institutional reality in the world history of politics. It creates a very powerful nation and state — the former by encouraging nationalist sentiments, thereby tightening the associational bonds among its inhabitants, and the latter by strengthening the state's institutions, extending their reach across society and centralizing the sources of power and legitimate authority within its hierarchical structure. To generate the power to do these things nation-states necessarily relied on free markets, which inevitably gave other nonstate actors wealth and power that in turn emboldened them to resist the political sovereign. This led to a complex struggle between these rival powers, in order to work out the rights and duties of all the parties. These struggles lasted centuries, and out of them, in some places, emerged liberalism, or more precisely the liberal state.

Liberalism embodies a genuine advance in our political imagination in modernity — the political idea that the state is a stopgap, not a failed church (or even less a successful one). This idea has a very old theological provenance, going back to the New Testament anxieties about empire, but only in the eighteenth century does it emerge in explicitly *political* discussions. Liberal democracy recognizes and is troubled by the absolutist claims that most political structures throughout history made upon their inhabitants, and acknowledges the deepening of this problem due to the rising power and reach of states in the sixteenth and seventeenth centuries. Out of this recognition, one of the main tasks liberal democracy takes on is to resist the state's encroachment on human identity, both institutionally and conceptually.

The liberal state is self-limiting in two ways. First, it is structurally self-limiting, both due to its belief in the importance of having a written constitution and due to its cultural commitment to the "rule of law," to the idea that *no one*, not even the political authorities themselves, is properly not subject to the constitution. This permits both a judiciary insulated from direct control by the sovereign and externalized legal basis for sovereignty, against the state's potentially limitless claim to absolute rule.

Second, and to my mind more ambivalently, the state is self-limiting conceptually as well, by expressly insisting on the inviolability of the individual person. This is conceptualized differently — for example, in terms of conscience or privacy — but it is essential. This has condensed over the past century into the liberalism of privacy, the idea that individuals have at their core the right not to be controlled by another, that not just politically but in more extreme formulations metaphysically they are to be left alone to create themselves.

The liberalism of privacy and the more simply laudable insistence on individual inviolability both emerge from a core suspicion at the root of liberalism, a suspicion about the potential of any and every political (and by extension, cultural) system to reduce people to a role in some immanent system of political or cultural power — that is, to say that people are "nothing but" their function or role in some system. Liberalism calls such reductionisms "totalitarianisms," and has set itself from its beginnings against them. Whether the nascent and primitive totalitarianism of the divine right of kings, the wholly modern and awesomely powerful totalitarianism of communism and National Socialism, the narrow but dagger-sharp totalitarianism of fundamentalist terror, or the thin and dimmed-down totalitarianism of absolute marketization — totalitarianism is what liberalism fears and sets itself up to oppose. This "totalitarianism" is, in religious terms, precisely the absolutization and theologization of the state, its tendency to begin to present itself as a god to its inhabitants. To counter that, liberalism requires strong citizens able to resist the state's siren song of absolutization. And clearly, for all its faults, religion has been *the* source of such rival energies. Healthy liberal societies recognize this and understand themselves as necessarily drawing strength from those nonliberal, even illiberal, religious traditions that their citizens confess, and try not to draw them into liberalism's too-warm embrace; for that is death for them, and then for liberalism too, in the long run. (The toleration, even nourishment, of nonliberal communities in a liberal polity is one of liberalism's defining characteristics.)

So since the liberal state should, by its own lights and on its own principles, recognize and honor the nonliberal religious traditions of its citizens, perhaps in return this understanding of liberal political society should be wholeheartedly supported by Christians, since it so clearly needs their involvement.

Unfortunately this is not so. Christians cannot simply accept and endorse the liberal case for traditional Christian belief and take it on board without any trouble; to do that would lead inexorably to the absolutization of the language of political liberalism itself, something Christians should not permit (nor, on its own lights, should political liberalism). Furthermore, because of the provisionally absolutist nature of the Christian language, that would allow Christianity to be "placed" subservient to another way of looking at the world — namely, the "liberal" one. Christians should not be good citizens for the good it does the liberal state; they should be good citizens because it is part of God's calling to us in this time and place to be such.

But what about liberal worries that Christianity can be totalizing in just the way that liberals fear? That may be a danger. But the totalization is crucially different, because it injects an eschatological leaven into the mix, insisting on the "not yet" character along with the "now." So Christians stand in a complex relation with this liberalism, supporting its suspicion of and hostility to apocalyptic determinations by worldly powers yet insisting on the ultimate truth of one such determinism, albeit one whose final application is eschatologically deferred.

Christians have good reasons to be critical of much of what passes for "liberal" political thought and language today. Some thinkers have attacked the modern notions of privacy, individualism, and associated concepts as conceptually incoherent, morally pernicious, and theologically impious. They complain that these categories seduce their users into accepting a radically autistic "interiorism," encourage a moral egoism, and insinuate an essentially Pelagian picture of God's relation with the world. I think these charges convey a great deal of truth; after all, the concept of privacy is rooted etymologically in the Latin word *privatio*, privation, which for much of the Christian tradition is the defining ontological mark of evil.

But the attacks can be pressed too far, and leave us bereft of the valuable work these resources do for us, or — as is more likely — leave us unable to acknowledge how we rely on these resources even if only provisionally, and so plunge us into a situation of bad faith, which is always to be avoided.

Strategically it is better to exploit these liberal languages, for they are practically quite useful. First of all, liberal democracy shifts the locus of political sovereignty from the ruler or the political community to the individual humans who populate that community. Complaints that in modernity humans have been taught to be fundamentally selfish, to not think beyond their own parochial good, may be true, but this was not the intended effect of the transposition of the locus of sovereignty, of the fundamental political subject, from the ruler to the people. That intended effect — and the accomplished one — was to undercut the prince's, or king's, claim to be the anchor of politics. Individualism has many pernicious effects, but no one today will deny that it had the rather large benefit of acknowledging that the selfishness of the many is at least far better than the many being ruled by the selfishness of the one. (And the fact that we universally agree with this sentiment is itself part of its success — it provoked a revolution in our values as much as if not more than in our institutions.)

Second, liberal democracy teaches that the nation is not the summum bonum, not the final frame of any human's moral identity. Liberal states explicitly and intentionally resist the tendency toward theo-political idolatry, a tendency that can only end in a state's conversion into, in Robin Lovin's phrase, a "failed church." The reach of our moral vocabulary has historically outstretched the reach of our political identity (so that we could have obligations to those who were not part of our polity, for example), but liberalism was the first to pay serious attention to this disjunction and make it a foundational part of political imagination. The liberal imagination recognizes that the comprehensive human good should not be sought centrally in, or pursued directly through, the arena of politics. Liberal states implicitly recognize in their institutional structures that they are fundamentally designed to manage wholly mundane problems and projects; they are the first political institutions explicitly to acknowledge the peril of the (perhaps necessary) theological pretensions of politics, and they seek structurally and institutionally to eschew the theo-political ambitions inevitably latent in political life itself.

Naturally this acknowledgment is a theoretical one, often violated in practice: while citizens and governors of these states may have more theological or eschatological ambitions for their political communities, the institutional structures are designed to stymie the implementation of those ambitions, and to vex their political development in the first place. This means that built into liberal political institutions is a negative, critical function at least as deep as its positive, constructive one. As the American political thinker Ian Shapiro has said, liberal democratic states are institutions designed not so much to *achieve* goals as to *hinder rule* — the subordination of some by others.

Historically, these institutions and civic-cultural developments first appeared in the seventeenth and eighteenth centuries, in the Netherlands and Great Britain. But the United States is the first state designed from the beginning to be less than the sum of its parts, designed *not* to be a failed church, but a device for managing the complexities and conflicts of life, for allowing its citizens to get on with the pursuit of flourishing life, and for giving them a way of participating in public life that would be part of the flourishing life. It was designed to restrain sovereignty in order to short-circuit what history had taught the Founders was the government's inevitable aggrandizement of power. As James Madison said, "[t]he great desideratum in Government is such a modification of the Sovereignty as will render it sufficiently neutral between the different interests and factions, to control one part of Society from invading the rights of another, and sufficiently controuled [*sic*] itself, from setting up an interest adverse to that of the whole Society." This is why, for example, the Constitutional Convention refused to make George Washington king, when that was what many of the people — including some of the Founding Fathers — wanted. This is what Abraham Lincoln was urging on his audience when he called America the "almost-chosen people." The aim is to resist the all-too-human desire to worship something palpable and large — something like the idea of America itself.

The United States may be the first state so conceived, designed to honor individuals in this distinctly liberal way. But America's culture works against this institutional anti-apocalypticism, and has been doing so almost from the beginning. Even in the Founders' own time, their elite vision of an enlightened and moderate citizenry, informed by cool reflection on their interests rather than driven by their passions, was a minority view. And since their era, American civic life has become far more populist, religious, and vigorously polemical — more like a punk rock concert than the minuet that some of the Founders imagined. Much of the history of the United States has been about a struggle between the institutions and the people living within them, with both sides changing and neither wholly in the right.

Understanding the "back story" to our contemporary situation offers us some helpful conceptual and institutional resources to understand how to be a citizen and not put absolute faith in the political order. But how, precisely, are we to do that?

IV. Confessing Citizenship

In fact, Christians are particularly well suited to participate in public life in ways that will benefit both their polities and their spiritual development, and modern liberal democratic states make it even more suitable. Both Christian and liberal political thought recognize that civic life is fraught with deep and abiding tensions, and both traditions, at their best, refuse to offer false pseudoresolutions to those tensions. Christian faith goes further than most liberal political thought, I would argue, in suggesting that those tensions are not only deep and abiding but also potentially productive. By living into their rival theological and political fidelities, Christian citizens can enrich their political life and deepen their faith. And because contemporary civic life in liberal democracies is surprisingly structurally welcoming to those who wish to live in that tension, this is an especially good time to be a Christian citizen.

This section explains how to be such a citizen. First, it talks about how to be faithfully engaged for the good of one's polity; second, it talks about how Christians ought to think about identity more broadly still, and how their civic activity can help in their ascetical practices of identity constitution. Central to both is the practice of confession. The key is the concept of confession, and the consequential recognition that the citizen, qua citizen, exists *under judgment*. I explain what that means in what follows.

A. How to Be a Citizen

It is odd to look to Augustine for help on these matters. "Citizen" is not a category he would have understood to apply to the politics of his age. Historically he knew about citizenship, but he thought its age had passed. He thought in terms of subjects, not of citizens. So we must beware of applying his political thought directly to our world. Yet there is a way in which his thought helps us grasp the full meaning of liberal citizenship and, for Christian citizens, to connect it to deep theological and ascetical practices intrinsic to Christian faith. For to be a liberal citizen means to consider yourself *under judgment*, and the Christian narrative, as exegeted by Augustine, should cultivate such a mind-set in a powerful way.

Augustine basically understood politics — which he took to be the complicated ordering of public life at times by force — to be a consequence of the fall. It is not a vehicle for building the kingdom of God on earth, and if it is not that, he assumed, it can be nothing more than a remedial structure for securing some modicum of peace and relative justice in a fallen world, until Christ's return inaugurates the only truly just polity, the reign of God. Therefore the core civic virtues for Augustine are pretty passive: they revolve around instrumental commitment to the stability of the civic order, for the sake of the goods provided by that order, which are basically structure, security, and stability for the sake of the continuance of the churches' liturgical life. Whenever he speaks of politics, he continually returns to the dangers inherent in political life, the dangers of pride, idolatry, *glorying* in power, all of which get summarized for him by the phrase *libido dominandi* — and the vices and evil deeds that stem from them. All in all, Augustine's picture of the moral promise of politics is at best grimly minimalist.

But there is another side to Augustine's views. For life in this world can be led as a form of training in virtue for the life to come. And the civic virtues are themselves, in a way, the theological virtues in a strange land. Engagement in civic life — just like every other part of our ordinary, mundane lives — is fruitful for cultivating our character; engagement in the earthly city helps fit us for the heavenly city to come. This is the aspect of Augustine's thought we can develop further here.

We can begin by thinking about the precarious way in which we ought to inhabit the role of "citizen." Even today, on the terms of the liberal state itself, we should see it as an unstable and provisional category — one enabling some things and disabling others. On this interpretation liberal citizenship is not a kind of quasi-religious identity, not a total and absolute identification with some political community, outside of which one cannot imagine one's life. That would be a picture of citizenship where the person "within" the citizen is exhausted by her political identity, wholly identical with it. As we have seen, the liberal state shuns so total an identification. (The tradition of civic republican political thought, a significant undercurrent in modern political thought, is tempted to more directly affirm that equivalence, but even there not every civic republican theorist succumbs to that temptation.) Liberal citizenship is more basically a negative reality than a positive one, as liberals see politics as a necessity, not as an intrinsic good. A liberal citizen has as one of her duties the obligation to be a watchman, jealously guarding her rights and independence against the monarchic tendencies of the state, and even against her own wholesale reduction to the identity of "citizen" itself, by a too-total "politicization" of her identity. Liberal citizens are citizens, but only in part, and they insist that they are *more* than, and not just *other* than, citizens. (This is why politics can seem of secondary import in liberal societies.) Liberal citizenship takes up a category that has historically been a totalizing, absolutist one, and uses it to resist just those totalizing and absolutist tendencies in modern political life. Civically, the liberal citizen is in an endlessly tense relationship with the state, other citizens, and even herself, as all these entities act vigilantly upon and sometimes against the citizen. So the state always tends to encroach on her autonomy, but it not infrequently asks for her legitimate service; simultaneously, other citizens monitor her individual encroachments upon them and her usefulness to them as fellow guardians against the state; and she herself checks to see if she is doing right by protecting her individual existence from the state's tendency to make absolute claims on her. There is, then, a constant monitoring of various scales of commitment and autonomy, and in all these dimensions the citizen must be vigilant as regards both her own integrity and the integrity of her commitment to the polity. The liberal-democratic citizen exists *under judgment*, politically speaking, and cannot hide from that fact, because she knows she will be held to account in explicitly liberal-democratic terms for the quality of her vigilance against the enemies, foreign and domestic, of liberal democracy. Being so under judgment, the citizen must act accordingly.

But if she is a Christian citizen, she lives under *theological* judgment as well; theologically the citizen is under judgment because, simply as a citizen, she claims to share in sovereignty — to share in the absolute and bottomless well of the power to decide. While the hubris of the citizen, in claiming such sovereignty, is often overlooked, religiously it is hard to avoid; and religious citizens' particularly emphatic recognition of this hubris, among other traits, can make them especially beneficial for a polity.

Furthermore, Christian citizens not only complicate and enrich the liberal polity as individuals; they do so in their communal life as well. After all, they are members of another community to which they ascribe political import, a community that claims their allegiance as well, and in a higher and more total way than can the liberal state. And so Christian citizens appear not only as citizens but also, in an indirect and complicated way, at least in civil society, as assembled into churches. In this way religious faith constantly disrupts and disturbs the polity's tendency toward narcissistic idolatry. In civic terms, we can say that by splitting our loyalties, refusing to allow them slothfully to resettle on one worldly axis of value and privileging a radically different end over patriotism, churches and other religious associations constantly disrupt the polity's tendencies toward absolutism.

But there is another, better way to put this that is harder for the state to affirm, and that is this: the churches are social bodies whose existence is tacitly subversive of the human's institution-building desire in general. The church is founded by Christ; "we the people" have nothing to do with it. The Promethean pretensions of liberal polities — their conceit that the people are absolute masters — smack of a profound irreligiosity. In theological terms, we can see such absolutism as the setting up of a false idol. In some sense, even the liberal state still smacks of Babel for the church — an effort by humans to organize their lives in profoundly self-contained, and self-regarding, and self-mastering ways. Tacitly for those who cannot directly hear its good news, and hopefully explicitly for those who can, the churches are always a standing rebuke to the hubris at the heart of the human endeavor to live together without direct and immediate governance by the one true Sovereign.

In properly theological terms, the churches do this by understanding themselves not as something begun by humans ex nihilo, but as things begun by someone else — namely, God. The church's Declaration of Independence is the gospel, and its Fourth of July is Easter morning; but God gave the church the gospel, just as God raised Christ on Easter morning. The church as a community is not most fundamentally an enactment of human will, but of an enabling power that gives the church the will to go on, to continue to be the body of Christ on earth.

Most essentially, the church is a body that is self-consciously *under another's judgment*, namely, God's. The church is a communal activity of receiving God's judgment, of hearing God's word, spoken against its illusions and spoken for its improvement. The church is a community where dynamic human beings learn that their dynamism is not all there is, that their dynamism is enframed and enabled by their receptivity of God's gracious dynamism, a dynamism so profound that it even creates the conditions of its own reception in humanity. Part of what it means to learn to be the church is to learn to be a community standing under judgment, and to hear that judgment for what it is — in its condemnation of the community for its arrogance and straying from God and for its indifference and cruelty (which are the same thing) to all of humanity and all of creation; and in its affirmation of the community, despite its sins, as the place through which God has chosen to inaugurate the redemption of God's creation as a whole. To hear judgment, negative and positive, God's condemnation and God's mercy, is just to be the recipient of God's constitutive act of creating an audience for the divine word, in all the theological senses that that term connotes.

In itself this is a powerful thing. But the church may exemplify something that is powerful in new ways as well. The theologian Jennifer McBride has argued that the churches can serve as a powerful example in contemporary societies of a community that accepts moral responsibility, where most are fleeing it at all costs. The churches can model the right kind of being human by modeling what it means to be fallen, what it means to beg for forgiveness, and by doing so rendering the community it inhabits graciously capable of redemption. In our culture — a culture so powerfully terrified by moral fault that even Nietzsche would be surprised — such a model could serve no end of good.

But as sites of receptivity more fundamentally than activity, the churches are not simply rebukes; they exemplify a positive alternative as well. For their existence says that the polity's fantasized destiny, its teleology, is misunderstood theology — a real longing, but not in the way our political vocabulary will let us express. The churches proclaim, that is, that politics expresses extrapolitical longings. So Christian faith, lived vigorously in community, keeps politics honest, because the eschatological dimensions of such faith oppose the apocalyptic dimensions of politics, which must inevitably move in the direction of false (that is, idolatrous) consciousness. Faith lets us see that there are no "final solutions" in politics, that there is no end to politics, not in this life.

By doing this, faith keeps politics properly "political," and playful. One of the dangers of politics is its ineluctable tendency to draw people in and suffocate their belief that there is anything beyond or outside politics. Such suffocation causes two things to happen. First, people lose the sense of joy, the sense of the depth and richness of life, that should suffuse our existence today. Existence becomes a joyless struggle to defeat others, out of fear that lest you do, they will do the same to you — a kind of vicious parody of the Golden Rule. When life becomes nothing but getting and spending — or worse, seeking to obstruct another's getting and spending — all joy disappears. Second, anything becomes legitimate to get one's way. The collapse of all into politics means, inevitably, the collapse of any sense of a higher moral order, which would serve to hold our more ruthless tendencies in check.

This playfulness extends beyond the centrally political dimensions of our life. And politics helps in this expansion, because in politics we find that our commitments and positions are not, and cannot wholly and honestly be, identified with ourselves. They are not necessarily "personal," as *The Godfather* would have it; it's "business." The gap between ourselves and our views that this distinction gives us is useful for learning more from public life — yet still sufficiently relevant to our lives to encourage us to take from it lessons about our lives. Because of this, politics can serve as a useful forum for self-improvement, and can even deepen our faith. The next section explains how.

B. Politics' Ascesis for Faith: Confessing Our Identity

Politics benefits faith because — if it is openly, honestly, confessionally undertaken — the vexations of public life constantly remind us of our real condition, and the distance separating that present condition and the state we aspire to in the kingdom of heaven. For example, articulating the "faith-based" way we came to these views, publicly and nondefensively, has several advantages. In doing so, we are trying, as best we can, to be honest about how we came to these beliefs, confessing the contingent and fragile path whereby we reached our conclusions. This honesty may, one hopes, provoke others to recognize the contingent and fragile character of their own beliefs, and lead to a more humble and modest dialogue. But such political consequences are not to be counted on; we should do this rather for the way it makes us more humble about our own situation. Honest assessment of one's beliefs makes one aware of the deep precariousness of some of those beliefs — and also, and always, makes one aware of how narcissistic it is to imagine that one has gained these beliefs simply by one's own effort. They help one realize the gift-character of one's beliefs, indeed of one's entire mind.

Furthermore, and more importantly, the experience of confessing faith gives us an inescapable reminder of our tragic condition. For while such public expressions are meant to bring us together, to put us more in communion with one another, they not only do that but sometimes they also estrange us in important ways from one another; they teach us again that what I see as a suitable cause for believing in a policy, or a position, you see as noise, and what you see as evidence for a program of action, I did not see as evidence of anything at all. Public expression of belief teaches us over and over again the inescapable idiosyncracies of our minds; it reminds us that we are irreducibly ourselves, and by doing that it teaches us to be less impatient and to expect less immediate consensus and understanding from our interlocutor.

Finally, in these ways and others, confessing faith reminds us that we are not *wholly* faithful, that we have a long way to go before we can claim confidentially that we genuinely possess, and therefore truthfully represent, the faith we purport to proclaim and confess. Our beliefs are far more fragile than we imagine, and are marked by our own quirkiness in surprising ways. We cannot imagine that we have reached decisive resolution on these matters at any time. This is civic life's deepest ascesis for faith.

What practical difference do dialogue, humility, and awareness of the tragic condition make, and why are these in particular so important? They help faithful citizens honestly live out their identity. That is to say, genuine engagement in public life promotes honest recognition of our situation: we need to discern our stories, yet we cannot do so without having lived our full stories, so we are never properly in a situation to do so short of our final "determination" in death (and arguably not even there). While we face this perhaps most obviously and immediately in the political realm, in fact this is a general truth about human life. We should inhabit this condition gracefully, by acknowledging that determination, and faith, is our inescapable condition, yet not one over which we are our own masters. Our saving grace is that true faith, genuinely inhabited, is relational — faith in something outside ourselves. True relational faith directs, orients, and opens us, in a way that will be resolved only eschatologically. In the meantime we must learn to face the terror of an open, yet-to-be determined identity. As children, we go where we will; but when we have a mature faith, we will be girded and taken where we do not want to go.

How can we do that? Part of the answer that Augustine urged on us is to understand our faith as *in Christ*. When we have faith in Christ, we put our faith "in" another: in a person whose story we affirm, and it is determinate for us, though we do not fully know yet how it is determinate. We *participate in* Christ's "faith," Christ's relation to the Father, and so it is not finally our own wholly private faith, nor even the communal faith of the church; it is a genuine, achieved relation that the church can rely on, can trust. It is not my faith but Christ's faith, not my identity but the identity Christ enables me to have, that is crucial.

Here is one way to talk about how the sacrifice of Christ is the key to our own identity. What Christ gave up was not only life, but a whole self-understanding that was shown to be the wrong one — the false messianism expected by many of his disciples. Because Jesus is the one, true, and sufficient sacrifice for the whole world — inaugurated on the cross but consummated only at the end of time — we need not imagine that our identity requires us to undertake any sacrifice on our own. Instead we must try to copy that earlier sacrifice in our own lives, and thereby participate in it.

Furthermore, Jesus' own call for fidelity transfigures the idea of sacrifice itself, and through it, our identity. "It is mercy I desire, not sacrifice" (Matt. 9:13 and 12:7), he says, quoting Hosea; what he seems to mean is that God asks not for devotionals made of blood, but for expressions of fidelity and commitment that partake of the dynamic forgiveness that God enacts — a forgiveness that enlivens all of us in order to become something new in the future, to move beyond the stale husk of what we had been. This dynamic forgiveness is manifest in and through graceful acts of mercy to others, just as we receive God's acts of mercy to us. To be properly faithful is to continue in the path of discipleship, of following Christ, and this means partaking in Christ's sacrifice. Our faith is Christ's faith, and the core and primordial sacrifice of this faith is Christ's sacrifice, which we reenact by sacrificing the idea that we properly possess our final "true" identity even now. Our faith, and our identity, will be redeemed if we have faith in Christ's resurrection; our faith, and our identity, has an eschatological dimension.

Properly understood, then, faith, and the identity that it both confers and expresses, is truly possessed only in the eschaton. Until then all God offers us is the promise of a self, of an absolutely stable and secure identity. We go about our lives with a kind of "now and not yet" confidence: knowing we have been called into a new being and feeling that we have some provisional apprehension of what that new being is — but a sense ever-deepening as we strengthen our conviction that eye has not seen, nor ear heard, the fullness of that new mode of being. This faith serves as a check on our other loyalties, ensuring that we do not expect them to stay the same, to remain unshriven, in the new creation into which we are entering. And we can do this, we believe, because of Christ, the firstfruits of that new creation, wholly accomplished, securing for us the promise of what will be. In grace we have confidence in a stability outside ourselves. This lets us keep our self-understanding open to quite serious revision, without simply jettisoning the idea of a real self.

The practice of self-exposure — of witness, if you will — required here is what Augustine described with his word *confessio,* or confession. Confession is a complicated term. First of all, it is a double confession — both a confession of one's sin and of praise of God — given to a double audience — composed both of God and of one's fellow humans. The primordial theological activity of confession, that is, is profoundly public and political. But this is not simply a new technique for political life; Augustine aims for an affective revolution that would transfigure politics. We must not think that "confession" here means what we typically take it to mean; it is not fundamentally an exhibitionism, the sort of thing ones sees in television talk shows, but is more an orientation than any communication of autobiographical data. In it we find ourselves *decentered*, no longer the main object of our purposes, but participating in something not primarily our own. This confession, then, is itself a turning to the other, not in the interests of mutual narcissism — which makes the other only a consolation prize for having to be already ourselves — but as an openness to transforming, and being transformed by, the other.

But "confession" for us means even more than the above. It also means to find yourself in Christ's story, so that your narrative gains meaning in the Gospel narrative and your life finds a role in the story the Gospels recount. Maybe you are like Peter, faithful but clueless, or Matthew, corrupted and knowing (and hating) it, or Martha, burdened with having a better sister, or Paul, holier than thou. Probably we are all of these people, and then some. But no matter: in finding a "place" in the story, you find a route to uncover deeper parts of yourself, revealed in the various characters' lives and responses to Jesus' call. On the other hand, it means to find Christ in your story — to come to understand your own life story as marked by Christ's mastery of your story, not only as an event in your story but also as the frame of it. Here you find the story as a God-haunted one, and you come to understand your desires, your struggles, and your failures as all shadowing a larger pursuit, Christ's pursuit of you, a pursuit that has revealed some tentative conclusion in the very act of finding this story as your own — but that also can now truly be lived, and truly begun.

A confessional identity has several relevant components. First of all, a confession is not a triumphalist genre. Originating in Roman law, the term *confessio* designated the act of publicly giving witness, before a court; it then gained the distinct connotation of the act whereby a martyr would give evidence of her faith — moving in this latter sense from merely verbal expression to the actual act of accepting and undergoing one's martyrdom. She who confesses today, then, is offering her story to another — not imposing it on another, but laying it at another's feet, for another's adjudication. Furthermore, she is presenting her testimony not as an author of that evidence, but more as a witness of it, more a bystander to the events than their instigator. To confess, then, is a humble act, and a humbling one. You do not pretend to know what your confession ultimately amounts to, or how it will count; you are simply trying to be as honest as possible about what was involved in your life. It is also an incomplete act of self-offering, for it elicits and waits upon the response of another. To understand oneself confessionally, then, is to understand oneself as attempting to explain oneself to another, as though one were a witness to one's life, without an absolutely privileged grasp of what that life means.

There are many things to say about confession as a mode of self-understanding. But for our purposes one crucial aspect of it is the way that such a confessional identity works to resist, on multiple levels, our humanly inescapable desire to judge, and ultimately to *be* the judge, to be the author of our own story, to be God. This is part of what the serpent offered Eve, the condition of being like God. It is one of our strongest temptations, actually inherent in our very mode of being after the fall: for to tell our story is to judge for ourselves what is our true story. But this judgment is inevitably presumptuous and duplicitous, for we change these stories with astonishing regularity and rapidity, though we never acknowledge that fact. The danger of this presumption is the danger of "knowing already" what I will ultimately be; it refuses to be open to the transforming presence of God's grace. This presumptuousness is, in Christian terms, perhaps the deepest and most pernicious form of sin that we possess — or that possesses us. We presume we are our own authors, because we presume that we are the root cause of ourselves, our own explanations, our own creators.

A confessional approach attacks this presumptuousness at its heart, and enables us to see our lives as much less intelligible than we usually think they are, both positively and negatively. Negatively, we are to come to see the absolute unintelligibility of our sinful lives as sinful: we must unlearn the false explanations we give of our corruption, and we must come to be shocked that we are as corrupted, as messed up, as we are — and we must come to be humbled and mournful about it. Positively, we should be bewildered by the sheer gratuitousness of our bare existence, by cultivating our recognition of our inability to explain our existence as "merited" by anything else: we must unlearn the false explanations of our existence, the stories we tell ourselves about how we got to be the way we are, and see our lives instead as a great gift to us, wholly unmerited by anything we have or could have done — and we must come to wonder in gratitude at the sheer gift of our existence. In undertaking this quest for greater self-understanding, we discover that instead we gain a deepened *in*comprehension of our lives, in a certain way: not a total disorientation, but an orientation toward mystery. Both our sins and our salvation are realities that we must learn to acknowledge, but not comprehend. In this new orientation we meet the surprises that invariably attend our life not fundamentally as threats against which we must be armored, but as gifts we must learn to accept.

Many worry that such a confessional mode of life simply provides theological legitimacy to the narcissism that seems so pervasive in our lives today, and reinforces a tendency that is already too widespread. There is a danger of such misuse here. But, as ever, something's *misuse* does not speak at all to its proper use; in fact, I would argue that this confessionalism, in its emphasis on humility about the self and openness to others' views about the self, is actually the great enemy of narcissism.

Conclusion: A Republic, If You Can Keep It

Dr. James McHenry, one of Maryland's delegates to the 1787 Constitutional Convention, recorded in his notes a scene that occurred at the close of the convention, on September 17. As Benjamin Franklin left the hall in Philadelphia, a woman waiting outside asked him, "What kind of government have you given us, Dr. Franklin?" He replied: "A republic, if you can keep it."

This exchange should be taught in every school civics class and inscribed above the lintels of every public university, first of all my own. For Franklin's reply is addressed not only to his questioner, but to all the citizens who have come after them. Franklin, after all, knew the government he had worked to design would not be for him, and after constitutional government began on March 4, 1789, he was able to live in the United States just over one year, dying on April 17, 1790.

The challenges and obligations of citizenship in a republic are manifold. Most of the challenges are in fact the obligations, and most of the time we take too little cognizance of them. We are happy to get by with a minimal attention to our civic duties; most of us are content, even proud, if we vote. But voting is not the fulfillment of our duties as citizens. In fact, it is one of the easiest of those duties. There are many more. Being a citizen of a republic is a difficult challenge.

Religious faith, at least of the Christian kind, does not relieve those difficulties. If anything it magnifies them. For it teaches us to make our commitment to our common republic complicatedly ambivalent. It is not simply a matter of antagonism, as if faith is necessarily reflexively hostile to political commitment; nor is it simply a matter of chastening, as if faith's job is like that of a proctor at a high school dance in the 1950s, keeping a prudent open space between the dancers' bodies; nor is it simply a matter of reinforcing or amplifying that commitment, as if faith were simply a political vitamin. It can be any of these at any time. At all times it is at least one of these. Almost all the time it is more than one.

And yet even from the wholly secular perspective of the republic, such ambivalent commitment ought to be respected. After all, the great danger, historically speaking, of republican government is idolatrous fanaticism, leading to imperialism, leading to moral decay and eventually the republic's collapse; this fanaticism was caused by the state asking too much of its citizens, and its citizens providing it. Republicanism may not be unique in having its vices be defects of its virtues, but it seems especially susceptible to those virtues' straightforward reversal into vices. It was the genius of the eighteenth-century liberal republicans to urge that a certain ambivalence be leavened into the republican spirit, lest it too easily curdle into a simple will to power, a *libido dominandi* that exults in the dominance of one's own community over all others. And it was those liberal republicans' great good fortune to find, in the religious consciousnesses and institutions of their fellow citizens, a collection of energies and convictions that enabled that ambivalence.

The challenges for religious believers in liberal-republican polities, and for polities populated in part by such religious believers, are manifold. In both directions misunderstandings are likely to occur. Religious believers' actions may confront a certain kind of "political illegibility" — a certain misunderstanding of their purpose, or even an incomprehension of what they are, by the state and their more secularly minded fellow citizens; a failure, from time to time, to see their actions as attempts at genuine political action. Conversely, the behavior of those more secular citizens, and the words and deeds of the state, may encounter a certain kind of "religious illegibility" in the minds of believers. In both cases the "illegibility" is caused by many complicated forces, but its effects are clear: it obscures or obstructs the efforts of both sides to live in genuine political community with one another — to see one another as partners in a series of this-worldly challenges. Some of these challenges arise simply from the complexities attendant on any effort to live together; others emerge, perversely, out of the opportunities for good enabled by that coexistence; in all cases they are issues of common concern, even if they are construed by different citizens in very different ways.

In such situations — which is to say, in almost any situation in which most Christians are likely to find themselves in the first world today — Christian citizens must learn, as we have heard Reinhold Niebuhr put it, "to do justice to the distinctions of good and evil in history and to the possibilities and obligations of realizing the good in history; and also to subordinate all these relative judgments and achievements to the final truth about life and history which is proclaimed in the Gospel." This general maxim generates distinct obligations, but these are different in different settings. Today I think there are three obligations, or challenges, that Christians have especially to undertake — one fundamentally affirmative, one fundamentally critical, and one that is both.

First, the fundamentally affirmative obligation is simple. Christian citizens must always agitate for, and publicly demonstrate their recognition of, the infinite value of the human being as bearing the weight of the *imago Dei*, the image of God. This is something churches do practice today, albeit not entirely in concert with one another; concerns about abortion, about torture, about the treatment of prisoners and the poor and the weak are all manifestations of these concerns, in different and partial ways. It is not just a matter of affirming this in private; Christians must *show it forth*, as Augustine said in his sermon on judging: "restore to God the image of God in the human being, just as the image of Caesar on the coin is restored to him." Establishing what is the appropriate mode of "showing forth," and the appropriate ranking of causes to agitate about, is and will continue to be disputable; that such affirmative agitation is required is not to be denied.

Second, more critically, Christians must resist and actively counteract all attempts to avoid the real moral difficulty and confusion of our condition. Christians must be Orwellians, against "moral clarity." It is not that Christians should be against real moral clarity. But we should recognize that real moral clarity produces a true approximation of the situation, and after the fall, the situation is always morally ambiguous. Real moral vision does not make things clearer, but rather more vividly ambivalent. The danger all of us, believers and unbelievers alike, face here is the ruthless simplifying energies of our own egos, amplified by the ideologies and identity politics of the day. A true hermeneutics of charity slows you down, makes you resist too-easy moral judgment. What Christianity should offer is *moral obscurity*, moral difficulty. Life, after all, is not easy, nor is it simple, and most of the clear choices we must make are clear only because they are trivial. Christians should be known for their capacity to be, from time to time, angst-ridden, confused, and uncertain.

Third, and most complicated, is the question of pluralism, of the challenge of people with very different beliefs living together in community. How should Christians address this challenge? What virtues should Christian citizens cultivate to confront it? Christians have thought about this for a long time, and the polity as a whole, including non-Christians, can learn from that history how this condition can be a fruitful one.

A pluralistic setting undercuts religious belief's "taken-for-grantedness" and makes such belief no longer an unquestioned background assumption but something that one is reflectively aware of as contingent. If one is to affirm one's beliefs in this setting, then one must *actively* affirm them. Religious believers, some would say, should cultivate the ability to see their own belief in alien guise, as it were — to see it from the perspective of one who does not share it, perhaps. This demands a great deal from any human being. But it has its benefits. Most importantly, having this skill gives believers a crucial principle whereby they can judge the extent to which hypocrisy or idolatry enters into their convictions. It is hard to overestimate the value of skeptical challenges to one's beliefs; believers should welcome such challenges as a healthy scouring of their beliefs.

On the other hand, it is morally and epistemologically equally useful, I would argue, for unbelievers in a pluralistic society to learn to see things from a religious person's perspective, and to try as best they can to understand what they are seeking to say. Part of the reason for this is simply the value of enlarging one's mind that comes with the encounter with those with different convictions. But another part has to do with the particular path that secularism has traveled in our era. The secularism of modernity is quite different from the secularism of late antiquity — of Augustine's own age, for example, which had its share of secularisms (and certainly was quite pluralist). The loudest voices of contemporary secularism are marked more by a more drearily reductionist materialism than the secularisms of earlier eras — a materialism that reduces humans to something far less than what we seem to ourselves to be. Another way of saying this is that modern secularism has been entwined with a certain kind of modern scientism, in a way that late antiquity would find incomprehensible. And because of this, modern secular thinkers are often underequipped to think about the breadth and depth of human experience. The religions can remind them of the full scope of human existence, the multiple dimensions of human life — not simply for matters of political significance, but also for all matters of human significance in its full existential shape — and challenge them to find structural analogies in a secularist vernacular for these missing dimensions. This may be a fairly romantic vision of the secular significance of the religions, to be sure, but one should not discount it for that. To be acquainted with the religions is to be acquainted with a dizzying array of ways of being human, and even on secularists' own terms, such acquaintance is to be sought, dare we say, devoutly.

Finally, one of the best things about genuine pluralism is how deeply it confuses the categories through which we try to manage it. For after all, these categories of "believers" and secularist "unbelievers" are far too fixed. Most of the things believers and unbelievers believe are the same

— that any two newspapers from a pile of fresh newspapers will contain the same news; that you can put letters in mailboxes and, if they have stamps, they will be picked up and delivered to where you said they should go; that if you turn the car key it will start the car; that if you drop change from your hand you should look down, not up, for it; that the Cleveland Indians will never, ever win a World Series again; that your wife and your children will walk through the door at the end of the day, unharmed by villains or vehicles. And most of the time, as regards religious faith, most people are at some point on the continuum of belief and unbelief. (The exchange between Felix Frankfurter and Reinhold Niebuhr, after a sermon by the latter, nicely captures this: Frankfurter, a lifelong atheist, said, "Reinie, may a believing unbeliever thank you for your sermon?" Niebuhr replied, "may an unbelieving believer thank you for appreciating it?") Recognition of these facts will be encouraged by life in a pluralistic society, and that offers yet one more opportunity for growth by Christians who inhabit it.

Religiously faithful citizens, if they remain faithful, can still successfully contribute to their polities today. Theirs is a difficult task, to be sure. But all republican citizenship is difficult, and at least they will be a bit more alert to the challenges than some others might be. And as no one ever said the vocation of a believer was easy, so no one can say that the vocation of a believing citizen should be simple. If faithful Christians are to be citizens, something like this complicated minuet with Caesar is required. Difficulty, if truthfully explicated, is no reason for forgoing the effort, and Christian faith asks no less of its adherents, and their polities can expect no more. To accomplish this difficult task, all we citizens will need is what we always and everywhere need — the grace of God, shed abroad in our hearts, to give us the ability to delight in God's will and walk in God's ways, to the everlasting glory of God's most holy name.

CHAPTER 7

Hope and Political Engagement

⌒*ᴍ*⌒

Stagger onward rejoicing

W. H. Auden, "Atlantis"

O nce upon a time, I had dinner with Adam Michnik, one of the
foremost Polish dissidents of the 1970s and 1980s. It was a wonderful occasion for many reasons, as far as I can recall. (Central Europeans really can drink more than Americans.) But one moment remains
crystal clear for me, and will do so until I die. Michnik recalled a joke
that was told in Poland in the 1980s: "What would have to happen to
make the Soviet Union's troops leave Poland? Well, there are two options — one rational, the other miraculous. The rational option is for St.
George the Dragon Slayer to come down from heaven on a white horse
with a flaming sword, land on the banks of the Vistula, and chase the
Soviets away. And the miraculous option? That's if they leave by themselves."

Hope may seem ungrounded, even fantastic, today. But in such situations it is worth remembering 1989, and what changed that year. It is
hard for us now to remember how intractable the conflicts of that time
seemed then — how permanent the divide between East and West
seemed to be. But those conflicts found resolution and those divides
were overcome. Such episodes can help us remember that greater miracles than we need have occurred. Our world is no more perilous than
the world we faced during the Cold War, and though our civic resources

may be somewhat more dissipated today, they still give us enough reason to hope we can have a future fit for our children.

Why does this book end with hope? Traditionally the highest of the virtues is love, and with good reason: faith looks back to the past, hope looks forward to the future, but love refers to our present participation in genuine presence, the thing to which faith looks back and hope looks forward. But as I have said, our lives as we live them today are deranged, and each of the virtues faces challenges distinct to it. And the challenges to the virtues of faith and love are, in important ways, rooted in a certain sort of challenge to our hope. We are tempted to profane love by our hopeless presumption that we can delight now, and we are tempted to idolatrous faith by our hopeless presumption that we know already who we are and what we rely upon. So it seems to me that, speaking civically, our deepest challenges today are challenges to hope — more specifically, the challenge we feel from our common despair.

The irony here is deep. After all, ours is the age of human achievement, human power. We have powers never imagined by previous generations — powers to remake ourselves and our world in fundamental ways. Given this, it is somewhat paradoxical that, in an age in which we are more powerful, more in charge of our destiny than ever before, we seem to be most afraid, even despairing. We do not trust ourselves. And for good reason. Michel Foucault put it well: "[f]or millennia man remained what he was for Aristotle: A living animal with the additional capacity for a political existence. Modern man is an animal whose politics places his existence as a living being in question." As the old *Pogo* cartoon has it, we have met the enemy, and he is us.

We have a very incomplete grasp of hope, and it has a very incomplete grasp on us. We know what it is to have faith in something, or someone, however misplaced that faith may be; we know something of what it means to love someone. But hope is more mysterious for us. Often we suspect hope is illusory. We think living in hope is to live in a shadow world; we think hope is otherworldly. But this is just an expression of our despair. For what we think of as reality is really the shadow world — realities derived from other, more fundamental ones — and it is that realization that escapes us in our despairing impatience of waiting.

Hope is not about looking away, but to look and see what is really there, to live most fundamentally "in tune with the world," in Josef Pieper's apt phrase, not radically in contradiction to it, as we sometimes seem to believe. Hope is *engaging*, not *escaping*; it does not seek a wholly other life, but this life in its fullness, "life abundant." Yes, there is a thoroughly eschatological conviction at the core of hope; there is a longing for more than what we have today. Yet it is not "escapist" or "otherworldly." We think we are alive now, but in fact we live in a living death, not fully alive. Hope is the true realism. Hope is the joy of waiting for life abundant: that is the theme of this chapter.

It offers a direct and general reflection on what this all means for how Christians should live their lives today — which is to say, how they should live in hope, which is the mode in which Christians properly live in history. Part I details the various contemporary deformations to which our hope is prone, and roots them in their proximate causes in our current situation and in their ultimate causes in the human condition, east of Eden. Part II describes the fundamental disposition through which Christians have historically cultivated hope, and explores some of its promise and perils. Finally, part III depicts the fundamental liturgical practice whereby this disposition is cultivated in us, and part IV defends the extension of that cultivation to the manifold practices of civic life in which we are engaged.

I. Against Apocalypticism

Hope is so hard to inhabit today in large part because we are tempted toward apocalypticism. Apocalyptic language and frameworks are popular, even among those who vocally disavow them. Examples of them are legion; we can name only a few here. But we are tempted toward apocalypticism not only because of its popularity in our historical moment. The temptation of apocalypticism, properly understood in all its richness, is actually an illuminating way to specify the primordial human flaw, our original sin. One good description of original sin is simply hastiness, and the whole history of the human race may be usefully seen as a struggle against such hastiness and the apocalyptic attitude it engenders. Through this we can come to see why and how the Augustinian political theology here articulated is fundamentally organized around defusing our tendencies toward apocalypticism, by offering a different, and better, eschatological stance.

Recall the difference between the "eschatological" and the "apocalyptic" imaginations. The "apocalyptic" imagination is the temptation we feel to assume we know already what is going on and what will be going on. It is based on the presumption that we already know in detail how things will turn out. In contrast, the eschatological faith that Augustine urges on us confidently confesses that it knows that "all will be well," but it also humbly confesses that it does not foreknow *how* all will be well. It requires us to look and see what is going on in the world, not to presume we know already. It does not seek to lure us from attention to the world; it demands that we scrutinize it all the more assiduously.

This contrast between the apocalyptic and the eschatological imaginations may seem sheerly stipulative, even arbitrary. But in fact it is deeply practical for our world today.

First, in both its political culture and its religious culture, as chapter 6 suggested, the United States is a profoundly apocalyptic nation, perhaps the first such nation in world history. Its money proclaimed a new order for the ages *(Novus Ordo Seclorum)* well before the first President Bush announced a "New World Order," and in reading the letters of some of its more fervent founders, such as Jefferson, one has the same sense of the generation just after Paul, expecting the parousia at any moment. And then, immediately after the founding generation, a religious revival swept the nation, profoundly altering its culture and infusing it with a kind of millenarian republicanism whose implications are now felt on every continent. Even today, Americans' political views, whether secular or religious, are likely to be informed by apocalyptic expectations. Much of our political discussion takes place in apocalyptic terms, and among the largest best sellers of recent years is the *Left Behind* series. In this setting we do well to reappropriate Augustine's resistance to seeing the "signs of the times" either too literally or too clearly.

On the other hand, many wholesale critics of America are also apocalyptic. In fact, it is fair to say that anti-Americanism in general is really little more than the latest version of this apocalyptic. Much of the violence riddling the world today in the form of terrorist and other nonstate actors takes on the form of what Anthony Cordesman strikingly called "eschatological warfare." The messianism of Marxism has been well documented, and often the post-Marxist forms of sociopolitical complaint employed by contemporary antiglobalization activists continue to rely on the same sorts of arguments and rhetorics once used by straightforward Marxists.

Many of the critics of America present their criticisms as if they are somehow essentially related to the particular character of American politics or culture, or to the particular course that history has taken to bring America to its position of preeminence today. And even those who do not focus their ire on America in particular but on more abstract things such as "globalization," still present the problems we face as if they are ultimately the product of some contingent configuration of our societies or a contingent effect of our history — as if, that is, they are not permanent figures of human existence. All these critics write as if they think that the full scope of our misery will disappear with the particular historical institutions or social systems with which they are concerned.

Both American jingoist millenarians and anti-American apocalypticists imagine that our challenges can be simply "solved." Each imagines that there is a cause fully within history for all the maladies of history, and so the human condition is itself not inextricably intertwined with the pathologies of power and suffering that mark our lives. Each, that is, has an apocalyptic view of our historical situation, one that anesthetizes the need for action, deflates the desire for new information or insight, and encourages in its stead a lazy, passive, and fundamentally spectatorial attitude toward what is to come.

I do not mean simply to castigate all such political imaginations as fundamentally flawed. I also mean to call attention to the pervasiveness and depth of the apocalyptic temptation in contemporary political culture. In fact it is deeper than the explicitly political — it is part of a larger technological mind-set, pervasive in our culture, a mind-set that is itself messianic, seeking a magical miracle cure for all our maladies. So apocalypticism is latent in, and perhaps intrinsic to, modernity itself.

In such an age, the idea of a life built around deep and profound hopes — hopes that mobilize but do not expect to be realized, hopes that spring from a settled, joyful receptivity to what we are given by one another, through creation and ultimately by God — has little purchase on our culture's imagination, and increasingly no purchase even on those most intentionally dedicated to realizing it. Consumer culture makes it very hard for us to understand ourselves as having longings insatiable in this life — longings to which our only real response can be hope. And so our lives become increasingly a matter of momentary appetites, disconnected from any larger arc of significance.

But it is delusional to blame this problem merely on the contingencies of recent history or the accidents of particular cultural configurations. For Augustinians the problems are fundamental to the fallen human condition itself. For what they have in common is *escapism* — a desire to be altogether elsewhere, a negative relation to the real. They are all fundamentally forms of despair. Certainly they are shaped by the particularities of their place and time, but the core challenge remains the same. Political apocalypticism presumes to know already what will happen, so that it need not ask any more questions. Cultural apocalypticism imagines the world as a site for settling our desires once and for all, and sees our continued longing not in positive terms but as a problem to be solved conclusively, a lack to be filled once and for all. Both forms seek to be at the end already — to no longer have to bear the waiting. They cannot see the passage of time as itself a good thing. At their heart there is a resentment that things continue, that we have not yet reached the end. And at the heart of that resentment is a wish — rarely explicit, normally unconscious, never totally exhaustive of our heart — that time would stop, that the world would end, that, in short, we would die.

The Christian tradition understands this. It sees apocalypticism as a useful description of our sinful condition. Traditionally we think of sin as fundamentally a form of pride, of the enormous and grotesque expansion of the self to elbow out all others. Certainly there is something to this. But over the past forty years, feminist and liberationist thinkers have drawn attention to the limitations of this image, to which they attribute (not without merit) debilitatingly conservative and authoritarian effects. Their work has led to a richer and more nuanced account of sin. They insist on recognizing a kind of sin born out of despair. Interestingly, this has resonances with a very old and venerable way of describing sin, going back at least to Irenaeus in the second century A.D. This account depicts sin as hastiness, apocalyptic hastiness. On this tradition, we despair of God helping us when we want God to, and so we begin to want to be *sicut Deus*, like God, and that means to master time, to no longer be in the condition of having to receive time. We want to be the creator of time, the author of history. To be in thrall to the apocalyptic imagination is just to wish to be in control.

We can combine this account with the traditionally popular one, and depict sin as a wild shuttling back and forth between pride and despair, with these being two sides of the same coin — the inexplicable refusal of humanity to share in the joys of their God-given destiny. But the obscurity of the cause does not obscure for us the vividness of the effects: it traps the human in a ceaseless, wild oscillation between a brooding, solipsistic isolation and a frenzied, desperate immersion in the world.

Augustine captured these two poles of sinful humanity's course in his discussion of sin as both privation and perversion. On one level sin is an emptying out of the self, an abandonment of its genuine loves, leaving a vacuity at the heart's core. But on another level this emptying out can manifest itself somewhat paradoxically, in the most extreme, debauched pursuit of worldly pleasures, as an attempt to fill that vacuity, to find real and lasting happiness in the transitory goods of this transitory life. These two acts are complementary, two sides of the same coin, but they are also modes of being that the person can only sequentially make visible. The oscillation between them is understandable: as Samuel Johnson famously said, "he who makes a beast of himself gets rid of the pain of being a man." But one can never finally stay bestial, for our desires for immaterial things are just as fundamental as our desires for material ones. The heart and the mind are as real as the belly. And so as fallen humans we are trapped, bouncing between the two poles, never able to find the central stability we seek.

All of this is very nice, I imagine you saying. But haven't we gone off track? Weren't we talking about hope and the challenges it faces today? Well, we're not off track. For it is just this oscillation between escapist retreat and frenzied immurement that is our life, absent hope. For consumerism is nothing but this immurement, punctuated (albeit infrequently) by the lethargic dolor of remorseful solitude. And both extremes are forms of despair: in seeking our joy in the world we despair of finding it in God, and in eschewing that quest we come face-to-face with our despair, and know it for what it is — a deep lack of loyalty to God, curdled into a desperate aggrandizement of the self, in lieu of any real worship of God.

Yet even despair is displaced hope; we would not despair if there were nothing to despair *of*; so despair itself is a good sign, a sign that we are not irredeemably lost. Furthermore, apocalypticism *is* a temptation just because the world is occasionally perforated by grace or divine presence. After all, we must always keep alert to the "signs of the times," and ever-available proleptic perforation of our fallen world by the coming reign of God. Real miracles *can* happen — they happen all the time. We are constantly confronted with the proleptic realization of some small fragment of our hopes, some "little apocalypses." It would be a perverse eschatology that functioned as a sleeping pill for its adherents on the night that Christ returns. Instead, it must make us eager to hasten to the bridegroom when the wedding is begun.

A proper eschatology is not just, that is, a negative doctrine, content to critique utopian apocalypticism. A proper eschatological hope eagerly searches through the world, seeking out *the real*. In contrast, one large problem with the apocalyptic imagination's desperate searching for "signs of the times" is that this actually is a way of ignoring the full complexity of the real, filtering out almost everything and seizing on just a few things.

Hope is what we lack when we wear such blinders. And hope is what we have when we recognize the blinders for what they are, and take them off. Hope is first seen not as directly possessed as our own attitude, but as a diagnosis of our condition. And it diagnoses us as sinfully escapist — failing genuinely to live in the world for what it is, refusing to let the world be creation, God's creation, and insisting instead that this world is nothing but what we say it is, and so all we have, and can have, in existence as a way of living, as a site for our flourishing. But it can never be that site, and hope shows us a better way to live in it, shorn of that illusory graspingness.

How do we cultivate hope? How should we confront the problem of our latent apocalypticism? That is the subject of the next section.

II. The Pilgrimage of Our Affections

So we live in a culture profoundly shaped by apocalyptic energies. In this setting, we should cultivate a mode of life that resists apocalypticism — that leaves the task of determining the end of time up to God and treats the time we are given not as a burden to overcome but as a mixed blessing, to be delighted in and to be endured, as our preparation to be citizens of the kingdom of God. Contrary to some perceptions, such an eschatological approach is not antijoy, but instead teaches its adherents to learn to see that all has at its core a mysterious gift.

But there is a problem with seeking a mode of life that cultivates eschatological patience. How do we get patience? How can one expect the unexpected? What does that mean? How can hope be cultivated? We have a clue in that very question. It cannot be created, only cultivated. There is no technology by which we can acquire it. It is there in us already, for our despair was never total. So we must cultivate its slender presence. And we do this best by enduring it, by enduring hope.

It sounds odd to talk about enduring hope. But recall, from chapter 1, the comic theologian John Cleese: "No, no, you don't understand anything! It's not the despair I mind, it's the hope I can't stand!" Hope is hard to stand; it is as much an experience of painful estrangement as it is a consolation. To be hopeful, that is, is to be on pilgrimage. Hope is not a destiny but a journey.

Hope so understood lets us see our lives as a pilgrimage, not by disparaging what is around us as second-rate, but by instilling in us the conviction that this world is not fully realized yet — that what we now see are only the firstfruits of a far more joyful and *just* world to come. A pilgrimage is a journey, of a peculiar sort: one where the pilgrim is as much passive witness as active traveler, as much (if not more) changed by his travail as by changing his location. It is not an aimless wander or walkabout, nor simply an instrumental trip; on a pilgrimage, time and space are sanctified or they are recognized as sanctified, in relation to the desired end.

But how do we translate these pretty thoughts about hope, and this grandiose metaphor of pilgrimage, into some concrete practices of inhabiting the world more hopefully? Following Augustine, I suggest that we should orient all our loves in the world to God, so that we love all things *in* God, and in a way listen to our longings' dissatisfactions in the present — learn to be "trained by our longings" to seek a certain eschatological consummation, and none before then. Augustine talks about this as an experience of growing into the *distensio animi*, the "distension of the soul," that is our lot in this life. Living in the *distensio* shows us the meaning of hope.

In Latin *distensio* originally referred to torture: to the suffering of a body when stretched out on a rack, like a rubber band. Augustine used it to capture the experience of the "stretched-outedness" of the human, our longings and desires, in time. These desires are truly temporal, in the sense that they stretch through time and reach beyond time. To recognize our *distensio* is to recognize our temporal extendedness, to realize that we are not a series of utterly discrete punctual moments but a whole whose boundaries are nothing less than birth and death (and for Augustinians, a great deal more than that). Furthermore, it is to insist that our experience as so distended gets at something real about the character of our life — our experience of constantly living not fully in the present but of "reaching back" into the past and "reaching forward" into the future. Stretched out in the present by memory and expectation, we are never fully present. To live in the *distensio*, that is, is just to live in time, to learn ever more fully to feel our lives as pained by our *distensio* across time.

Distensio sounds bad. Does it not just destroy whatever real goods we could experience now? Is not hope simply expressive of an escapist animus toward the world, corrosive of our ability to "be here now," and thereby of our ability to be at all? Is not hope, in short, antilife? No; hope simply means to see what you see and recognize that there's more beyond what you see, beyond the immediate, and to long for that — to refuse to allow things to be determined by their immediate, historical, concrete density. Their meaning is spiritual, their literality is spiritual. It lets us appreciate goods for what they are. It is not antijoy, but antisatisfaction, anticonclusion. It is an eschatological practice, performed in this life.

Some will remain skeptical here, wondering whether this response fully confronts the worry they feel. The heart of their worry is simple: Augustine's proposal raises suspicions for many people that our love for one another is cruelly restricted — that, for example, I cannot fully love my daughter, that somehow my love for her should be guarded, qualified, constrained as love "in God," or love as God loves her. This sounds like I'm loving her with a second-rate or derivative love, as if she could not be loved for herself.

There is something right about this worry: this faith, and hope, and love wreak havoc on our received understanding of who we are to love and how we are to love them. Augustine, for example, talks explicitly about the paradoxes of a faith where one is enjoined to "love the enemy" and to "hate one's father and mother and wife and children." To begin to see God's will for you as normative for your life will inevitably disrupt your habituated affections in manifold ways. Sometimes it can seem that this God is the enemy of this created world.

Yet at the same time, on this account, those we do love can be sources of joy and even metaphysical wonder for us — even as we resist our sinful desire to have them be apocalyptically satisfactory for us, a desire that will always leave us frustrated and disappointed by their failure, and hence resentful of the conditions of our world. After all, we should love one another. Our love of one another is not a bad thing, and it is tempted toward idolatry only because we are supposed to be the vehicles of God's love for one another. That is to say, having a worshipful sense of another person is precisely what God wants us to have, as God means to call us into God's own inner life. This, after all, is the destiny that the tradition has captured in the language of deification or *theosis*, the process of our becoming "godlike." This is precisely why idolatry is so powerful a temptation — for it is not far off the mark: loving another as God wants another to be loved is quite close to loving another *as* God.

What, then, should we say? Should we hate the world and all its works? How can we fulfill the two great commandments, to love God with all our being and to love our neighbor as ourselves? The answer is straightforward, but profound. These two loves — in our example, my love of God and my love of my daughter — only conflict if we understand God and my daughter to be rivals for my affection. This is how we, sinful humans that we are, are prone to see things. But in fact, occasionally we get glimpses of another way of seeing things. As regards my love for my daughter, what Augustine is ruling out is quite precise. On his understanding, I certainly may glory and delight in her presence in the world, which always has a transcendent character, provoking wonder. Genuine attention to those persons and "things" closest to your heart makes it most manifest that they, above all, always escape capture — always "open out" in the most wonderful and terrifying way. In all these ways I can find her a cause of joy, happiness, and delight for me. But there is another attitude toward her to which I am prone. (Any parent can tell the difference between these two.) This other attitude is grasping, jealous, clinging, comprehending, seeking control. I should not seek to find my flourishing — that is, to live — through my daughter. Such an attitude places too much existential weight on her; it "leans on" her too heavily, even were she an adult. You cannot ask anyone else to be your Supreme Good, to provide you with your basic meaning in the world. Yet this jealous love is in me too, and it will never, in this life, go away. In the tension of wonder and frustration, we experience again that *distensio animi.*

Yet this living into the *distensio* is not the end of the story. We must still leave space for moments of more. For we do experience some moments of "real presence," of genuine, full contact. And this contact enables us to see beyond immediate experiences to a mystery within and beyond them. This is a descriptive, not a prescriptive, claim: I want to argue that anyone who has loving relations with others can, or should be able to, simply *see* this transcendence. "Mystery" is far from the blank incomprehension from which we begin. (If you experience something as a mystery the first time you meet it, you have experienced something that you already recognize as having a claim on you — something to which you are already related in a profound way.) The more we know someone, the more we love that person, the more mysterious he or she is to us. Mystery and transcendence are at the heart of being, and realizing a person's proper mystery is an achievement, a goal. Our deepest loves have a transcendence to them, a longing and wonder that are both positive and negative, a presence and an absence, an answer and an ongoing question.

Hope is the name we give to the recognition of this mystery, and the expectation that it will be fully given to us in the eschaton. We cannot overcome this estrangement, but should simply acknowledge it and cultivate its implications. This is why Augustine says we will be truly happy in this life only through our hope. Furthermore, while we may think we are always "in pursuit" of true happiness throughout history, at the end of time it will round on us and pounce. And then we will fully know how joyfully terrifying is the thing all along that we have thought we were pursuing.

This hope is not just an expression of one's inner attitude; it implies a picture of reality itself, a metaphysics of hope. This metaphysics suggests a new understanding of creation itself, as not yet fully real, as waiting to be fully realized in the eschaton. Augustine seems to have thought something like this — "that God brought creation into existence can even be interpreted in a future sense. That God created light may be understood as an event to take place when Christ rises from the dead. For it is only at the moment when he separates the immortal from the mortal that he truly separates the light from the darkness." Hope is not simply about a positive attitude, it also reveals to us a New World.

This may sound pretty esoteric. What does it matter if our metaphysics changes? It matters a great deal, actually. For your metaphysics is your picture of reality — and when that changes, your behavior changes also. But how does it change? How does our new metaphysics change our beliefs? What does it shape us for? What does it make us pursue? Toward what end are we straining? What is the eschatological aim? In life today that means refusing finality, refusing to allow anything to have the "last word" for us. We turn to explaining that next.

III. Eucharist: Training in Longing for the Time Being

So sin is most usefully understood, for people in situations such as ours, as stemming from a bad apocalypticism. To do better, we should undertake the journey of hope as a pilgrimage of affections, a training in longing. But how can this attitude be cultivated? How are we to long, to keep desiring? How is it intentionally, socially, and practically cultivated?

The general answer of the Christian churches has historically been that the main device for such cultivation is liturgy. The hopeful disposition we commend is cultivated by Christian liturgical practices, and especially the most fundamental such practice, the Eucharist (which some Christians call Communion or the Lord's Supper). We must be careful here; liturgy, "the work of the people," is not most fundamentally a set of outward rituals (at least as "ritual" is typically understood), but rather a set of practices, inner and outer, whereby people come to shape their experience of the world in fundamental ways. Liturgy, to borrow a line Ezra Pound originally applied to literature, is "news that stays news" — a form of experience whose revelatory power is always potent and forceful. In contrast, so much of what passes for news in our world today is actually a device for confirming us in our prejudices — a device, that is, for helping us avoid reality, with all the painful adjustments that such an encounter would entail. Liturgy is, in some essential way, the life of the church, the process of coming to be transformed into properly formed children of God, to be taken up into the divine life.

Furthermore, the transformation it most immediately seeks to work is the transformation of perception. In the passing of the peace after the confession of sin, for example, one comes to see all those around one as no longer strangers sitting uncomfortably close to one another in pews, but now as fellow members of the hospital of grace, gathered to receive Christ's medicinal mercy.

The change that should happen to the participants consists largely in learning to see the world as always "more of the same," in contrast to our pervasive desire, accentuated by modernity, to see our world in apocalyptic terms. Its goal is twofold: First, it means to help us see the proper transformation of human agency, from seeing ourselves as primarily active to seeing ourselves as primarily passive. This is a change in the story we tell ourselves, from one in which we appear to be the kinds of creatures who make our lives happen by the actions we undertake and the decisions we make to a story in which we are the kinds of creatures who are, in Martin Luther's phrase, "more acted upon than acting," creatures more shaped by events and circumstances outside ourselves than shaping those events and circumstances by a preexisting self. Second, and related to the first, it means to help us see the transformation of the direction of flow, as it were, of value and desire in our lives — to see us transformed from those who fundamentally desire to those who are fundamentally desired. The Christian liturgy does this in three large moments.

First, the enactment of the liturgy gathers the people together. The agency here is important: we do not gather, but we are gathered, invited, brought into the feast by the messengers of God. The liturgy begins before we get there; it begins in the act of summoning us itself. We are collected together, brought to a common point in space and time, by God, who gathers the community and calls each out by name. The extent of the gathering may well be universal; there is certainly no created limit to God's call. And confession is our response to this achievement, however partial, of community. We confess we have been led here, or brought here, by God. People talk about "finding themselves" in church, and the double entendre there captures something of this.

Once the community has been gathered, it is named by God — given a collective identity as the body of Christ and, in a way, each one given an individual story within that collective identity. This must be described with real care, for fear of implying that the collective is more primordial than the individuals. That is not true. But the individuals are no more primordial than the collective, and God is more primordial than both. Both the community and the individuals that constitute it need each other to be real. Furthermore, this naming is not simply an affirmation of ourselves by God. Our identity is not determined by us; we *receive* it. Christ does not answer our questions on our terms but refuses to let us have the last word on who we are; instead, he makes us surprises, even to ourselves, genuinely new beings whose being is found in gift. The response of the laity to this naming is the passing of the peace, when in our newfound identity we turn to see each other and recognize each other.

Both of these acts are promises of the third, the most fundamental, gifting. In fact, the whole of the liturgy is premised on the most profound gift of all, the gift of God's real presence, God's self. Most immediately this is the gift of God's life for our own, in Christ's sacrifice. But our recognition of this is itself a further gift that God gives us. And the gift is also a gift of God's presence, in Christ, for it is only as the community formed by God — the body of Christ — that we can receive this gift. This gift creates in grace the possibility of its own reception; it is wholly gift, for it gives a gift and the possibility to receive that gift as well. (The triune analogies here are not inapt.) And this gift is the gift of God's very self, the gift of Jesus' life. Through the liturgy, in the liturgy, and as the liturgy, we become the gift that God has given us.

The Eucharist, for instance, begins with the presentation of the "gifts" at the altar as a giving to God of God's own gifts to us — bread and wine, nourishment for our bodies. But God accepts these gifts, and they are "taken up," transfigured, and then returned to the earth, as nourishment for our souls as well. Their original "earthly" form is not renounced but rather transfigured and enriched by God's gracious acceptance of our gifts. Just so, we the people gathered for this liturgy are also taken up, broken, transfigured, and regiven to us and the world as our old selves, but more than that as well.

In the central ritual of the Christian liturgy — the eucharistic meal — we see a symbol and an enactment of this radical transformation of agency. For where once we imagined we were the ones eating, consuming the flesh and blood of the Lord, slowly we come to see that in our eating we are eaten — we have become food for God's meal. For in digesting *we* are digested, and we become part of the body of Christ, the church.

Here are revealed the mystery and transcendence that Christianity proclaims are at the heart of being: for just as bread and wine, among the simplest forms of human nourishment, are transfigured into the body of God, so too we the people, in all our pettiness, foolishness, and clumsiness, will be transformed as well into an instrument of divine harmony. The Eucharist, and the liturgy in general, teaches us to see that the world is charged with the transcendent grandeur of God. The world is meant to delight us, not finally and fundamentally to be merely a means of our satiation, but a provocation to exult.

In all of this, we are mistaken if we see the liturgy as a resolution, or a sheer achievement. In fact, what these practices do is accentuate the tension between our "now" and the eschatological "not yet." By so increasing the tension around our experience of the transfiguration of this world, the practices of the liturgy challenge us as to our participation in God's kingdom.

This is perhaps most clearly seen in the doctrine sometimes known as the "real presence" of Christ in the elements of the Eucharist. For it looks as if we face here simple bread and wine, simple pieces of our wholly mundane world. But the liturgy tells us that in the liturgy they become something more, something higher or deeper than what they were, the body of God. (This would have been even more powerful in the early churches, for which the Eucharist was not just a "symbolic" ritual but a real meal, providing literal physical nourishment.) This is the most accentuated point of our *distensio*. It is also one of the most fraught topics of inter-Christian argument; debates about the liturgy (and especially the Eucharist) have split Christians for a very long time. (It is also a topic that can give rise to great skepticism about the faith in general; after all, the word "hocus-pocus" is a parody of the Latin *Hoc est corpus meum*, "this is my body," an essential part of the Eucharist.) The Eucharist is, therefore, the most exquisite point of contact between the two conditions of our being, the mundane and the transfigured.

During the world, hope is our mode of recognizing our *distensio*, our experience of tantalizing incompleteness that we confess we exist in at present, while at the same time proclaiming we will be healed in the eschaton — and we must recognize both our own incompleteness and the way that it tantalizes us. All this the liturgy is meant to teach us, to give us the most exquisite "training in longing" we could imagine, in order to sculpt our souls into the right shape, to turn our minds toward contemplation of God's incomprehensible goodness, to stretch our hearts back to the size they were meant to be in the first place. It teaches us how to live faithfully, to be sure, and lovingly, but for our purposes most pointedly it teaches us how to live hopefully: a proper hope seeks a middle ground between the impatient, too-complacent apocalyptic immanentism of the resigned or self-righteous and the impatient, too-complacent apocalyptic escapism of the embittered or smug.

The world as we have it now is not completed; it still has its surprises for us. God has made us for Godself, and our heart is restless until it rests in God, so no worldly dispensation is adequate. Yet this dispensation matters; the violations and injustices here are not simply accidental or immaterial, and its joys and sorrows will finally be taken up into God and transformed into their full reality.

But how do we live *now*, before the eschatological communion of the eucharistic feast? How should we *long* for paradise? A concrete example might help here. We can turn to the two stories Augustine tells in the *Confessions* (in books 7 and 9) of his experiences of the full presence of God. In the first, Augustine engages in philosophical meditative contemplation and finally perceives, in some obscure way, the God of sheer being — "I am He who is" — but he cannot stay in this vision, and instead falls back to earth. In the second, after his conversion, catechesis, and baptism, in an upper room waiting for their return to Africa, Augustine and his mother Monica "talk" their way to God, to God's presence, "touching" God with their hearts before falling away again in sighs and further, deeper longing.

Typically the latter of these stories is understood as the achievement that was denied Augustine in the former. Most readers of the *Confessions* see this culmination as a conclusion, a realization of what Augustine has sought all along. But it is equally a continuation of the same pattern of temporary intimacies, fleeting achievements, whose fleetingness serves only to increase Augustine's hunger and longing for God. We fail, as Augustine did in the first experience, if we become fixated on locating the story's significance as the achievement of a definite *experience*, a dense and discrete "event," whose inner character, immediately accessible to the participants, exhaustively determines the meaning of the experience itself. But this is not so; rather it is better understood as a moment in an entire life — which has the only real "integrity" that human existence allows, and a quite limited and leaky integrity at that — and gains its full meaning in terms of its place in the larger narrative, especially in terms of how Augustine responds to it in the moment, and how he retrospectively interprets it much later.

After this latter episode — both immediately afterward in book 9 and most certainly in the "authorial present" of Augustine as he is writing the *Confessions* — he sees it, unlike earlier ones, not as a failed lunge at eternity, a botched attempt at an immediate, immanent experience whose value is in itself (and therefore essentially nontemporal), but as a foretaste, glorious in itself but still a foretaste, of a later and far greater blessing in heaven. Now, dissatisfaction no longer leads ineluctably to a sense of failure; incompleteness no longer leads to self-recrimination. It is not part of a larger project of *apprehensio*, of grasping apprehension. Augustine has given that up; his new hope, in this life, is only for *attingere*, touch.

Augustine's new perspective gave him the ability to be patient with his life, a more relaxed attitude than he had permitted himself before, habituated as he was to expect the complete comprehension of previous foretastes. Immediate comprehension — itself a form of resolution — is now no longer Augustine's aim; instead, he is willing to allow an event's significance to emerge over time, indeed, to emerge beyond time. His understanding will be, as it is in the whole *Confessions*, essentially retrospective. History is not a series of failed attempts at reaching union with the divine; it is one long lesson in (because it is one extended act of ascesis for) what that union will one day, at the end of days, be revealed to be. (Though even that will not be the sort of conclusion we wish, in our sinfulness, for it to be.) In the meantime our life is a matter of learning to feel the *distensio* of worldly existence, and to long properly for the homeland of "rest" to come. Where once he expected to find resolution, to find answers — where his attitude was essentially (if implicitly) apocalyptic — now he sees that his life will be lived in deepening awareness and acceptance of the real mysteriousness of God's providence. As Augustine says, such knowledge "is sought in order to be found all the more delightfully, and it is found in order to be sought all the more avidly."

To us this sounds like an uncomfortable task, but its discomfort is due to our sinful desire to know and control the course of our lives. In surrendering his will to grace, Augustine no less surrendered his intellect; it was given back to him not with answers to the questions he had asked but with those questions transfigured and transformed. Now he can begin to live, not first of all by seeking knowledge — whether the knowledge of good and evil or the knowledge of God and the soul — but instead by inhabiting an ever-deepening sense of wonder and praise.

This way of life — this "hope" — may sound to us escapist and otherworldly. After all, it can sound as if political life is all about us getting better, and merely *using* others for our "spiritual" betterment. But this suspicion reflects the despair we feel at being (we assume) wholly on our own, unsponsored by the universe, with our hopes and longings simply projections of what we would like to be true. We do not believe we have any right to hope. The audacity of Christian hope lies in its semi-immanence, how it tortures us with its tantalizing possibility. And if we — when we — "surrender" to its temptation, we will not have willed this surrender but simply ceased to attempt to seize control for ourselves. We do not achieve hope, we acknowledge it. It is inextricably part of a complex theological project: the ongoing, always only just-begun practice of articulating our gratitude for the gratuitous gifts of a loving God. It is, in fact, the dismissal of such hope that is unworldly, because it refuses to admit that its pull on us speaks of something real.

IV. Citizens of the Kingdom of God, during the World

These days, many books in Christian theology end with discussions of the church, with the idea that building up the church is today's most pressing theological task. This book has emphasized the importance of Christian concepts, practices, and institutions for the shaping of believers' lives. But I want to end not in the church, but in the world. God so loved the world, recall, that God's only-begotten Son was given for it. While it is always centrally anchored in the Eucharist, then, the liturgy that the church most basically is, is not in fact most basically an inward-looking activity. The liturgy that the church most basically is, is that set of activities that cause Christians to reach out to the non-Christian world, and be transformed beyond the church doors — so that we carry it out into our lives beyond our Sundays.

But how? Given that hope can be so cultivated, how should it shape Christians' public engagement — and how in turn should that public engagement enrich and challenge faith? This hope offers a kind of critique, with real sociopolitical power, because it flows from the larger communal practices of the ecclesial community. If we have hope at all, it springs from prayer, prayerful action, and prayerful reflection upon such action. But it does more than that for politics; it offers a vision of the Beloved Community beyond what the world by itself would warrant, and in so doing infuses us with energies undreamt of by mundane imaginations. Conversely, this hope is trained by civic engagement, purified of its more mundane trappings and misapprehensions, until it is something far greater. This final section of the chapter talks about both of these.

A. *How Hope Shapes Political Life*

Hope mobilizes people's energy for civic change, both because of what it negates and because of what it affirms. It affirms the inchoate assent to creation that is part of every human's existence; it says that our deepest hopes about the goodness of this world are true, and that, more than that, those hopes are if anything not hopeful enough, not good enough for what is coming. Eye has not seen, nor ear heard, the joys that hope tells us are on the way.

But hope also opposes the various stultifying deceptions we collectively tell ourselves in order to dull or numb that affirmation. After all, we are wary of letting hope have too much of us, for fear of being crushed when it turns out to be untrue. Hope resists this resistance, undoes our cynicism acknowledging our salutary wariness, but insisting that it is nonetheless worse and more fantasy-ridden to refuse to acknowledge the realities to which hope refers.

Hope's power, that is, lies as much in its resistance as in its recognitions. In both ways it resists our "worldly" temptations toward a wholly mundane understanding of our world and especially of our civic order. Hope is both realistic and fantastic, true vision and powerful imagination. It sees clearly the true situation because it resists our attempts to anesthetize the intellect by distracting us from what is really there, interposing our wishes and our needs. When these drop away, we see clearly.

Yet this refusal of self-deception is not simply a matter of clear-sightedness; it is also a powerful act of imagination: for we know that things are not meant to be the way they are now. Hope empowers in part because of the vividness of the dreams it gives us, because of how it helps us imagine a "counter-polis," an antipolitics of the mind, and by imagining it we work to transform reality closer to the image of our imagined world. Such was the work of the civil rights campaigns in the United States in the 1950s and 1960s, the movements in Eastern Europe in the 1970s and 1980s, and the struggle in South Africa from the 1960s to the 1990s. Through hope, we know that no political order in this life is apocalyptically final. The energy of hope is not a utopian loan, a promissory note that our hopes will be validated by the millennium. Hopeful dissatisfaction with "the way the world is" is necessary, but we should beware lest it curdle into despair.

So this hope is deeply chastening, in two senses. First, it does not promise that our hopes will be realized, but rather that the will of God will be accomplished; so it always insinuates a slight gap between our concrete expectations and its promised end, a gap that encourages us always to be open to the new, without deflating our energies for action. Second, it urges us to see beyond the immediate worldly political goals we pursue and appreciate the *iconic* character of our political engagement; hope insists that political ends are not in themselves adequate, nor finally complete, but always also express and in some way symbolize deeper aims beyond themselves in the eschaton.

In all such hopeful engagement, several tactical insights are repeatedly emphasized. We should acknowledge the need, value, and legitimacy of social structures, but we must not grant them their apocalyptic pretensions. Our world is more than these systems permit it to be — though that "more" cannot be exhaustively articulated in the present dispensation. Human beings and their actions transcend bare literality, and the eschatological hopefulness of the churches emerges in part through their refusal to take the nation-state system with ultimate seriousness. What the state lays claim to is not its proper possession; it is on loan, as it were, from the heavenly kingdom; and sooner than the state thinks, that loan will be called due. We must recognize the limits to the systems we inhabit — to the political form of the modern nation-state, to the economic form of liberal market capitalism, and to the sociocultural form of liberal individualism, among others. We best recognize these limits not simply by proclamation, but by witnessing to what gets lost when these systems ignore their own limits.

Churches can call everyone's attention to the "remainders" that such systems inevitably leave behind: the lost, the forlorn, the discarded in society, the homeless, the perpetually unemployed, the abused, the impoverished. The churches recognize the limits of political citizenship by critiquing nationalism and demanding care beyond worldly citizenship — through the sanctuary movement, care for migrants, transnational understanding, and many other routes. Ever since Abraham, his children, adopted or not, have been immigrants; our condition today "at home" in some nation should not make us blind to the pains and discomforts of those who are more newly arrived in our lands. And political states will be held eschatologically accountable to these standards, and found wanting: a fundamentally negative judgment by God upon the pretensions of Caesar stands within all the churches' other proclamations, a basso profundo counterpoint to the higher notes. To recognize the value and necessity of such civic commitment alongside its nonultimacy: that is what Christian hope demands. However "inevitable" such discarded lives may be for fallen human societies, attention must be paid, and aid must be provided, for they may well be the gatekeepers when we come to the entrance of the kingdom.

Yet hope's civic face is not simply negative, not simply a scolding frown, angry at the nations for being imperfect. It is also affirmative, joyously proclaiming liberation, calling politics beyond itself. Most immediately, it persistently presses beyond the contractual language of the state toward a deeper, covenantal language. We do not know fully what our obligations are; we are not fully in control of them. Citizenship is not a simple contract, drawn up between fundamentally autonomous interlocutors; it bespeaks a covenant, a deeper relationship, a commitment that begins in the here and now but inevitably extends back in time, as we take responsibility for our polity's past, and across political boundaries, as we see political divisions as ultimately not final divisions. While civic membership in some polity here is essential, for believers it is ultimately derivative; our primary citizenship is in heaven. What we call "citizenship" in this world is just a political imitation of the real thing.

Inevitably, this understanding of citizenship ironically invests more in the concept than any worldly polity will want to allow — in large part because the investment is beyond that worldly polity's control.

In this way hope reveals that politics in our world is not about only mundane matters. It is our attempt, in our fallen condition, to achieve the Beloved Community. And its aim is not simply a way to get along with others — mostly by tolerating or ignoring them — in this life. Rather its aim is true community, a community of genuine care.

In this life, of course, hopes of this sort cannot, will not, ever be fully met. Struggle toward true community is unending. History does not finally move toward any simple resolution, with the multitudinous trajectories of the cacophonous past finding a happy harmony in a perfectly reconciled utopia. There is a rupture between the history we inhabit today and the kingdom of God promised in Scripture. The kingdom of God will come like a thief in the night, with no clear signs of progress, no readily visible clue to its proximity. Our struggles do not hasten its arrival. And yet the time before them is worthwhile. The next and final section says how.

B. How Political Engagement Shapes Hope

How can this hope be deepened by public engagement? The answer is straightforward: by being vexed. In public life, history's recalcitrance to our expectations is most visibly, even glaringly, displayed; our actions never have quite the effect we command them to have, and so our engagement with "worldly matters" inevitably results in losing control of our fate more than gaining control of it. For all the talk about "empowering" people to engage in public life, what those so engaged repeatedly report is not simply empowerment; alongside that experience — and sometimes, indeed, inside it — is a deepened sense of their own smallness, even their own powerlessness, of the complexities of the issues involved and the power of unforeseen and unforeseeable accidents and consequences to warp one's actions. This is not a fact only about modern public life; as Sophocles and Thucydides taught 2,500 years ago, it is in public affairs that *nemesis* is most palpably present.

Hope is deepened by being repeatedly recalled to the tension between that fact and our continuing confidence that history's ultimate destiny is what we partially and provisionally glimpse today in joy. Engagement in public life can work as a graceful brushfire, clearing away the choking undergrowth of our indulgent delusions so that we can know more fully the ironic lesson of the perverse swervings of public life and the urgency of our engaging it.

This is not a little ironic. We think of hope as deeply comforting, encouraging, and empowering. But it may be just as easily disturbing. It may be a judgment on our anxieties and a fearful insistence that we know what will happen. Hope forbids and implicitly condemns any too-determinate expectations of the coming order.

But hope's chastening does not demoralize or de-energize, because it is governed by affirmation. It is liberating precisely *as* judgment, for it frees us from the fantasy that we are in control and lets us use the enormous psychic energies dedicated to sustaining that fantasy for other, more fruitful tasks — responding freely and freshly to the surprises God sets before us every day, playfully and delightedly rejoicing in the gift. It is the angel announcing the good tidings, announcing the birth of the new in and by which we are made new. It is the dream of the new Jerusalem, the joyful kingdom of God on earth. And it is not an achievement but a gift: this kingdom, after all, is presented in the book of Revelation as "coming down" to a sanctified humanity, and humans do not rise up from the earth to reach it but "go forward" on the ground to enter into its gates (Rev. 21:2; 21:26).

Nonetheless, as we have emphasized throughout this book, that annunciation evokes terror as well as — in fact, *within* — joy, and this dual experience of terror and joy is the deepest ascesis of hope. In public life this struggle with terror is most clearly manifest through hope's prophetic dimension. Politics is constantly tempted toward the sinful prescription of self-sufficiency, toward the presumption that politics' goals are legitimately immanent and self-enclosed ends in themselves — that somehow the sphere of the political or the "social" has an integrity and coherence of its own. Hope works against this complacency by insisting, obtrusively, that our politics falls short of our hopes, in two distinct ways. First of all, it falls short on its own terms: the poor are not clothed, the hungry not fed, the homeless not housed, the righteous not rewarded, the wicked not punished. It is an essential part of the prophetic imagination, itself grounded in hope, to remind us, as did Amos, of the covenant we continually fail to keep, of the need for justice to flow like a river, and righteousness as a mighty stream. But this call for justice is only one prophetic task. God has demands on us beyond justice; God wants more of us than merely for us to "play fair." Prophetic hope challenges the pretension that humans are fundamentally aiming at ends achievable by politics at all — that humans' ends are fundamentally this-worldly. Hope calls politics beyond itself, and reveals politics' ultimate inadequacy. Hope calls us beyond the mundane, reminds us that our lives are not simply about the outcome of our actions, but flourish most profoundly in conversation and communion with a God whose ways are not our own.

But that public life is insufficient does not imply that it is irrelevant. Politics is one way God speaks to us; beyond its mundane literality, worldly action has an iconic character. We see all semiotically, and we act as *semeia*, signs of God. This is how Abraham Lincoln, in his Second Inaugural Address, "read" the American Civil War as God's judgment on the people of the United States, "North and South," as punishment for their collective complicity in the sin of slavery. Along with justice, then, the prophets insist that public life has a destiny beyond justice, but it is a destiny that will transfigure our mundane life, not renounce it.

Public life for Christians, then, when properly undertaken, inevitably leads its participants to contemplate the mysteries of providence and the sovereignty of God, and thereby to cultivate the holy terror that is integral to true piety. By hopeful engagement in public life, the public sphere itself becomes the forum for an ascetical inquiry whose aims it cannot itself, in this dispensation, comprehend. By so gracefully enduring hope, we are better shaped more fully to receive God's grace.

Conclusion

In all that I have said about hope, I may sound as if I think hope can stand on its own as an autonomous virtue. But this is not so. Without the other virtues, in fact, each virtue is imbalanced and leads to various kinds of deformation. If you emphasize hope while ignoring faith and love, you will instrumentalize religion for politics. If you emphasize faith while ignoring hope and love, you will encourage an undue hostility toward the state and a self-delusional, self-aggrandizing emphasis on purity. If you emphasize love, you can't quite forget faith and hope but you will be tempted to conceive of love as a simple emotion, which will lead to a kind of lame, atemporal sentimental idealism. All three go together, and collectively they constitute a whole way of life, a way of *living in time*, of living as longing beings, in a world that would like us to forget time and history altogether.

And yet this is no finally stable way of life. It is in fact always ramshackle, always about to fall apart. A hopeful way of living, to be sure, is better than an unhopeful one, but better is far from perfect — even, to be frank, far from good. To live in hope is not to live like a person contemplating, with complacent smugness, one's imminent triumph; it is to live in the hope that, whatever happens, one needn't count only on one's own resources to see it through — that we can lean on the universe, on the confidence that the cosmos is neither against us nor indifferent to us.

In all this we see again the importance of appreciating the irony that hope creates. The poet Charles Wright once wrote that "happiness happens, like sainthood, in spite of ourselves." It happens despite ourselves, and by happening, it spites us — annoys us. Recognizing this is key to truly living in our world, which is to say living ironically in it. Irony lets us delight in the surprises of history, and is a manifestation of how the New Thing always escapes even our expectations of it, showing us as well to have been trapped in the past. For after all, we are saved *despite* ourselves. The danger with most appreciations of hope is that they are far too earnest. In appreciating hope's irony, we come yet again to appreciate, while not exactly empty, in a certain way how shallow are our hopes for our own achievement of goodness and happiness. In coming to see this, we learn something of what God knows about us, and begin to become sanctified in that knowledge.

Learning to Begin

⌒*ℳ*⌒

We, too, will be legends for future generations, because we once lived, and our words will mean more than we care to admit today.

Adam Zagajewski

Analogies between one time and another are always dangerous. Prone as we are to self-aggrandizement and self-congratulation, we must remain suspicious of enrolling other ages in our struggles. They had their own battles to fight, their own challenges to confront. To assume that there is any straightforward and easy way to say "we're like them" or "they're like us" is invariably to do them historical damage and us immense intellectual harm. The more we know about another age, the less plausible sounds any parallel to our own. Each era is so inescapably itself, each life is so dyed in its own distinct hues, that it seems the height of historiographical impiety to join together what God has put asunder. Perhaps we should just let the dead lie.

But humans work by thinking comparatively. After all, for all their violence, comparisons sometimes do bring some light, along with their inevitable accompanying heat. Comparison can sometimes be illuminating. And anyway, it is unavoidable.

Augustine's age was very different from today. But there are some real similarities between then and now. In fact, in several senses we are closer to Augustine's age than any intervening era has been. An era of rapid, and tumultuous, cultural change; an era in which the character of the known world is transforming itself rapidly; an era of vast and pluriform pluralism, religious and otherwise; an era of profound anxiety for Christian believers: these are all defining characteristics of Augustine's age, and of our own.

In such ages Christians have two basic tasks: they must witness to the gospel and communicate that witness to others, and they must retain the faith that was handed on to them and hand it on to the next generation. In service of those tasks they must recall things that are in danger of being forgotten altogether, and they must think further along the lines that their elders laid down, thinking forward in the traditions they inherited, in order to hand them on to coming generations in workable order.

This book has tried to do those things. It is a link in a chain letter that reaches far back in the past, with Augustine's *City of God*, if not before. Repeating the words of past books is an important task. It is meet and right, perhaps even our bounden duty, so to do. But those books' words must, from time to time, be updated.

In Augustine's time much ink was spilled on the ideas of honor and glory. Above all things, Romans sought glory. Augustine thought glory was a real thing, and definitely to be admired, but he believed all glory was first and foremost to be ascribed to God, and only secondarily to human achievements; the Romans erred in trying to rise up and seize glory for themselves — an effort that spoke more to their titanic egos and despair of reliable divine comfort. So one crucial issue for Augustine, in the *City of God*, was demystifying the Romans' absolute worship of *gloria*, the glory they thought they could win for themselves by great deeds done for the Senate and people of Rome. Hence, for the first word in the *City of God* he chose *gloriosissimam* — "most glorious" — though he applied it to the city of God, not to any human achievement. He tried to show, that is, that true glory accrues to God, and derivatively to those who follow God's path. He tried to say, that is, that the longings of his time and place were real longings, and perceived and pursued real goods, but they misconstrued the origins and final character of those goods, and so were in need of reorientation. He argued that his contemporaries were not pursuing demonic goods, but real goods tragically misunderstood; those goods did not warrant final rejection, but transformation. He did not renounce; he converted.

And so should we. Perhaps we lack a single category with the power that *gloria* had for the Romans. But we have some strong contenders. Perhaps the one that comes closest is our deep commitment to freedom. But what is the sort of freedom we pursue? Too often it is not freedom for the future, but rather simply freedom *from* — freedom from the past. We want not to be determined by what has come before; we kick at the past as if it were the entangling arms of an octopus, trying to drag us back into the deeps. This makes it easy for us to be escapist, to see freedom as flight, from the world, from our pasts, from our neighbors, from ourselves.

But this is not the only approach to freedom we can take. To turn responsibly toward the past, to accept it for a gift and see how we can build on it — that would be another, more responsible, and perhaps less reactionary way to think about freedom. Here freedom is not imagined as a magic potion, some sort of technology (which is, after all, just an updated potion). We will be more history's recipients, and less sheerly history's creators. We will live *in* history, in time, in the world, and not let the difficulty of that condition curdle into resentment at it.

Today — as is the case every day, in our fallen world — such a frank recognition that our condition can easily cause resentment may well make some perceive in my proposal an apparent escapism and hostility to our finite condition. This book's emphasis on longing and lack has been an attempt frankly to face up to these accusations, in order to see what they amount to. (In a world roaring with consumerism and overspending, even when many others have little, I would suggest that accusations of antimaterialism are more curious than we often realize. But let that lie.) This emphasis is counterbalanced by our equal insistence that, on the best construal of the Christian tradition, humanity's destiny — let's call it "heaven" — is not an escape from our created condition, or from our bodies, but rather a full and final possession of our embodiment, in flesh and in time, in all its glorious and multitudinous complexity. This is what belief in the resurrection of the body means. If we are going to call such a position "otherworldly," it is an oddly pro-creation otherworldliness, one where escape is not a longed-for aim, but that wants us to recognize a presently inhabited condition — a more or less permanent situation, until the second coming.

In all this there is likely to be something disappointing. Isn't our situation today apocalyptically different? We think so; we are convinced that this moment is the *kairos* time, the time of crisis, the time of decision, the day of salvation. But this is just our version of the same old apocalypticism against which Augustine warned us, sixteen hundred years ago. Perhaps the deepest disquiet, and the newest news, that an Augustinian perspective can provide for us is just this insistence that, in some basic way, an Augustinian look at empire today, for all its differences in detail, is little more than more of the same.

*   *   *

A dark time is coming. It always is. As Reinhold Niebuhr put it, the crises of history will mount, not resolve themselves, over the course of history. At times of hopelessness and terror, profound oppression of body and spirit, there have always been those who refused to despair. They have been believers and unbelievers, atheists, cosmopolitan polytheists, moralists, immoralists, and antimoralists. Among this multitude there ought to be at least a few Christians.

In this setting we must be witnesses and prophets. But what does such witness, such prophecy, look like? As ever, it will be contingent on the exigencies of the place and time. But opportunities for it arise every day. I began this book with one story of a teacher and his students. I will end with another, similar story. On the morning of Monday, April 23, 2007, I was preparing for my large "Comparative Religious Ethics" class. It's a big lecture class that introduces students to the ethical thought-worlds of the Abrahamic traditions — Judaism, Christianity, and Islam. I will occasionally interrupt the class to mention interesting things of the day. Well, this day there was an interesting thing. Boris Yeltsin had just died. Before class, I quickly read the news reports on various Web sites. Then I gathered my notes and walked to class.

On the walk I remembered one weekend in August 1991, the weekend of the Soviet old guard's coup, when the fate of the Cold War seemed to hang on whether or not some apparatchiks could get to Yeltsin and kill him. I remembered watching television, transfixed, with his bodyguards holding up briefcases that doubled as bulletproof shields; him standing on a tank, then on the portico of the Parliament building, addressing the crowds, crowds that seemed to go on forever; and him finally, fully accepting that he had become the leader of the nation, of the motherland, and had to lead it into a new millennium, and a new political dispensation. Yeltsin's drunken fumbling through the rest of the nineties faded away in my mind. All I saw was that one heroic gesture — a gesture that meant more than anyone can tell, and not just to Russians, or the other peoples in the USSR. By the time I got to my classroom, I knew what I would say to them.

"Once upon a time," I began, "there was a thing called the Soviet Union. And people like me, who were born into a world where it existed, grew up in an era called the Cold War. You may not remember it, for the USSR died ignominiously when you were small children, and the Cold War ended with it. But for many of us it was a great and powerful reality — a near-physical presence in our lives, in many ways. I grew up believing that there were better than even odds that there would be a nuclear war between the United States and the Soviet Union. And I remember when it collapsed. We never believed it could happen. But we were wrong.

"Now we live in another age, another age of fear, of wars and rumors of wars. But I prophesy to you today, here, that one day you will tell people much younger than yourselves — your students, perhaps, or your children or grandchildren — a similar story. 'Once,' you will say, 'there was a thing called al-Qaeda, and a war called the War on Terror.' And I hope that when you begin to tell that story — the story of our times — you remember this day, and what I told you here."

I meant it then. I mean it still. Wars we will always have with us; worries and terrors, anxieties and uncertainties: these are our lot in life, after the fall, east of Eden. But we must never allow the terrible pressures of today to make us forget that today is not all there is. The pressing exigencies of the parochial present can and will afflict us with their promise of total answers, complete conclusions, final solutions. But an honest apprehension of the world teaches us that its challenges will not end before its blessings do, nor vice versa, and that this day is always followed by another, until the end of time. These are the facts of our situation. Our disappointment at these facts is real, and genuine, and it is itself another fact of which we must take account. Were we to live in full and honest recognition of our ambivalent, paradoxical, contradictory situation — in the world yet not of it, joyful yet accepting of reasonable sorrow, seeking an end that will never be ours in this life — we would be what we are supposed to be: "impostors, yet true; unknown, yet well known; dying, and behold — we are alive."

To learn to inhabit that condition is to learn, in a way, what it is to begin to be alive. To learn this lesson is the terrible, graceful vocation of all humanity. It is a lesson that Christians are called upon to inaugurate in their lives here and now. The shape that that lesson takes in our world will be, I fear, and I believe, inescapably political, but its point is far more profound than our political languages can bear. If I have taught you something in this book, I have meant it to be something about the sacramental possibilities of a political life. But the details of my own proposal are relatively insignificant before this more fundamental task. We may need to find new languages to speak of our lives; we may need a new way of living in old languages; we may need to recover words long forgotten, or long misused. We probably need all these things, and more. But these tasks are ones we can no longer defer. Now is the acceptable day. Now is the day of salvation. Now we must begin.

References and Further Reading

⁓✍︎⁓

Introduction

For a nice discussion of Barth's "Theological Existence Today," and its original context, see Timothy Gorringe, *Karl Barth: Against Hegemony* (New York: Oxford University Press, 1999), especially pp. 20-23.

The C. S. Lewis quotation (and the title of my introduction) comes from his address "Learning in War-Time," in *The Weight of Glory, and Other Addresses* (Grand Rapids: Eerdmans, 1965 [1939]), pp. 43-54, at p. 44.

The Reinhold Niebuhr quotation comes from his *The Nature and Destiny of Man*, vol. 2, *Human Destiny* (Louisville: Westminster John Knox, 1996 [1941]), p. 198.

The Edward Teller story is reported in Larry King and Emily Yoffe, *Larry King* (New York: Simon and Schuster, 1982), p. 156.

Chapter One

The William Gibson quotation comes from "William Gibson, Shifting from Cyberspace to a Spooky Reality," *Washington Post*, September 6, 2007, p. C4. The Václav Havel quotation comes from his *The Art of the Impossible: Politics as Morality in Practice*, trans. Paul Wilson (New York: Knopf, 1997), p. 104.

The passage from Gregory of Nyssa is from his *Commentary on the*

Song of Songs 7.933M, p. 235, ll. 3-5 (Langerbeck ed.), on Cant. 4:4, cited in A. Rousselle, "Parole et inspiration: le travail de la voix dans le monde romain," *History and Philosophy of the Life Sciences*, sec. 2, Pubblicazioni della Stazione zoological di Napoli 5.2 (Naples, 1983), pp. 129-57. But this citation was itself found in Averil Cameron, *Christianity and the Rhetoric of Empire: The Development of Christian Discourse* (Berkeley: University of California Press, 1994), p. 15.

For the Walter Benjamin text, see Walter Benjamin, "The Storyteller," in *Illuminations: Essays and Reflections*, trans. Harry Zohn, edited with an introduction by Hannah Arendt (New York: Schocken, 1969), pp. 83-109. Quotations are on pp. 86 and 89. For a more information-heavy (and rather unironic) assessment of some of these matters, see Philip Tetlock, *Expert Political Judgment: How Good Is It? How Can We Know?* (Princeton: Princeton University Press, 2005).

For very stimulating broad views on the challenges facing us in the twenty-first century, see Timothy Garton Ash, *Free World: America, Europe, and the Surprising Future of the West* (New York: Random House, 2004); Pierre Manent, *A World beyond Politics? A Defense of the Nation-State*, trans. Marc LePain (Princeton: Princeton University Press, 2006); and Bernard Henri-Levi, *War, Evil, and the End of History* (New York: Melville House, 2000).

On the "crisis of humanitarianism," see David Rieff, *A Bed for the Night: Humanitarianism in Crisis* (New York: Simon and Schuster, 2003).

On terror in the twentieth century, see Tzvetan Todorov, *Hope and Memory: Lessons from the Twentieth Century*, trans. David Bellos (Princeton: Princeton University Press, 2003), and Hannah Arendt, *The Origins of Totalitarianism* (New York: Harcourt Brace Jovanovich, 1973 [1951]), especially her "Epilogue: Ideology and Terror."

On the changing nature of human beings in modernity, I am drawing especially on the work of Charles Taylor; see his *A Secular Age* (Cambridge: Harvard University Press, 2007), but see also Anthony Giddens, *The Consequences of Modernity* (Palo Alto: Stanford University Press, 1991); Frederic Jameson, *Postmodernism; or, The Cultural Logic of Late Capitalism* (Durham, N.C.: Duke University Press, 1991); and Adam Seligman, *Modernity's Wager: Authority, the Self, and Transcendence* (Princeton: Princeton University Press, 2003).

For evidence and interpretation of the decline of violence in modernity, see Eric A. Johnson and Eric H. Monkkonen, eds., *The Civilization of Crime:*

Violence in Town and Country since the Middle Ages (Champaign: University of Illinois Press, 1996); Norbert Elias, *The Civilizing Process*, 2nd ed. (Cambridge: Wiley-Blackwell, 2000); and A. O. Hirschman, *The Passions and the Interests* (Princeton: Princeton University Press, 1977). For the argument that the burst of wars at the end of the Cold War has obscured the decline of major war in the twentieth century, see John Mueller, *The Remnants of War* (Ithaca, N.Y.: Cornell University Press, 2004), p. 162, for summary of findings on this. For more see Mueller, *Retreat from Doomsday: The Obsolescence of Major War* (New York: Basic Books, 1989), and the *Human Security Report* project; see the web site at: http://www.humansecurityreport.info/.

For a good study of the linguistic career of *imperium* and *imperator*, see Richard Koebner, *Empire* (Cambridge: Cambridge University Press, 1961). For some good works on the recent history of empires, see Niall Ferguson, *Empire: How Britain Made the Modern World* (London: Penguin, 2004); Uday Singh Mehta, *Liberalism and Empire: A Study in Nineteenth-Century British Liberal Thought* (Chicago: University of Chicago Press, 1999); Sankar Muthu, *Enlightenment against Empire* (Princeton: Princeton University Press, 2003); Jennifer Pitts, *A Turn to Empire: The Rise of Imperial Liberalism in Britain and France* (Princeton: Princeton University Press, 2005); Anthony Pagden, *Lords of All the World: Ideologies of Empire in Spain, Britain, and France, c. 1500-1800* (New Haven: Yale University Press, 1995); Peter S. Onuf, *Jefferson's Empire: The Language of American Nationhood* (Charlottesville: University Press of Virginia, 2000); Anthony Pagden, *Peoples and Empires* (New York: Modern Library, 2003). For Christian thinking on empire, see Oliver O'Donovan, *The Desire of the Nations: Rediscovering the Roots of Political Theology* (New York: Cambridge University Press, 1996), and Cameron, *Christianity and the Rhetoric of Empire*.

Chapter Two

For deaths in auto accidents after 9/11, see Gerd Gigerenzer, "Dread Risk, September 11, and Fatal Traffic Accidents," *Psychological Science* 15, no. 4 (2004): 286-87.

I quote from Augustine's letters 23, 87, 88, 93, 105; his *Homilies on the First Epistle of John* 1.12; 10.10; and his *Enarrationes in Psalmos* 49.2.2. The phrase "love and do what you will" is found in *Homilies* 7.8; the idea of being "trained by longings" comes from *Homilies* 4.6.

The quotation from Christopher Henzel is from his "The Origins of al Qaeda's Ideology: Implications for US Strategy," *Parameters* (Spring 2005): 69-80, at p. 77.

The quotation from Gilles Kepel is from his *The War for Muslim Minds: Islam and the West*, trans. Pascale Ghazaleh (Cambridge: Harvard University Press, 2004), p. 112.

The passage of Bruce B. Lawrence is from his introduction to *Messages to the World: The Statements of Osama bin Laden* (New York: Verso, 2005), p. xxii.

On the revealing memos from within al-Qaeda, see Sebastian Rotella, "Within al-Qaida, a Numbing Bureaucracy: Captured Papers Show Obsession over Details, Infighting," *Baltimore Sun*, April 20, 2008.

On terrorism's history, see David C. Rapoport, "The Four Waves of Modern Terrorism," in *Attacking Terrorism: Elements of a Grand Strategy*, ed. Audrey Kurth Cronin and James M. Ludes (Washington, D.C.: Georgetown University Press, 2004), pp. 46-73; David C. Rapoport, "Fear and Trembling: Terrorism in Three Religious Traditions," *American Political Science Review* 78, no. 3 (September 1984): 658-77; and Gérard Chaliand and Arnauld Blin, eds., *The History of Terrorism: From Antiquity to al-Qaeda* (Berkeley: University of California Press, 2007). On contemporary terrorists, see Marc Sageman, *Understanding Terror Networks* (Philadelphia: University of Pennsylvania Press, 2004); Daniel Byman, *Deadly Connections: States That Sponsor Terrorism* (New York: Cambridge University Press, 2005); Alan B. Krueger, *What Makes a Terrorist? Economics and the Roots of Terrorism* (Princeton: Princeton University Press, 2007). More specifically see Peter Bergen and Swati Pandey, "The Madrassa Scapegoat," *Washington Quarterly*, Spring 2006, pp. 117-25. See also Terry McDermott, *Perfect Soldiers: The Hijackers; Who They Were, Why They Did It* (New York: HarperCollins, 2005), and "Cracks in the Foundation: Leadership Schisms in al-Qa'ida from 1989-2006," available from the West Point Combating Terrorism Center at http://www.ctc.usma.edu/aq/aq3.asp.

For the origins of modern radical politics, see Michael Walzer, *The Revolution of the Saints: A Study in the Origins of Radical Politics* (Cambridge: Harvard University Press, 1982 [1965]). I still find this book astonishingly prescient about the structures of al-Qaeda. On the changing nature of Islam, see Patrick Haenni, *L'Islam de marché: L'autre révolution conservatrice* (Paris: Seuil, 2005). For fairly optimistic studies of European Muslims, see Jytte Klausen, *The Islamic Challenge: Politics and Religion in Western Europe* (New York: Oxford University Press, 2006), and Jonathan Laurence and Justin Vaisse, *Integrating Islam: Political and Religious Challenges in Contemporary France* (Washington, D.C.: Brookings Institution Press, 2006). On Islam in the Middle East, see Olivier Roy, *The Politics of Chaos in the Middle East*, trans. Ros Schwartz (New York: Columbia University Press, 2008). See also Fawaz Gerges, *The Far Enemy: Why Jihad Went Global* (New York: Cambridge University Press, 2005); Christopher Henzel, "The Origins of al Qaeda's Ideology: Implications for US Strategy," *Parameters* (Spring 2005): 69-80; and Michael Scott Doran, "Somebody Else's Civil War: Ideology, Rage, and the Assault on America," in Rose and Hodge, *How Did This Happen?* (New York: Council on Foreign Relations, 2001). On the nascent "post-Islamist" movement in the Islamic world, see Asef Bayat, *Making Islam Democratic: Social Movements and the Post-Islamist Turn* (Stanford: Stanford University Press, 2007), and on movements in Europe, see Tariq Ramadan, *Western Muslims and the Future of Islam* (New York: Oxford University Press, 2005). On humiliation and resentment in parts of the Islamic world, see Peter Bergen and Michael Lind, "A Matter of Pride: Why We Can't Buy Off the Next Osama bin Laden," *Democracy Journal* 3 (Winter 2007): 8-16. On the legitimation crisis of the Islamic authorities, see John Kelsay, *Arguing the Just War in Islam* (Cambridge: Harvard University Press, 2007). On changes in understandings of jihad, see Faisal Devji, *Landscapes of the Jihad: Militancy, Morality, Modernity* (Ithaca, N.Y.: Cornell University Press, 2005), and David Cook, *Understanding Jihad* (Berkeley: University of California Press, 2005).

On Augustine and the Donatists, see W. H. C. Frend, *The Donatist Church: A Movement of Protest in Roman North Africa* (Oxford: Clarendon; New York: Oxford University Press, 2000); T. D. Barnes, "The Beginning of Donatism," *Journal of Theological Studies* 26 (1975): 13-22; and, famously, P. L. R. Brown, "Saint Augustine's Attitude to Religious Coercion," *Journal of Roman Studies* 54 (1964): 107-16. More recently see Frederick H. Russell, "Persuading the Donatists: Augustine's Coercion by Words," in *The Limits of Ancient Christianity: Essays on Late Antique Thought and Culture in Honor of R. A. Markus*, ed. William E. Klingshirn and Mark Vessey (Ann Arbor: University of Michigan Press, 1999), pp. 115-38, and two essays by Neal Wood: "African Peasant Terrorism and Augustine's Political Thought," in *History from Below: Studies in Popular Protest and Popular Ideology in Honour of George Rudé*, ed. Frederick Kranz (Montreal: Concordia

University Press, 1985), pp. 279-99, and *"Populares* and *Circumcelliones:* The Vocabulary of 'Fallen Man' in Cicero and St. Augustine," in *History of Political Thought*, vol. 7 (1986), pp. 33-51.

For more on Augustine and evil, see my *Evil and the Augustinian Tradition* (Cambridge: Cambridge University Press, 2001).

Chapter Three

Quotations from Jerome come from his letters 123 and 127, and his commentary on Ezekiel (1, pref.).

The exchange between Augustine and Marcellinus is comprised of letters 136 (Marcellinus to Augustine) and 138 (Augustine to Marcellinus). For Augustine on Roman virtue, see letter 138 and his very late *Against Julian* 4.26, though the famous discussion is really in *City of God* 5.

The essay by Mark Haas that I discuss here is Mark L. Haas, "A Geriatric Peace? The Future of U.S. Power in a World of Aging Populations," *International Security* 32, no. 1 (Summer 2007): 112-47.

The quotation of Lord Salisbury is from Christopher Layne, "From Preponderance to Offshore Balancing: America's Future Grand Strategy," *International Security* 22, no. 1 (Summer 1997): 86-124, at p. 123.

The quotation of Stanley Cavell is from his "The Avoidance of Love: A Reading of *King Lear*," in *Must We Mean What We Say? A Book of Essays* (Cambridge: Cambridge University Press, 1976), pp. 267-353, here pp. 344-45.

The quotation of Christina V. Balis comes from her "Contrasting Images, Complementary Visions," in *Visions of America and Europe: September 11, Iraq, and Transatlantic Relations*, ed. Christina V. Balis and Simon Serfaty (Washington, D.C.: Center for Strategic and International Studies, 2004), pp. 203-23.

The quotation from Nicole Bacharan is from Roger Cohen, David E. Sanger, and Steven R. Weisma, "Challenging Rest of the World with a New Order," *New York Times*, October 12, 2004.

The quotation from an unnamed "Asian Ambassador in Washington" comes from Kurt M. Campbell, "Possibilities of War: The Confluence of Persistent Contemporary Flashpoints and Worrisome New Trouble Spots" (discussion paper prepared for NIC 2020 project), p. 16; available at: http://www.dni.gov/nic/PDF_GIF_2020_Support/2004_05_25_pa-pers/possibilities.pdf.

The quotations from Ivan Krastev are all from his "The Anti-American Century?" *Journal of Democracy* 15, no. 2 (April 2004): 5-16. For more on anti-Americanism, see Tony Judt and Denis Lacorne, *With Us or against Us: Studies in Global Anti-Americanism* (New York: Palgrave Macmillan, 2005).

Ernst Renan's lecture "What Is a Nation?" is found in *Becoming National: A Reader*, ed. Geoff Eley and Ronald Grigor Suny (New York: Oxford University Press, 1996), pp. 41-55.

For an optimistic view of Europe's prospects, see Mark Leonard, *Why Europe Will Run the 21st Century* (New York: PublicAffairs, 2006). For more worried views, see Larry Siedentorp, *Democracy in Europe* (New York: Columbia University Press, 2001), and Alberto Alesina and Francesco Giavazzi, *The Future of Europe: Reform or Decline* (Cambridge: MIT Press, 2006).

For a good overview of China's rise in Asia since 2001, see David Shambaugh, "China Engages Asia: Reshaping the Regional Order," *International Security* 29, no. 3 (November/December 2003): 22-35. For a discussion of the challenges China faces as it "rises to greatness," see Jeffrey W. Legro, *Rethinking the World: Great Power Strategies and International Order* (Ithaca, N.Y.: Cornell University Press, 2005), pp. 173-78. On "crony capitalism" in particular, see Minxin Pei, *China's Trapped Transition* (Cambridge: Harvard University Press, 2006). For China's influence on East Asia see David Shambaugh, *Power Shift: China and Asia's New Dynamics* (Berkeley: University of California Press, 2006). On demographic challenges to rising powers, see Nicholas Eberstadt, "Growing Old the Hard Way: China, Russia, India," *Policy Review* 136 (April/May 2006), and Valerie M. Hudson and Andrea M. den Boer, *Bare Branches: The Security Implications of Asia's Surplus Male Population* (Cambridge: MIT Press, 2005).

For demography, see Nicholas Eberstadt, "What If It's a World Population Implosion? Speculations about Global De-population," Global Reproductive Health Forum (Harvard University, 1998; available at www.hsph.harvard.edu/Organizations/healthnet/HUpapers/implosion/depop.html).

For useful discussions of U.S. hegemony, see Colin S. Gray, *The Sheriff: America's Defense of the New World Order* (Lexington: University Press of Kentucky, 2004), and Michael Mandelbaum, *The Case for Goliath: How*

America Acts as the World's Government in the Twenty-first Century (New York: Public Affairs, 2005). See also David H. Levey and Stuart S. Brown, "The Overstretch Myth," *Foreign Affairs* 84 (March/April 2005): 2-7; William E. Odom and Robert Dujarric, *America's Inadvertent Empire* (New Haven: Yale University Press, 2004); Robert Kagan, *Of Paradise and Power: America and Europe in the New World Order* (New York: Knopf, 2003); also Kagan's *Dangerous Nation: America's Foreign Policy from Its Earliest Days to the Dawn of the Twentieth Century* (New York: Knopf, 2006).

On how America's history shapes its presence in global politics, see George McKenna, *The Puritan Origins of American Patriotism* (New Haven: Yale University Press, 2007); Nathan Hatch, *The Democratization of American Christianity* (New Haven: Yale University Press, 1989); Mark Noll, *America's God: Jonathan Edwards to Abraham Lincoln* (New York: Oxford University Press, 2002); William R. Hutchison, *Errand to the World: American Protestant Thought and Foreign Missions* (Chicago: University of Chicago Press, 1987); and Josef Joffe, *Überpower: The Imperial Temptation of America* (New York: Norton, 2006). In contrast, Anthony D. Smith, *Chosen Peoples: Sacred Sources of National Identity* (New York: Oxford University Press, 2003), shows that the United States' messianic self-understanding is not as unusual historically as many suggest it is.

For American moralism and militarism, see James Morone, *Hellfire Nation: The Politics of Sin in American History* (New Haven: Yale University Press, 2004), and Fred Anderson and Andrew Cayton, *The Dominion of War: Empire and Liberty in North America, 1500-2000* (New York: Viking, 2005).

For the military face of America's foreign policy, see Dana Priest, *The Mission: Waging War and Keeping Peace with America's Military* (New York: Norton, 2003), and J. Anthony Holmes, "Where Are the Civilians? How to Rebuild the U.S. Foreign Service," *Foreign Affairs* 88, no. 1 (January-February 2009): 148-61.

For the changing nature of the American military's presence in the world, see Thomas P. M. Barnett, *The Pentagon's New Map: War and Peace in the Twenty-first Century* (New York: Berkeley, 2005); *American Military Culture in the Twenty-first Century*, CSIS International Security Program Report (Washington, D.C.: CSIS, 2000); Ole R. Holsti, "A Widening Gap between the U.S. Military and Civilian Society? Some Evidence, 1976-1996," *International Security* 23 (Winter 1998-99); and Center for Strategic and International Studies, *American Military Culture in the Twenty-first Cen-*

tury (Washington, D.C.: CSIS, 2000); David Kilkullen, "New Paradigms for 21st Century Conflict," locatable at: http://usinfo.state.gov/journals/itps/0507/ijpe/kilcullen.htm#2; Barry R. Posen, "Command of the Commons: The Military Foundation of U.S. Hegemony," *International Security* 28, no. 1 (Summer 2003): 5-46.

Chapter Four

The Iris Murdoch quotation comes from her "Metaphysics and Ethics," in *Existentialists and Mystics: Writings on Philosophy and Literature*, ed. Peter Conradi (New York: Penguin, 1999), pp. 59-75, at p. 75.

The H. Richard Niebuhr quotation comes from his *The Kingdom of God in America* (Middletown, Conn.: Wesleyan University Press, 1988 [1938]), p. 193.

On changes in culture in the contemporary world, see David Harvey, *The Condition of Postmodernity* (Cambridge, Mass.: Blackwell, 1990); Arlie Russell Hochschild, *The Commercialization of Intimate Life: Notes from Home and Work* (Berkeley: University of California Press, 2003); James Davison Hunter, *The Death of Character: Moral Education in an Age without Good or Evil* (New York: Basic Books, 2000); James Nolan, *The Therapeutic State: Justifying Government at Century's End* (New York: New York University Press, 1998); Zygmunt Baumann, *Liquid Modernity* (Oxford: Polity, 2000); Richard Sennett, *The Culture of the New Capitalism* (New Haven: Yale University Press, 2006); and Eyal Chowers, *The Modern Self in the Labyrinth: Politics and the Entrapment Imagination* (Cambridge: Havard University Press, 2004).

On consumerism, see Colin Campbell, *The Romantic Ethic and the Spirit of Modern Consumerism* (New York: Blackwell, 1987); Lizabeth Cohen, *A Consumer's Republic: The Politics of Mass Consumption in Postwar America* (New York: Knopf, 2003); Vincent Miller, *Consuming Religion: Christian Faith and Practice in a Consumer Culture* (New York: Continuum, 2004); Thomas Hine, *I Want That: How We All Became Shoppers* (New York: HarperCollins, 2002); and Nicholas Boyle, *Who Are We Now? Christian Humanism and the Global Market from Hegel to Heaney* (Notre Dame, Ind.: University of Notre Dame Press, 1998).

On the language of choice, see Peter Berger, *The Heretical Imperative: Contemporary Possibilities of Religious Affirmation* (New York: Doubleday,

1979). For a study of the psychological dissatisfactions of a "choice-centric" life, see Barry Schwartz, *The Paradox of Choice: Why More Is Less* (New York: HarperCollins, 2004). For a very deep sociological account of the social implications of choice, see Edward C. Rosenthal, *The Era of Choice* (Cambridge: MIT Press, 2005). For a historical study of the infiltration of the language of choice across all facets of society over the course of the twentieth century, see Lawrence Meir Friedman, *The Republic of Choice: Law, Authority, and Culture* (Cambridge: Harvard University Press, 1990), and Tim Kasser, *The High Price of Materialism* (Cambridge: MIT Press, 2002).

On the cultural changes in religion, see Robert Wuthnow, *The Crisis in the Churches: Spiritual Malaise, Fiscal Woe* (New York: Oxford University Press, 1997); Dean Hoge, William Dinges, Mary Johnson, and Juan Gonzales, *Young Adult Catholics: Religion in the Culture of Choice* (Notre Dame, Ind.: University of Notre Dame Press, 2001); Wade Clark Roof, *A Generation of Seekers: The Spiritual Journeys of the Baby Boom Generation* (New York: HarperCollins, 1993); and Joel Shuman and Keith Meador, *Heal Thyself: Spirituality, Medicine, and the Distortion of Christianity* (New York: Oxford University Press, 2003). See Wade Clark Roof, *Spiritual Marketplace: Baby Boomers and the Remaking of American Religion* (Princeton: Princeton University Press, 2005); Peter Berger, "Religion and the West," *National Interest*, no. 80 (Summer 2005): 112-29; Wendy Cadge and Lynn Davidman, "Ascription, Choice, and the Construction of Religious Identities in the Contemporary United States," *Journal for the Scientific Study of Religion* 45, no. 1 (2006): 23-38; and the Brookings Institution roundtable on "Faith and Youth in the iPod Era," available at: http://www.brookings.edu/events/2005/0411religion.aspx.

On the link between studying rational choice economics and selfishness, see Robert H. Frank, Thomas Gilovich, and Dennis T. Regan, "Do Economists Make Bad Citizens?" *Journal of Economic Perspectives* 10, no. 1 (Winter 1996): 187-92. For a skeptical view, see Bruno S. Frey and Stephan Meier, "Are Political Economists Selfish and Indoctrinated? Evidence from a Natural Experiment," *Economic Inquiry* 41, no. 3 (July 2003): 448-62.

On cities see Saskia Sassen, *The Global City: New York, London, Tokyo* (Princeton: Princeton University Press, 1991); Witold Rybczynski, *City Life: Urban Expectations in a New World* (New York: Scribner, 1995); Joel Kotkin, *The City: A Global History* (New York: Modern Library, 2005); and

Deane Neubauer, "Mixed Blessings of the Megacities," *Yale Global Online,*
September 24, 2004, available at http://yaleglobal.yale.edu/display.arti-
cle?id=4573. On suburbs see Kenneth Jackson, *Crabgrass Frontier: The
Suburbanization of the United States* (New York: Oxford University Press,
1985). For an excellent attempt to grapple with the ambivalent implications of suburbanization — to see the real goods as well as the (more
frequently bemoaned) damaging consequences — see Robert
Bruegmann, *Sprawl: A Compact History* (Chicago: University of Chicago
Press, 2005).

On global aging, see Joel E. Cohen, "Human Population Grows Up,"
Scientific American, September 2005; Peter G. Peterson, *Gray Dawn: How
the Coming Age Wave Will Transform America — and the World* (New York:
Times Books, 1999); and Rachel A. Pruchno and Michael A. Smyer, eds.,
Challenges of an Aging Society: Ethical Dilemmas, Political Issues (Baltimore:
Johns Hopkins University Press, 2007).

On changes in population morbidity, see Robert W. Fogel, *The Escape
from Hunger and Premature Death, 1700-2100: Europe, America, and the Third
World* (New York: Cambridge University Press, 2004), and James C.
Riley, *Rising Life Expectancy: A Global History* (New York: Cambridge University Press, 2001). John Maynard Keynes saw this; see "Economic Possibilities for Our Grandchildren," in *Essays in Persuasion* (New York:
Norton, 1963 [1931]), pp. 358-73.

For more on our distorted notions of joy, see Tibor Scitovsky, *The Joyless Economy: The Psychology of Human Satisfaction,* rev. ed. (New York: Oxford University Press, 1992). For a theological reflection on joy, see Josef
Pieper, *In Tune with the World: A Theory of Festivity* (Notre Dame, Ind.: St.
Augustine's Press, 1999 [1965]).

On Augustine's idea of *distensio,* look at G. J. P. O'Daly, "Time as
Distensio and St. Augustine's Exegesis of Philippians 3, 12-14," *Revue des
Études Augustiniennes* 23 (1977): 265-71.

On the centralization of political life and concomitant diminishing of
opportunities for citizens' engagement, see Theda Skocpol, *Diminished
Democracy: From Membership to Management in American Civic Life* (Norman:
University of Oklahoma Press, 2003).

On political polarization, see Cass Sunstein, *Republic.com 2.0* (Princeton: Princeton University Press, 2007); William A. Galston and Elaine C.
Kamarack, "The Politics of Polarization," A Third Way Report (Washington, D.C.: Third Way, 2005); Stefano DellaVigna and Ethan Kaplan, "The

Fox News Effect: Media Bias and Voting," *Quarterly Journal of Economics* 122, no. 3 (August 2007): 1187-1234; and Bill Bishop and Robert G. Cushing, *The Big Sort: Why the Clustering of Like-Minded America Is Tearing Us Apart* (New York: Houghton Mifflin, 2008).

On rights-talk, see Wendy Brown, *States of Injury* (Princeton: Princeton University Press, 1995), and Mary Ann Glendon, *Rights Talk: The Impoverishment of Political Discourse* (New York: Free Press, 1991). For an interesting study of rights discourse that emphasizes the particular historical conditions in which several different kinds of rights-claims (and visions of rights-talk) came to prominence, see Richard A. Primus, *The American Language of Rights* (New York: Cambridge University Press, 1999). For one interpretation of the political effects of our reliance on this language, see William Saletan, *Bearing Right: How Conservatives Won the Abortion War* (Berkeley: University of California Press, 2004).

Chapter Five

The quotation by Paul Ramsey comes from his *The Just War: Force and Political Responsibility* (Lanham, Md.: Rowman and Littlefield, 2002), p. 143.

The quotations from Augustine to Boniface are from letter 189. Augustine's discussion of Jesus' rebuke of Peter in the Garden of Gethsemane comes from his *Contra Faustem* 22.70.

The quotation from Hannah Arendt is from her *Eichmann in Jerusalem: A Report on the Banality of Evil* (London: Penguin, 1964), p. 298.

Christian thinking on war was not all sweetness and light; for an example of how off-track such reasoning could go, see Jonathan Riley-Smith, "Crusading as an Act of Love," *History* 65 (1980): 177-92; yet note the way that Augustine appears in this essay as an alternative, and arguably a critic, of the crusader ideology; see especially pp. 186-87. For more on just war, see Frederick H. Russell, *The Just War in the Middle Ages* (New York: Cambridge University Press, 1975).

For classical Christian discussions of the "threefold office" of Christ, see Thomas Aquinas, *Summa Theologiae* IIIa pars, though Aquinas talks about Christ's four roles: lawgiver *(legifer)*, priest *(sacerdos)*, king *(rex)*, judge *(judex)*; John Calvin, *Institutes of the Christian Religion* 2.15, and Karl Barth, *Church Dogmatics* IV/2 (Edinburgh: T. & T. Clark, 1958).

On Augustine's political thought in general, see Robert Dodaro,

Christ and the Just Society in the Thought of St. Augustine (New York: Cambridge University Press, 2004). On Augustine and authority, see Conrad Leyser, *Authority and Asceticism from Augustine to Gregory the Great* (Oxford: Clarendon, 2000). For an excellent collection of Augustine's political writings, including sermon 13, see R. J. Dodaro, ed., *Augustine: Political Writings* (New York: Cambridge University Press, 2001).

Chapter Six

The quotation from William Galston is from his book *Liberal Purposes* (Cambridge: Cambridge University Press, 1991), p. 225.

Eisenhower's quip is discussed in Patrick Henry, "'And I Don't Care What It Is': The Tradition-History of a Civil Religion Proof Text," *Journal of the American Academy of Religion* 49, no. 1 (March 1981): 35-49. (Perhaps Eisenhower knew his Gibbon, who famously claimed that "[t]he various modes of worship which prevailed in the Roman world were all considered by the people as equally true; by the philosopher as equally false; and by the magistrate as equally useful" [*The Decline and Fall of the Roman Empire*, vol. 1 (New York: Random House, 1995 [1776]), p. 22].)

The Melville quotation comes from *Moby-Dick, Billy Budd, and Other Writings* (New York: Library of America, 2000), p. 75.

The Newman quotation comes from *An Essay on the Development of Christian Doctrine* (Notre Dame, Ind.: University of Notre Dame Press, 1989), p. 40.

The O'Donovan quotation comes from Oliver O'Donovan, *The Desire of the Nations: Rediscovering the Roots of Political Theology* (New York: Cambridge University Press, 1996), p. 92.

The passage from James Madison about "the great desideratum in Government" is from his "Vices of the Political System of the United States" (the confederacy, pre-Constitution).

The quotation from Benjamin Franklin is found in the papers of Dr. James McHenry on the Federal Convention of 1787, which can themselves be found in Charles C. Tansill, *Documents Illustrative of the Formation of the Union of the American States* (Washington, D.C.: U.S. Printing Office, 1927); the exchange between Franklin and the woman is recorded on page 952.

The story of Reinhold Niebuhr and Felix Frankfurter is found in Arthur Schlesinger, Jr., *A Life in the Twentieth Century: Innocent Beginnings, 1917-1950* (New York: Mariner Books, 2002), p. 513.

The exchange between Pliny the Younger and the Emperor Trajan is found in Pliny's letters, book 10, 96-97. For a good analysis of pagan Roman views of the Christians, see Robert L. Wilken, *The Christians as the Romans Saw Them* (New Haven: Yale University Press, 1984). For a very nice discussion of sacrifice see George Heyman, *The Power of Sacrifice: Roman and Christian Discourses in Conflict* (Washington, D.C.: Catholic University of America Press, 2007).

On the topic of modern nationalism, see Benedict Anderson, *Imagined Communities: Reflections on the Origin and Spread of Nationalism* (London: Verso, 1983); Eugene Weber, *Peasants into Frenchmen: The Modernization of Rural France, 1870-1914* (Palo Alto: Stanford University Press, 1976). On the modern state see Perry Anderson, *Lineages of the Absolutist State* (New York: Schocken, 1979); Charles Tilly, *Coercion, Capital, and European States, AD 990-1992* (Cambridge, Mass.: Blackwell, 1992); Hendrick Spruyt, *The Sovereign State and Its Competitors* (Princeton: Princeton University Press, 1994); and Daniel Philpott, *Revolutions in Sovereignty* (Princeton: Princeton University Press, 2001). See Anthony Marx, *Faith in Nation: Exclusionary Origins of Nationalism* (New York: Oxford University Press, 2003), and Pierre Manent, "Modern Democracy as a System of Separations," *Journal of Democracy* 14, no. 1 (2003): 114-25.

For the church as the community gathered to hear judgment pronounced upon it, see Paul DeHart, *The Trial of the Witnesses: The Rise and Decline of Postliberal Theology* (Cambridge, Mass.: Blackwell, 2006).

Chapter Seven

The passage from Michel Foucault is from his *The History of Sexuality*, vol. 1, trans. Robert Hurley (Harmondsworth: Penguin, 1981), p. 143.

The passage by Anthony Cordesman comes from pages 17-18 in Anthony H. Cordesman, "Lessons of Post-Cold War Conflict: Middle Eastern Lessons and Perspectives," discussion paper prepared for NIC 2020 project; accessible at: http://www.csis.org/index.php?option=com_csis_pubs&task=view&id=1563.

Augustine's discussion of the oddness of loving one's enemy and hating one's family can be found in his *Commentary on the Sermon on the*

Mount 1.15.40. His discussion of creation ending with the resurrection of the dead is found in *Enarrationes in Psalmos* 47.1, but see also Augustine's creative reading together of Genesis and Revelation in *Confessions* 12. His discussion of the human as always seeking God is found in *De Trinitate* 15.2. The role of seeking in *Confessions* seems more explicitly articulated and addressed in *De Trinitate*, especially as that text is centrally organized around Ps. 105:4, "seek his face always."

The line of poetry by Charles Wright is from his *World of the Ten Thousand Things* (New York: Farrar, Straus, and Giroux, 1994), p. 193.

On apocalypticism, see Michael Northcott, *An Angel Directs the Storm: Apocalyptic Religion and American Empire* (London and New York: I. B. Tauris, 2004), and Amy Johnson Frykholm, *Rapture Culture: Left Behind in Evangelical America* (New York: Oxford University Press, 2004).

On the development of Christian pilgrimage as part of a spiritual life, see Jas Elsner and Ian Rutherford, eds., *Pilgrimage in Graeco-Roman and Early Christian Antiquity: Seeing the Gods* (Oxford: Oxford University Press, 2005); Maribel Dietz, *Wandering Monks, Virgins, and Pilgrims: Ascetic Travel in the Mediterranean World, A.D. 300-800* (University Park: Pennsylvania State University Press, 2005); and Georgia Frank, *The Memory of the Eyes: Pilgrims to Living Saints in Classical Antiquity* (Berkeley: University of California Press, 2000).

Some Useful Web Sites

United Nations Population Information Network is a good site for world demographics, historically, on present and future trends: http://www.un.org/popin/.

The U.N. Development Program: http://hdr.undp.org/en/statistics/.

The International Peace Research Institute, Oslo: http://www.prio.no/.

For a monthly analysis of economic data prepared for the Joint Economic Committee by the Council of Economic Advisors for the U.S. federal government: http://www.gpoaccess.gov/indicators/.

CIA World Factbook: https://www.cia.gov/library/publications/the-world-factbook/.

For a significant database of economic data from the United States, and one that also directs you to economic data from Canada, Britain,

Germany, the European Union, France, Italy, Russia, and China, look at EconStats: http://www.econstats.com/index.htm.

For a nice study of "European Values," derived from polling data from 1981 forward, look at: http://www.europeanvalues.nl/.

For a good study of the complexities of "political Islam," see: http://www.politicalislam.org/.

For a site on international jihad, see: http://www.jihadica.com/.

For information on ethnic conflict around the world, look at the "Minorities at Risk" database: http://www.cidcm.umd.edu/mar/.

A nice source on global migration is the Migration Information Source, a weekly online journal. Its Web site is: migrationinformation .org.

For information on the state of religion, religious belief, and religious institutions in the United States and worldwide, see the Association of Religion Data Archives Web site: www.theARDA.com.

For a good Web site on religion and public life, especially in the United States, see the Pew Forum: http://www.pewforum.org/.

Acknowledgments

This book began as one paper for a conference on Augustine at Princeton University in October of 2004, and as another paper for a Georgetown University Political Theory Colloquium in September 2006; it then took determinate shape as the MacKinnon Lectures at the Atlantic School of Theology, in Halifax, Nova Scotia, which I was honored to give in October of 2006. At Princeton, I thank Eric Gregory for hosting the conference and for the other participants, most notably Patrick Deneen, for discussions after my paper. At Georgetown I especially thank the respondent to my paper, Matthew Sitman, for his incisive and constructive comments, and again — oddly, come to think of it — my friend Patrick Deneen, for organizing it. At the Atlantic School of Theology I thank the audience for their patience and charity toward me, and especially Dean David MacLachlan, President Eric Beresford, Christopher Brittain, Alyda Faber, and the absent yet present Philip Ziegler. Dean MacLachlan's gentle criticisms of my excessively apophatic eschatology have helped me (I *would* write "in ways I cannot say," but one should avoid theological jokes). The lively academic and religious community at AST was palpable even in my short stay there, and I am deeply grateful and honored for the good will they showed toward me.

In 2005, I was fortunate to be invited by my friend and colleague Charles Marsh to be part of a theological writing seminar that his Project on Lived Theology was putting together, and the conversations in that group — lasting over the past few years — have been fundamental to shaping not just *what* I wrote but *how* I wrote it. This has probably been the one setting where I've actually learned something useful about writing and talking to an audience that is larger than other academics. Plus, being in the group provided me with the wherewithal to take a semester's extra leave from UVA, and dedicate myself to the heavy lifting of drafting this book. For all their assistance, their laughter, and the fun we have had, I am tremendously grateful to Charles and the other members of the group: Carlos Eire, Mark Gornik, Patricia Hampl, Susan Holman, and Alan Jacobs. Rebekah Menning and Kristina Garcia Wade, the two assistants for the project, were also essential to our functioning as well as we did. Giles Anderson, my agent, was enthusiastic about this book and effective in placing it with Eerdmans.

Colleagues and students, and some students who are now colleagues, and all of them friends, read this book, or parts of it, in several drafts. I thank especially Steven Bush, Zak Calo, Shaun Casey, Marta Cook, Emily Gum (*née* Raudenbusch), Karen Guth, Slava Jakelic, Paul Jones, Peter Kang, Philip Lorish, Betsy Mesard, Mary Moorman, Erik Owens, Kathleen Phillips, Bart Renner, Aaron Riches, Kevin Schultz, Keith Starkenburg, Chad Wayner, and, as ever, Joshua Yates, whose unpublished work and living thoughts I have borrowed from repeatedly. Luke Bretherton has been a long-distance correspondent on this book, and our occasional meetings, on my side of the pond or on his, have always given me new thoughts and greater enthusiasm for this project. A long time ago Katherine Pennock read an early draft, and gave very helpful advice; I am grateful for her acute thoughts and her enduring enthusiasm for it. Near the end, Amy Graeser helped me wrestle it into shape, and gave me the benefit of her meticulous mind, and scrutinizing eye, for both of which I am also very grateful. And last but not least, Mark Storslee undertook the arduous ascetical task of proofing the book and preparing the index, for both of which thankless tasks I am, paradoxically, most thankful.

An early version of some of the ideas that go into this book appeared in *Theology Today*, in an essay entitled "An Augustinian Look at Empire," *Theology Today* 63, no. 3 (October 2006): 290-304. I thank the journal and the editors for allowing me to reproduce some words from that piece here.

I worked seriously on this book over a sabbatical in Washington, D.C., during which the Pew Forum on Religion and Public Life gave me an office, an e-mail connection, and rights to a printer and a seemingly endless supply of peanut M&Ms, and I will be ever grateful for the director of the Pew Forum, Luis Lugo, Sandra Stencel, and the staff of that remarkable institution both for the material assistance they gave my arguments and for the deeply responsible and admirable way they proceed in researching and reporting on what are essentially explosive topics. While at the Pew Forum, also, several conversations with David Masci and Timothy Shah were very crucial to my argument. I thank Luis, David, Tim, and everyone else at Pew for their help.

Until her death in 2006, my mother, Martha Mathewes, helped with this book in innumerable ways. And throughout the book's composition my mother-in-law, Norma Geddes, was also invaluable for her love and insight.

As ever, my wife Jennifer Geddes read drafts of this and, what's worse, endured my innumerable attempts to try out various parts of the argument verbally. If anyone ever needed further evidence of her patience and love, this probably would serve as overkill.

What I know of love I owe in large part to my parents and my sister, and to Jennifer. What I know of adoration, I owe to Isabelle and Henry. Since adoration turns out to be central to this book, it only made sense to dedicate it to them.

Index

CPSIA information can be obtained
at www.ICGtesting.com
Printed in the USA
FSHW012158071221
86694FS

9 780802 865083